THE
WINE
AND
FOOD
OF
EUROPE

Peaches for sale in Eger, Hungary.

THE WINE AND FOOD OF EUROPE

An Illustrated Guide

MARC & KIM MILLON

Foreword by
JOHN ARLOTT

Webb&Bower
EXETER, ENGLAND

To our families

Published in Great Britain 1982 by
Webb & Bower (Publishers) Limited
9 Colleton Crescent, Exeter, Devon EX2 4BY

Designed by Peter Wrigley
Maps by Gill Embleton

British Cataloguing in Publication Data

Millon, Marc
   The wine and food of Europe.
   1. Wine and wine making—Europe
   2. Liquors   3. Cookery, European
   I. Title   II. Millon, Kim
   641.2   TP533
   ISBN 0-906671-35-3

Typeset in Great Britain by
August Filmsetting, Warrington, Cheshire

Printed and bound in Italy by
New Interlitho, SpA, Milan

CONTENTS

FOREWORD

John Arlott

The Wine and Food of Europe, written with obvious relish, and to be relished, is, in effect, an account of a gastronomic Grand Tour. Indeed, it is a survey of the heartland of an important region of civilization and of culture.

The author's study ground, the classic vineyard territory, has developed a particular feeling for the aspect of culture which may be called gastronomy. Many of the ordinary people of those countries, though, would recoil in mock amazement at the use of so pretentious a word for what is, for them, as natural as breathing.

The Nordic people, apart from Germany – and certainly the English-speaking nations – often tend to treat interest in food and drink almost as a form of depravity, leading men into idleness and gluttony and keeping them from their work. Hence the convenience foods; sandwiches, smorgasbord, mass-produced snacks – all easily prepared, always secondary to work, making no such demands of punctuality on the cook or time for relaxed enjoyment of the eater, as a well-cooked meal should always do.

A French wine merchant one day lamented, 'If only I could get my people to work an eight to half-past-four day with half an hour for lunch as you do in England, I would happily give them their midday meal and a half bottle or so with it: but no, they will have their full lunch at home even though some of them have to bicycle three kilometres each way for it.' Thus sacred remains the French *déjeuner*, even – and, surely, happily – now.

The basic fact is that wine has the unique capacity to lift some items of plain wholesome food to the standing of a meal, and a few carefully pre-pared, though simple, dishes to an experience which merits contemplation.

Of course, vines are grown and wine is made in the United States, Britain and Australia. None of those countries, though, has yet created a parallel culinary tradition, nor adopted the mental attitude which Brillat Savarin in *Physiologie du Gout* called '*gourmandise*'. Protesting against the failure of lexicographers to distinguish between that civilized awareness and the grossness of gluttony, he defined it as 'a passionate, reasoned and habitual preference for that which delights the palate'. It is, he went on, 'The enemy of excess' and, in a typically French peroration, 'morally it is strict obedience to the Creator who, having commanded us to eat in order to live, invites us with appetite, encourages us with flavour, and rewards us with pleasure.'

Again he asserts, 'Alcohol is the monarch of liquids; it lifts the palate to the highest degree of exaltation; and, in its various forms, has opened up new sources of pleasure.'

It is striking, and probably significant, that none of the nations dealt with here have suffered from obsession with prohibition or enforced abstinence (except Yugoslavia and Bulgaria under Muslim rule). Quite apart from geography – that factor which effectively excludes the United States and Australia from this survey – they and Britain have attempted in varying degrees to enforce teetotalism by law. In contrast, the countries of the European vine-belt accept wine as part of normal life. There can be no more conclusive evidence of the difference of attitude than the fact that a convict sentenced to penal servitude in Italy is entitled to a litre of wine a day. Since he probably is accustomed to drink twice as much as that, he may find the reduction a punitive deprivation, but officialdom would never consider denying him that fluid staff of Italian life.

Always the combination of wine and food has been significant. Wine undoubtedly induces the contemplative mood which enables food to be taken with a quietly critical enjoyment. It was, once more, Brillat Savarin who precisely indicated the difference when he wrote, 'Wine is the most delightful of drinks, whether we owe it to Noah, who planted the vine, or to Bacchus who squeezed the juice from the grape, it comes from the infancy of the world.'

Mr Millon's territory lies, too, and probably crucially, within a single land mass. Communications between the countries were always relatively easy, even for invaders. So the various cépages of grapes passed from one set of vineyards to another, and sometimes there was crossing; certainly different soils, climates, methods of growing, pruning and vinification produced wines through a wide range of different flavours and colours, some still and some sparkling – from, originally, the same grapes. So, too, foodstuffs – crops, meat, fish and fruits – passed across borders, and took on different characteristics in different weather, terrain, river or ocean. Ideas moved, too: foods were grown differently, cooked differently, garnished differently.

The modern view, which can hardly be challenged, is that the French cuisine is the finest in the world. It can be argued, though, that it has not always been so; and, also, that French cuisine is by no means purely French. In the sixteenth century, two Medici women became queens of France. In 1533 Catherine de'Medici married the Dauphin who was to become Henri II. She bore him ten children, three of whom became kings and two queens; in addition, she introduced the fork to France, but too soon; for another two centuries the French preferred to use their fingers. In 1599 Marie de'Medici replaced the childless Margaret de Valois as wife of Henri IV and produced six children, including the much desired heir. Importantly, however, both brought with them – significantly from Florence – a retinue of Italian cooks who included, then, the finest *pâtissiers* in the then world. Moreover, since they both survived to act as regents – and, therefore, effectively to rule the country – they were able to introduce, even impose on the court, Italian cooking methods which were then more sophisticated than the French.

That fits well into the pattern of European history; for Florence, the hub of the Etruscan civilization which was the springhead of European enlightenment, was also, later, the hub of the Renaissance. It is fitting indeed that it should also have been a major influence in the creation of the cultural facet of gastronomy.

Yet, even while such major exchanges of ideas and dishes went on, some of Europe remained gastronomically insular. As Mr Millon makes clear, the field of wine was sadly limited until relatively recently. Indeed, in many parts of Europe it remains so. The sabotage of vehicles, and rioting, which the southern French wine producers employed against the importers of Italian wines, were in direct violation not only of normal law, but also of specific EEC wine legislation. Even within France there remains a strong tendency for the people of Burgundy to drink only their own wines to the exclusion of Bordeaux, where they, too, drink almost solely their own: the Alsatians and the people of the Rhône and Loire are also determinedly locally minded in their drinking. Certainly the Champenoises often follow their own product with claret. On the whole, though, the French are, at best, regionally minded in terms of wine. They may well argue, too, that their own regional dishes are better than any others they could serve, not only on the basis of natural sympathy with the wine, but because of the freshness as well as the excellence of the basic local materials.

In the event, the United States and Britain, certainly through their wine merchants, but also in their cosmopolitan restaurants, have a wider choice of the gastronomic pleasures of Europe than most of the countries which produce them; though, of course, in the foreign markets, they must generally pay a higher price. That is especially true in the instance of wines, which the British and American governments choose to regard as sin and, in consequence, impose huge fiscal penalties upon them.

The inescapable conclusion is that, at all levels, from unsophisticated peasant life to intellectual and wealthy privilege, in these winelands, the effect of the balanced combination of local cooking and wine induces contemplation and the relaxed enjoyment of the pleasures of the table.

One of these meals, though, is never quite the same when served in another country, however authentic the materials or expert the preparation. It is often said that some wines 'do not travel', and there may, sometimes, be chemical reasons for the deterioration of a removed bottle. That is part – but, as a rule, only part – of the reason why the cherished bottle reverently brought back from an overseas holiday rarely tastes so good as the memory of it in its own country. It is only a partial explanation because neither food nor drink will ever be quite the same as in its own native climate, atmosphere and setting; every item of food and drink has a degree of its own *goût de terroir*.

Truly matched food and drink form a civilized – perhaps, indeed, an artistic – creation, in the world of gastronomy. For the catholic eater and drinker, not affectedly squeamish about snails, tripe, winkles or retsina, the world is his oyster; and a mightily tasty one.

The spice of food is adventure. For the European traveller from one of the 'outside' countries, there can be no more impressive experience than *huîtres Bordelaises* – Bordeaux oysters – when you take, first, a fresh cold oyster – a *fine de claire* from Marennes – then a bite of buttered brown bread; then one of the small local spicy sausages – *lou kencous* – and finally a taste of well chilled dry, white Graves, then begin the process all over again; the contrasts are the spice of life.

Marc Millon, though, here arouses all kinds of memory flavours; and the reader who can finish this book with his digestive juices unstimulated must be singularly dull of both appetite and imagination.

INTRODUCTION

What could be more enjoyable than munching grilled prawns while sipping a chilled *copita* of *fino* sherry? Eating oysters on the half-shell with a glass of Entre-Deux-Mers? Feasting on beef stewed in Barolo, accompanied by that king of Italian wines? Savouring hot, puffy cheese *gougères* and a brimming tumbler of Beaujolais *primeur*? Abandoning one's table decorum to the delights of Greek retsina and lamb *souvlakia*, *saltimbocca* and golden Frascati?

In Europe's wine regions, wine and food are inseparable. From the *bodegas* of Jerez de la Frontera to the steep green shores of the Moselle, from Portugal, Europe's westernmost edge, to the Thracian plain of Bulgaria, distinctive regional foods are natural and unselfconscious partners to the wines produced there. Our aim, in this European gastronomic journey, is to introduce the characteristic tastes and flavours of these wine regions, with the hope that authentic regional dishes will be re-created in the kitchen to be savoured at the table in conjunction with the wines of the land.

Indeed, we feel that this relationship between wine and food is basic and important. Our neighbours on the Continent have known it all along, and how we envy them. Wine over there, after all, is drunk daily, as essential to a meal as salt and pepper.

On the other hand, the great tradition of the wine trade in Britain places us in a peculiarly privileged position. For in the wine regions of Europe themselves, though wine can be relatively inexpensive, local prejudice (and protection of local and national interest) is so strong that it is sometimes impossible to find wine from another district, let alone another country. Stubborn Burgundians, for example, would never dream of drinking wine from Bordeaux. And you would be hard-pressed to find a bottle of Spanish Rioja in a Roman wine shop. Or a Moselle in Portugal.

Here in Britain, though, there is undoubtedly the widest selection of wines available anywhere in the world. And this is not limited to exclusive wine merchants, either: High Street supermarkets today offer a tremendous variety of good-value drinking wines.

One problem when discussing regional food and wine is that many distinctive products of a regional cuisine may not be available outside that region. In certain cases it is precisely these products that make a regional cuisine distinctive. White truffles are a rich and integral element in the *cucina* of Italy's Piedmont. A 'proper' *bouillabaisse* requires fish available only at the seafront market of Marseilles. Greek olive oil lends its inimitable flavour to the foods of that country, while goose lard is indispensable to the Bordelaise housewife. And true Hungarian paprika adds a pungent aroma and rich colour to goulash and paprika chicken that is unmistakable.

Though local produce from European wine regions cannot always be found in shops in Britain, nevertheless those same supermarkets that are today stocking such wide selections of wine are also carrying wider ranges of continental products and produce than ever before. Most of the recipes included in this book can be prepared with ingredients that are readily available. In addition, there are now numerous continental and specialist grocers to be found throughout the country that are well worth a visit. Sometimes it takes just a single characteristic ingredient to give a touch of authenticity to foreign tastes and aromas.

Wine is simply the fermented juice of grape, and yet what miraculous variety exists within that basic equation. From grapes, the land they grow in, and the skill of man come liquids as differing in character as the elements. For each of Europe's wine regions projects a distinctive personality that betrays local predilection, priority, and prejudice.

Equally varied and distinctive are the foods of each region, reflecting geographical and cultural differences, varieties in local produce, traditions, temperament, and tempo. Portugal, a nation of mariners and fishermen, spreads its colourful table with the fruits of the sea. The foods of Yugoslavia and Bulgaria have been influenced as much by historical factors such as centuries of Turkish domination as by indigenous forces. Provençal cooking is characterized by its liberal use of garlic, olive oil, tomatoes, and the wild herbs that grow in abundance on the scrubby hills of the south of France. And alpine Switzerland exists, to a great extent, on a diet of cheese developed by mountain herdsmen.

If the wine and food regions of Europe are remarkable in their diversity, there is one thing that unites them: a friendly, convivial attitude to eating and drinking that is disarming. For wine and food are more than just nourishment. Concern for the quality of food and the manner in which one partakes of it is so important to a concept of good living as to be a way of life —indeed, it is a ritual of well-being. The daily midday repast, whether taken at home or in a restaurant, is an important focal point for the family. It is usual in these regions for three generations to sit together to enjoy their meals. Children are propped up on pillows. They drink watered-down wine and learn to coax snails or mussels out of stubborn shells. They practise speech with parents and grandparents, learn to listen to them, and teach them something, too.

To gather the information and pictures for this book we have travelled thousands of miles in Europe. We met grape-growers, talked with wine producers and shippers, and observed loving cellar techniques. We met housewives and exchanged and discussed recipes, shared food and wine with families and new friends. We talked to restaurateurs and chefs, and people in bars, cafés, *tavernas*, *cantine*, and *gostilnas*. We lunched with workers in the fields—and we were chased off by them.

Through it all, from the singing wine festivals of Germany to the steamy Pannonian plain of Austria's Burgenland, through the maze of culinary terms and regional ingredients, to the litres of wine tasted (and sometimes swallowed), one fact clearly emerges: that regional wine and food in Europe is very much a living force, always playing an integral and omnipresent role in everyday life.

A NOTE ON MEASUREMENTS: It is difficult if not impossible to convert measures from one system into equally convenient measures in another. In those recipes where precision is important, we have tried to be as exact as possible. In many recipes, however, proportions of ingredients are more important than exact quantity, so it is essential to follow one system consistently.

FRANCE

CHAMPAGNE

R. La Vesle

Reims

Strasbourg

Molsheim
SYLVANER
PINOT NOIR
D'ALSACE

PINOT
MEUNIER
VALLÉE
DE LA MARNE

MONTAGNE
DE REIMS

Verzenay
PINOT
NOIR

Hautvillers

Epernay • Ay
Bouzy
BOUZY
Tours-sur-Marne

Châlons-
sur-Marne

CÔTE
DES
BLANCS

• Cramant
• Avize

R. Marne

CHARDONNAY

R. Aube

MÉDOC
St Estèphe •

Pauillac

St Julien •

SAUVIGNON

CÔTES DE
BLAYE

Blaye •

R. Gironde

CABERNET
SAUVIGNON
Listrac
• Moulis
Margaux

Bourg •

CÔTES DE
BOURG

R. Isle

HAUT-
MÉDOC

Fronsac •

Pomerol
Libourne
St Emilion

MERLOT

Bordeaux •

R. Dordogne

R. Garonne

Vayres •

ENTRE-
DEUX-
MERS

GRAVES

PREMIÈRES
CÔTES DE
BORDEAUX

BORDEAUX

Bassin
d'Arcachon

Barsac •

SAUTERNES

Sauternes •

Langon

LANDES

SEMILLON

St Nazaire •

Nantes •

MUSCADET
GROS PLANT

MUSCADET
DE SÈVRE-ET-
MAINE

R. Sèvre-Nantaise

R. Main

ANJOU-COTEAUX
DE LA LOIRE

Savennières

R. Sarthe

CABERNET D'ANJOU

Angers •

COTEAUX
DE LA LOIRE

ROSÉ D'ANJOU

COTEAUX
DE L'AUBANCE

COTEAUX
DU LAYON

Saumur •

Bonnezeaux •

SAUMUR

VOUVRAY
Vouvray

Tours •

Bourgueil •

Montlouis

COTEAUX
DE TOURAINE

Chinon • SAUVIGNON
DE TOURAINE

LOIRE

ALSACE

Obernai
TOKAY D'ALSACE
R. Andlau
Barr
PINOT BLANC
Sélestat
R. Fecht
Colmar
RIESLING
Ribeauvillé
R. Weiss
Riquewihr
MUSCAT D'ALSACE
VOSGES MTNS
Kaysersberg
EAU-DE-VIE D'ALSACE
R. Lauch
R. Thur
Guebwiller
VOSGES MTNS
Thann

BURGUNDY

R. Serein
Fontenay
Chablis
CHABLIS
CHARDONNAY
Auxerre
R. Cure
Dijon
CÔTE D'OR
CÔTE DE NUITS
Vosne-Romanée
Aloxe-Corton
Gevrey-Chambertin
Nuits-St-Georges
CÔTE DE BEAUNE
Volnay
Beaune
R. Saône
Puligny-Montrachet
Meursault
PINOT NOIR
Chagny
Rully
CHALONNAIS
Givry
Chalon-sur-Saône
Montagny
Tournus
Charolles
Cluny
MÂCONNAIS
Fuissé
Vinzelles
Mâcon
R. Veyle
Moulin-à-Vent
Fleurie
Bourg
Chiroubles
Brouilly
BEAUJOLAIS
Villefranche
GAMAY
Lyon

RHÔNE AND PROVENCE

Lyon
R. Rhône
CÔTE RÔTIE
Condrieu
CHÂTEAU GRILLET
Vienne
R. Isère
CROZES-HERMITAGE
Tain-l'Hermitage
HERMITAGE
Cornas
St Péray
Valence
CLAIRETTE DE DIE
Die
CÔTES DU RHÔNE
R. Rhône
Montélimar
R. Aygues
Gigondas
MUSCAT
Beaumes-de-Venise
Digne
CÔTES DE PROVENCE
Orange
Lirac
Châteauneuf-du-Pape
Tavel
ROSÉ
Avignon
R. Durance
Arles
Marseille

R. Loire
Orléans
R. Cher
Sancerre
SANCERRE
POUILLY BLANC FUMÉ
Pouilly-sur-Loire
Menetou-Salon
Quincy
Reuilly
Nevers

Haut-Koenigsbourg Castle, deep in the Vosges mountains.

14

ALSACE

Medieval villages with timber-framed houses; boxes of scarlet geraniums, and cobbled courtyards; towns with decidedly German names; people with vehemently French attitudes; a local patois that is neither; and, not least of all, a food and wine tradition inextricably linked to both cultures, but with a character all its own: this is Alsace.

Cut off from the rest of France by the Vosges mountains, separated from Germany by the Rhine, this slender and beautiful region has been one of the most fought over in Europe. The last century alone has seen Alsace caught in a miserable tug-of-war between France and Germany no less than four times. The area was ruled by Germany for fifty years after the Franco–Prussian War. An Allied victory in World War I brought Alsace back to France for a mere twenty years. But peace was short-lived, and this calm and idyllic land was under siege again when Hitler launched an offensive into the Rhineland to reclaim it. During the Second World War there were four years of intensive Germanization. But afterwards France once more asserted rights over this beautiful valley. Its history of turmoil, moreover, is not confined to recent times. At least as long ago as the ninth century, the region was bartered continuously—a prize for the biggest and strongest.

Constant conflict has contributed to the unique character of the Alsace. Many older people still speak German; others speak the Alsatian dialect. Here one goes into a *Weinstube*, with carved barrels and dark mahogany seats, instead of the usual Gallic café. In homes and restaurants classic regional dishes include *escargots*, *coq au Riesling*, and *foie gras*—but equally popular

are such hearty favourites as sauerkraut and sausages, and the rib-sticking Alsatian stew called *Bäckeofe*. Another indication of the Alsatian dual nature is that wine struggles for supremacy with lager beer. The best in France is brewed in this region, and its distinctive character is not dissimilar to Alsatian wine: crystal clean, fresh, and strong. Alsatian wine itself is curiously balanced between French and German: at once fruity and full of scent, yet firm, bone-dry, and remarkably crisp.

The Vosges mountains, as well as separating the province from the rest of France, act as a climatic barrier which catches much of the rain before it reaches the rich land of the Rhine. Summers are hot and long and dry. Because the majority of vineyards are situated along the foothills of the mountains, they are removed from the dense fog that forms along the river flatlands. The geological structure of these foothills is at once complex, varied, and rich.

The violent history of Alsace has had an important effect on the wine producer, too. Time and again, fields carefully nurtured and built up were destroyed by war. And changing governments put restrictions on growers regarding both methods of production and the varieties of grapes they could cultivate.

After the Franco–Prussian War, for example, the victorious Germans passed legislation compelling the growers in Alsace to make wine from common grape varieties for the purpose of blending. Because that government wanted growers in Germany's principal wine regions to produce quality wine for export, the Alsatian wine producers were needed to supply in quantity everyday table wine for German consumption. As a result, inferior vines that produced a substantially larger annual crop were planted. Unfortunately, from inferior grapes comes inferior wine.

When France reclaimed the region after World War I, growers were this time forced to strip vineyards planted with common vines, for the aim now was to encourage (if not compel) the production of quality wine. This decision was by no means a popular one, because it is much easier to tend and cultivate common grapes than it is to grow temperamental, noble

varieties. The growers nevertheless acceded to the latest mandate, and eventually settled well to the rigours of quality-vine cultivation. But then, after about twenty years of relative peace, Germany invaded the province once more, and Alsace was again under occupation for four hard years. Not only did continual wars damage the region profoundly, not only did changing governments' demands cause confusion and resentment among growers, as well there was the commercial hardship of having to adapt and readapt continually to different markets with remarkably different tastes and needs.

After the Second World War, the *Code du Vin* was passed, which outlined, among other things, legally acceptable standards for grapes used to make simple table wines as well as to make the more distinctive wines which today we associate with Alsace. Indeed, grape variety was always of primary importance here: as long ago as 1575 there were mandates specifying which varieties could be grown. Today, noble grape varieties with extremely different and distinct characteristics are cultivated throughout the region. Those which produce the best wines of Alsace are Riesling, Gewurztraminer, Muscat, Sylvaner, Pinot Gris (Tokay d'Alsace), Pinot Blanc (Klevner), and Pinot Noir.

The best Alsatian wines are single-grape varieties—that is, made entirely from one of the noble grape varieties. Indeed, so important is the individual character of the grape that the traditional wine-maker's goal, above all else, is to lose as little as possible of the grape itself—its unique fragrance, ripeness, and purity—during that delicate process of transformation of grape into wine.

The inference should not be drawn that the reason quality wine comes from Alsace today is because the region is now governed by France. An equally important debt is owed to German tradition. Undoubtedly the style of wine produced here bears resemblance to German types. The delicate balance between acidity and fruity aroma is of importance to wine producers in both areas. To stress the difference between wine produced here and in other parts of France, Alsatian *appellation contrôlée* wine is sold under the all-important grape name (Riesling d'Alsace

Choucroute alsacienne (Alsatian sauerkraut) in the Petite France district of Strasbourg.

Huge white cabbages become *choucroute*, a necessity of of the Alsatian table.

or Tokay d'Alsace, for example) while most other French quality wine regions are concerned with pinpointing in varying degrees the location from which grapes for a particular wine are grown (at one extreme, by simply naming the broad region, such as Bordeaux or the Côtes du Rhône; at the other, by naming the specific vine-yard that has given that wine, such as Le Cham-bertin or Château Margaux). Specific single vine-yards are rarely named in Alsace (when they are, it is always a sign of quality). Rather, since there are so many small *vignerons* here, wine made from single-grape varieties grown throughout the region is often blended. When buying

Alsatian wine, therefore, it is important to look for the particular grape variety, and also the name of a reliable producer or shipper. Another resemblance between Alsatian wine and German is that here quality wine is sold in the distinctive Alsatian *flûte*, a tall, narrow bottle that resembles the slender green-glass bottles of the Mosel-Saar-Ruwer.

Clearly, the influence of both cultures on wine goes deep. Equally important is the dual influence on the food of the region. If gastronomy throughout France is approached with nothing short of reverence, here in Alsace, Gallic high seriousness is balanced with a certain Germanic gusto. Food, foremost, is meant to be eaten and enjoyed—preferably in large quantities. Whereas sauerkraut in Germany can be a rather tedious and unexciting accompaniment, here *choucroute alsacienne*, a huge platter of sauerkraut garnished with delicious meats such as smoked pork chops, grilled Strasbourg sausage and *Knockwurst*, salted beef, pig's knuckle, and black pudding, translates into a feast. Delicate winy sauces are consorts to stolid, heavy-set (and heavy-sitting) stews cooked in pot-bellied earthenware. And light, rosy-cheeked *petits fours* are matched by down-to-earth nut- and raisin-laden *Kugelhopf*.

Bäckeofe is typical Alsatian fare, a one-pot stew that makes use of all the week's left-over meats and vegetables. Traditionally made in an earthenware crock, it contains Wagnerian portions of pork, beef, lamb, mutton, and potatoes, simmered in wine and herbs. One might normally expect to drink full-bodied red wine with such a hefty dish, but the Alsatians drink their firm, strong white wine with virtually everything, including game and red meat. There is no reason why such wines cannot stand up to these foods; it is usually only convention that decrees otherwise. Tokay d'Alsace, biggest of all Alsatian wines, has a steely backbone, and a dry disciplined firmness that allows it to partner a variety of full-flavoured dishes.

The only red wine produced in Alsace is Pinot Noir d'Alsace. Surprisingly, this pretty and pleasant wine is even more delicate than the great white wines of the region. Nevertheless, it is a fine, easy wine to drink on a picnic, or just for a change.

Another wine that is perhaps surprising is Muscat d'Alsace. Intriguingly heavy and fragrant, the wine promises the sweetness of fresh dessert grapes, yet is clean, crisp, and bone-dry. It is the perfect wine to drink as an *apéritif* at the start of an Alsatian meal.

Meals here often begin with the celebrated *foie gras*, goose liver embellished with the black truffle of Périgord. Geese are force-fed to develop enlarged livers, a practice that goes back to the Romans. These livers are rich, unctuous, prized for their compact, smooth texture, and intense flavour and aroma. Though Alsatian wine is essentially dry, in exceptional years rich, sweet

varieties are produced from late-picked grapes. Such wines are known as *vendange tardive*. A *vendange tardive* Gewurztraminer has an assertive and full character that can stand up well to the strong personality of this delicacy.

Gewurztraminer is an attractive introduction to the wines of Alsace, because it has a distinctive bouquet reminiscent of the herbs, grass, and wild flowers of the lower Vosges mountains where the grapes ripen. *Gewürz* means spice in German, and indeed it is a revelation of how intensely appealing wine can be: lingering, seductive—once tasted, irresistible.

Though Gewurztraminer is obviously popular, the king of Alsatian wine must be Riesling. In Germany, this hard, late-ripening grape provides in exceptional years some of the finest and

Stainless steel tanks ensure that Alsatian wine is clean and fresh, although the greater wines still spend time in wood.

sweetest dessert wines in the world. Riesling d'Alsace is racy, elegant, at once fruity, yet remarkably firm and full-bodied. Fermented completely, it is clean, dry, and relatively powerful, a wine that is ideal with food.

Coq au Riesling is a classic Alsatian favourite, totally different to other 'chicken cooked in wine' stews found elsewhere. The method here is to *flambé* the chicken in brandy, then cook the pieces slowly in a cream and wine sauce. This is always accompanied by buttered egg noodles and, of course, Riesling d'Alsace. *Matelote au Riesling* is a similar wine stew, using the delicious freshwater fish of the region: pike, perch, trout, and eel. Another typical way of preparing fish is *au bleu*, that is, poached in a vinegary *court-bouillon*, which causes the skin of extremely fresh fish to turn a striking shade of blue.

Snails are a pest generally found in wine-producing regions, and, whether the practice of eating them in a garlic and butter sauce originated here or in Burgundy, they are never more delicious than in an Alsatian *Weinstube*—crowded, laughing, informal—washed down with a carafe of Zwicker (blended Alsatian table wine), or perhaps a bottle of Sylvaner. Sylvaner, though lacking the depth, elegance, and body of Riesling, is a refreshing, forceful wine, particularly loved by the Alsatians themselves.

In these crowded *Weinstuben* located the length of the ninety-mile *Route du Vin* which extends from Marlenheim down to Thann, one can sometimes sample Alsatian food at its simplest and best. Alsatian onion tart, for example, is a delicious snack (and also excellent picnic fare), while a thick slab of pungent Münster cheese, sprinkled liberally with caraway seeds, is a welcome accompaniment to that ever-waiting, slender, green-stemmed glass of wine.

Apple tart and plum pie, still warm from the oven and dusted with powdered sugar, are tempting at the end of a meal. This is also the time to sample the famous *alcools blancs* which come from this versatile land. Aged in glass in such a manner that the result is as colourless as water, these eaux-de-vie d'Alsace are brandies made from fruit such as pears, wild strawberries, raspberries, plums, as well as from the *marc* (pressed grape skins, pips, stems) of noble grape

varieties (eau-de-vie marc de Gewurztraminer, for example). They are deliciously clean, fragrant, and exceedingly strong. Alsatians swear by their digestive and health-giving properties; some go so far as to begin each day with a 'tot' to accompany breakfast of *Kugelhopf*, the distinctive fruit bread so popular here.

An outdoor market in the old section of Colmar.

Alsace is old, Alsace is surprisingly unspoiled. Turmoil and strife are past now, and a deep sigh of relief has settled over the region. In the vineyards that carpet the foothills of the mountains where so much fierce fighting took place, the grapes, slowly, steadily, are ripening. Deep in cellars, naked green-glass bottles lie ready to be labelled, to be bought, to be uncorked, to be enjoyed. And in homes, restaurants, *Weinstuben*, cafés, or *brasseries* throughout the region, the past, if too painfully vivid to be forgotten, at least coexists silently with the happier reality of the present.

Riquewihr, one of the many beautiful and unspoiled Alsatian town nestles in some of the region's most prized vineyards.

RECIPES FROM ALSACE

Quantities where necessary are given in
Metric, Imperial and US measurements.

Tarte à l'Oignon

Onion Tart

4 rashers/slices of bacon
25 g/1 oz/2 tbsp butter
1 tbsp oil
3 large onions, peeled and thinly sliced
4 eggs
150 ml/¼ pt/⅔ cup cream
Salt
Freshly ground black pepper
Pinch of grated nutmeg
23 cm/9 in flan tin lined with half-baked
pâte brisée (see recipe)

Fry the bacon until crisp. Remove, drain, and crumble. Discard bacon fat and add butter and oil. Fry onions over a low heat until soft and golden. This will take about 45 min.

Meanwhile, beat eggs and add cream and seasonings. Crumble bacon into the half-baked *pâte brisée* case, and add cooked golden onions. Pour egg mixture on to this, and place on a baking sheet in a fairly hot oven, 200°C/Gas Mark 6/400°F, for 30 min., until it has set and the top turned a golden brown.

Serve hot or cold, with French bread and a salad.

Suggested wine:
Sylvaner d'Alsace

Pâte Brisée

This crust can be used for hors-d'oeuvres and for desserts. Fillings can vary from savoury mixtures of creamy onion and bacon to plums and golden apples.

100 g/4 oz/1 stick butter
175 g/6 oz/1⅓ cups flour
1 egg

Pinch of salt
2 tbsp cold water

Soften butter. Sieve flour into a large bowl, and add butter (cut into small pieces), egg, and salt. Rub in well with fingertips. Add cold water little by little until dough becomes moist yet supple. Form into a ball, and put into the refrigerator for at least 2 hr. Roll out pastry so it is about 3 mm/⅛ in thick, and line a buttered 23 cm/9 in flan tin.

Prick bottom of pastry at regular intervals with a fork. Butter the under-side of another smaller tin, and weight it down with dry beans. Place it inside the pastry case to prevent the bottom from puffing up while cooking.

Bake in a pre-heated oven, 200°C/Gas Mark 6/400°F, for about 10 min., or until the pastry has hardened. Remove the tin and beans, and again prick the bottom of the pastry. Return to oven and cook for another 3 min. until it begins to colour. Cool and fill.

Matelote au Riesling

Freshwater Fish Stew
Serves 4

1 kg/2 lb freshwater fish (mixture of e.g. trout,
perch, eel, pike)
1 onion, peeled and sliced
2 carrots, sliced
1 bay leaf
Sprig of thyme
Salt
Freshly ground black pepper
450 ml/¾ pt/2 cups Riesling d'Alsace
3 tbsp butter
3 tbsp flour
150 ml/¼ pt/⅔ cup sour cream
Freshly chopped parsley

Clean and dry fish. Cut eel into 5 cm/2 in pieces. Prepare a *court-bouillon* with onion, carrots, seasonings, and wine in a large casserole.

Bring to the boil, and allow to simmer for about 30 min. Add the fish one by one. The time needed for cooking each will depend upon type and size. Eel, for example, will take the longest time, perch the least. They will vary from 10 to about 25 min. While they are cooking, make a roux in a small saucepan with butter and flour. Leave to cook for a couple of minutes. When fish are tender, arrange them on a large warmed platter and keep warm while the sauce is made. Strain the *court-bouillon* and add slowly to the roux, stirring continuously. Gently bring to the boil, and allow to simmer for 10 min. This will reduce the liquid. Remove from heat, and beat in the sour cream. Adjust seasoning. Pour sauce over the fish, and decorate with parsley.

Serve with buttered noodles and a green salad.

Suggested wine:
Riesling d'Alsace

Coq au Riesling

Chicken in Riesling
Serves 4

1.5 kg/3 lb chicken
50 g/2 oz/½ stick butter
1 tbsp oil
2 tbsp cognac
2 shallots (or small mild onion), peeled and finely chopped
300 ml/½ pt/1¼ cups Riesling d'Alsace
150 ml/¼ pt/⅔ cup double cream (whipping cream)
100 g/¼ lb fresh mushrooms, sliced
Salt
Freshly ground black pepper
Freshly chopped parsley

Cut chicken into 8 pieces and fry in butter and oil until golden. Pour cognac into a ladle, warm, then set alight with a match. Pour flaming cognac over chicken; the flames will die down in a minute. Remove chicken pieces from pan and set aside. Add the shallots to pan juices, and fry gently for 1 min. Add wine, cream, mushrooms, salt, and black pepper. Stir until sauce is smooth, then return chicken pieces to pan. Cover and

cook over a low heat for about 45 min., until tender. Remove the lid and cook for another 10 min. until sauce is reduced. Adjust seasoning, and decorate with chopped parsley.

Serve with buttered noodles.

Suggested wine:
Riesling d'Alsace

Bäckeofe

Alsatian Meat and Potato Stew
Serves 6

350 g/¾ lb shoulder of pork
350 g/¾ lb boneless lamb shoulder
500 g/1 lb chuck steak
300 ml/½ pt/1¼ cups Alsatian dry white wine (Edelzwicker, Pinot Blanc)
2 bay leaves
1 bouquet garni
1 sprig of thyme (or ½ tsp dried thyme)
Salt
Freshly ground black pepper
2 garlic cloves, peeled and chopped
250 g/½ lb onions, peeled and thinly sliced
750 g/1½ lb potatoes, peeled and sliced

Cut meat into 5 cm/2 in cubes and put into a large bowl. Pour over wine and seasonings, and leave to marinate overnight.

Grease a large casserole and make alternate layers of onions, potatoes, and meats. Pour marinade over the top. Cover and cook in a preheated oven, 180°C/Gas Mark 4/350°F, for about 2 hr. or until tender.

Serve piping hot, with a salad and French bread.

Suggested wine:
Tokay d'Alsace

Choucroute Alsacienne

Sauerkraut and Braised Meats

Braised sauerkraut may be used as a bed for all kinds of sausages, smoked ham, and pork. The meats can be either cooked separately and served on the sauerkraut or braised with the sauerkraut in a large casserole. This dish is informal, so use ingredients that are available in quantities and proportions that appeal.

Serves 6

2 kg/4 lb sauerkraut (tinned can be used)
75 g/3 oz/6 tbsp pork, duck, or goose fat, or butter
1 large onion, peeled and finely chopped
8 juniper berries, crushed
5 rashers/slices of bacon, cut into small pieces
1 bay leaf
Salt
6 black peppercorns
1 tbsp caraway seeds
300 ml/½ pt/1¼ cups stock
150 ml/¼ pt/⅔ cup Sylvaner

Suggestions for meats:
4 smoked pork chops
2 ham knuckles
Frankfurters, Knockwurst, black pudding, and other German-style sausages

Rinse sauerkraut well under running cold water. Drain and squeeze out most of the water. Melt fat in a large casserole. Cook onion and bacon for about 10 min. Stir in sauerkraut, making sure it is well coated with fat. Add ham knuckles and any of the other meats that take a long time to cook. Add seasonings, stock, and wine. Bring slowly to the boil, cover, and simmer for a total of 3 hr. Add pork chops and sausages about 45 min. before sauerkraut is fully cooked.

Transfer sauerkraut to a large, warmed platter. Place cooked meats on top of this bed, and serve with boiled potatoes garnished with chopped parsley and butter.

Suggested wine:
Tokay d'Alsace or Sylvaner d'Alsace

Kugelhopf

Raisin and Almond Cake

Kugelhopf is the name of the distinctive earthenware mould used for this favourite Alsatian cake. Moulds can be bought in some shops selling French kitchenware.

To fill a 20 cm/8 in mould

150 ml/¼ pt/⅔ cup milk
25 g/1 oz dried yeast
175 g/6 oz/¾ cup butter
600 g/1¼ lb/4½ cups flour
Salt
2 eggs
75 g/3 oz/3 tbsp castor sugar
200 g/5 oz/1 cup sultanas soaked in kirsch
About 1 dozen whole blanched almonds
Icing (powdered) sugar

Warm the milk gently. Add yeast and butter to milk and mix well. Sieve flour into a large mixing bowl, and add salt, eggs, and sugar. Combine them and slowly add the warmed milk, butter, and yeast. Knead well for about 20 min. until the mixture no longer sticks to the sides of the bowl. The dough should be moist but not wet. Cover the bowl with a damp cloth, and leave in a warm place for about 1 hr.

Knead again, then add and work in the sultanas soaked in kirsch. Butter the mould well, and decorate inside with almonds. Pile dough into mould. Again, leave in a warm place until dough has risen to the top, 1 hr. or so. Bake in a pre-heated oven, 180°C/Gas Mark 4/350°F, for about 1 hr. Push a knife into the dough, and if it comes out clean the *Kugelhopf* is ready.

If it browns too quickly, cover with a sheet of greaseproof paper or silver foil. Turn out of mould, dust with icing sugar, and serve hot or cold.

Suggested drink:
Muscat d'Alsace (or eau-de-vie d'Alsace)

Kugelhopf and eau-de-vie; a typical Alsatian breakfast.

Tarte aux Pommes Alsacienne
Apple Tart

23 cm/9 in flan tin lined with half-baked pâte
brisée *(see recipe)*
1 kg/2 lb firm, sweet apples
1 tsp lemon juice
4 tbsp sugar
150 ml/$\frac{1}{4}$ pt/$\frac{2}{3}$ cup milk
150 ml/$\frac{1}{4}$ pt/$\frac{2}{3}$ cup cream
2 eggs
1 tsp vanilla essence

Peel and core apples, and slice them each into
about 8 pieces. Arrange them in the partially
baked pastry case in overlapping circles. Sprinkle
with lemon juice and half of the sugar. Bake in a
hot oven, 240°C/Gas Mark 8/450°F, for about 25
min. Meanwhile beat eggs and remaining sugar
together. Slowly add milk, cream, and vanilla
essence. When apples are slightly tender, pour
the mixture over them, and cook until set—about
another 10 min.

Serve warm, sprinkled with a little sugar.

Suggested wine:
Gewurztraminer (vendange tardive)

BORDEAUX

South-west France: vast stretches of unspoiled and windswept sand-dunes, and mile after mile of beaches and Atlantic coastline fenced off by protective barriers of pine trees; Basque country and the Pyrenees; the Dordogne, extending as far east as the Massif Central—rugged, rustic, yet naturally rich and luxuriant. And in the centre of it all, Bordeaux, and the famous region known as the Gironde which surrounds France's fourth largest city. To the west and north of Bordeaux are the gravelly slopes of Graves and the Médoc. To the south are wine communes such as Sauternes and Barsac, as well as lands between the Garonne and Dordogne rivers (literally *entre deux mers*), and those on the right bank of the Dordogne, around St Emilion and Pomerol.

This is rich, satisfying country. Bordeaux has the cosmopolitan *élan* of a city aware of its own worth. The allées de Tourny and the Cours de l'Intendance are at once fashionable, chic, and nostalgic; here, the shops with their grand eighteenth-century façades are as expensive and sophisticated as those in Paris. Elsewhere, too, in Pauillac, St Julien, or Margaux, in Sauternes or in St Emilion, the grand and even not-so-grand châteaux of wine producers, and rows upon rows of vines that seem almost to have received personal and loving manicures, exude an air of self-importance, of near-smugness. Even modest farmhouses have that indefinable sense of well-fed prosperity that is apparent in the look of the chickens pecking and scratching in the courtyard; in the well-tended beds of roses standing bright against stolid, stone-grey walls; in the fact that there is always smoke rising briskly from chimneys on autumn and winter days; or in irresistible aromas emanating from country kitchens.

Rich and self-satisfied though this region is, it is at the same time generous and remarkably welcoming. Even the most famous wine châteaux take time off to welcome casual visitors and strangers. Samples of fine wine are offered to people who might never otherwise be able to taste such wines. And in small wine towns, in Bordeaux itself, or in coastal resorts or isolated villages deep in inland forests, the dinner table may be set, but there is always room for one more, friend or stranger alike. Here, truly, there is plenty for all. The sand and pine stretches of the Landes contribute *foie gras* (fattened goose liver) and *confit d'oie* and *canard* (cooked goose or duck preserved in its own rendered fat). Goose fat is the favoured cooking oil, and adds its characteristic flavour to all food prepared with it. *Huîtres* (oysters) are farmed in the Arcachon basin, while the Atlantic yields mussels, scallops, shellfish, and other seafood. Black truffles and wild edible mushrooms come from the Dordogne, while raw *jambon de Bayonne* and a taste for piquant foods come from the Basque country to the south. Simply cooked beef and lamb satisfy workers, businessmen, and wine merchants alike, while salt-water fish and lampreys from the Gironde (the wide north-flowing estuary that forms when the Garonne and Dordogne meet north of Bordeaux) are as popular as freshwater trout, salmon, and shad from the region's many rivers. And, of course, in this biggest quality-vineyard in the world, there is never a shortage of wine.

That is not to say, however, that one opens a bottle of Château Latour or Lafite whenever the mood strikes. It is not only a matter of money (or, for most of us, the lack of it), but also a question of attitude, for such great wines deserve to be drunk only on special occasions, when they will be appreciated and remembered for having contributed to a memorable time. Indeed, it is reassuring to realize that, great though the wines of Bordeaux are, the everyday wines drunk here are rather more modest. Bordeaux is a great wine region in this sense, too, for she also produces vast amounts of reliable table wines that are relatively inexpensive. And finally, Bordeaux is a great wine region because of her remarkable versatility. Not only are some of the finest,

longest-lived, and most complex red wines in the world produced in the Haut-Médoc, St Emilion, Graves, and Pomerol; not only are solid everyday red and white table wines produced throughout the region; in addition, this relatively compact area offers those precise conditions required to produce some of the most unctuous, richly textured, and greatest sweet wines in the world, in the communes of Sauternes and Barsac, among others.

Wine, in the Gironde, is clearly a way of life, not least of all because so many here earn their livelihood from it. Indeed, it has probably been so since Roman days at least. As early as the first century AD wine from Bordeaux was exported to other parts of Europe; gradually the strategic port increased in importance as a centre for trade. When, in 1152, young Henry Plantagenet married Eleanor of Aquitaine (Aquitania, meaning land of waters, was the Roman name for the region) a peculiarly fond relationship between the British and the *bordelais* was forged which continues even today. For, just two years after the marriage, Henry was crowned King of England, and thus the prized vineyards of Bordeaux became British possessions. Soon the Englishman's beloved claret (which simply means red Bordeaux wine) was flowing into English ports. Though Aquitaine was subsequently lost in 1453, a love affair was firmly and unquestionably established.

Claret is loved today throughout the world, and judged by many to be the greatest, most complex, or challenging of all wines. Because of its great reputation, however, it can also appear

Château Margaux, home of a great wine.

Tending the vines in winter is an essential part of the year's work.

over-complicated and unapproachable. It is important, therefore, to understand in some fashion the way wines in Bordeaux are named and labelled.

Many bear château names, but it is always important to discern the *appellation d'origine contrôlée* to which each wine is entitled. The commonest is simply Bordeaux. Bordeaux *supérieur* refers to wine that is marginally stronger in alcohol. These general names can apply to wine produced from grapes grown throughout the approved Bordeaux region, although they must still be produced from approved grape varieties following strict rules of production. These rules include density of planting, pruning of vines, maximum yield, and minimum alcoholic strength. The next step up the ladder are wines produced within a specific but broad region, such as the Médoc, for example, which is a large area north of Bordeaux, or Entre-Deux-Mers, an area that lies between the Dordogne and Garonne rivers. Within these large but specific geographical areas, there can be further sub-divisions. The Haut-Médoc, for example (that part of the peninsula closest to Bordeaux), is superior to the upper section closer to the Atlantic; thus a bottle of wine with the *appellation* Haut-Médoc, as opposed to simply

Médoc, can generally be assumed to be the better one. Better still is a more specific *appellation* within the Haut-Médoc, pinpointing the commune from which a particular wine comes: Margaux, St Estèphe, Pauillac, St Julien, Listrac, or Moulis. And finally, there are individual vineyards within each specific commune that produce the best (or at least the most expensive) wines of all. The system basically works on the principal that the better the wine, the more exactly its origins are both pinpointed and recognizable in the character of the wine itself.

Naturally, not all bottles bearing a château name are as good as others. The word itself implies a certain grandness, but in fact, many 'châteaux' are no more than modest farmhouses. Nevertheless, the fact that a wine is château-bottled (*mis en bouteilles au château*) is a guarantee of quality and authenticity. Moreover, the best wines will bear specific *appellations* (Pauillac or Pomerol, for example) rather than broad ones. Additionally, there are important classifications which recognize an accepted hierarchy of superior wines. No overall classification covers all the wines of Bordeaux, but individual classifications for certain regions are important.

The assumption behind the classification of 1855 (the most important and famous: it classified the red wines of the Médoc, one red Graves, and the white wines of Sauternes) was that higher prices consistently paid for wines are an indirect but generally true indication of superior wine. Thus, an important list of fine wines was established that, with some variations, still stands today. When someone speaks of a 'classed growth claret' (*cru classé*) he is probably referring to a wine on this list. Five levels of superiority were then given, from *cinquième cru* (fifth growth) to *premier cru* (first growth). All sixty or so wines on this list can be considered fine or very good wines, though there are of course variations in quality of even the best, from year to year. Today there are five *premier cru* clarets: four from the Médoc (Château Lafite-Rothschild, Château Margaux, Château Latour, and Château Mouton-Rothschild) and one from Graves (Château Haut Brion).

The classification of Sauterne was drawn up

Oyster beds in the Arcachon basin.

at the same time. It placed the famous Château d'Yquem in a class of its own, *grand premier cru*, while other consistently excellent wines were designated *premiers crus*. The best wines of St Emilion were similarly classified in 1955 into a two-tier hierarchy of *premier grand cru classé* and *grand cru classé*. On the other hand, the wines of Pomerol, arguably as fine as any in Bordeaux, have never been classified. And in the Médoc, to confuse matters even more, some wines that were not classified in 1855, but are consistently good, have been designated *bourgeois crus classés*. These are sub-classified further into *crus exceptionnels, grands bourgeois*, and *crus bourgeois*.

This complex grading of wines may at first seem baffling, but a certain knowledge of such classifications is rewarding. For one thing, these names may be encountered on wine labels, and it is beneficial to know what they mean in order to know what one is paying for. They also serve as

Oyster stands in the Gironde are as common as newspaper kiosks elsewhere.

Shucking oysters calls for a strong knife and stronger hands.

So simple yet so delicious – raw oysters and chilled Entre-Deux-Mers.

St Emilion, a town with a centuries-long tradition of producing fine claret.

points of reference, allowing fascinating comparisons to be made among wines of different communes and classes. It is precisely because so many great wines with distinct personalities are produced within this relatively compact region that the wines of Bordeaux are considered so challenging.

Drinking wine, however, is not simply an intellectual exercise, and Bordeaux wine, like any other, can be appreciated on a basic and satisfying level. Indeed, much Bordeaux wine is relatively uncomplicated, and should be accepted as such, void of fuss or pretension.

Red Bordeaux is produced primarily from the Cabernet Sauvignon, with some blending of the Cabernet Franc and the Merlot grapes. The Cabernet Sauvignon is a tough, firm, deep-purple grape that produces wine with a correspondingly tough and at first unforthcoming and aggressive character. The wine is high in tannin (a group of organic substances drawn from the skin, pips, and stalk of the grapes) and though this is a necessary component for long bottle-ageing, it at first appears unattractive and mouth-puckering. It softens with age, however, and at the same time allows great wines to develop subtle nuances in bouquet and flavour. Some producers blend a higher proportion of Merlot and Cabernet Franc in their wines, since these grapes (particularly Merlot) are somewhat softer in temperament. It is partly for this reason, for example, that the red wines of Pomerol and St Emilion are generally more immediately forthcoming and perhaps easier to appreciate than the great wines of the Haut-Médoc. Simple red Bordeaux, however, does not need years of bottle-ageing. Even in youth it is a balanced, bracing and fragrant table wine; honest, straightforward, and warm—the sort of drink that enhances a simple meal without dominating food or company.

Likewise, the dry white wines of Entre-Deux-Mers, Graves (which produces both red and white wines), or Bourg and Blaye (which both also produce red and white), are made customarily from the Sauvignon and Semillon grapes, and have a character that is at once crisp, firm, fresh, and immediately appealing. Though there are some eight *crus classés* dry white Graves,

the dry white wines of Bordeaux do not generally reach the levels of greatness or complexity the finest red wines of the region attain. Still even the humblest Bordeaux *blanc* or Entre-Deux-Mers is reliable—a balanced partner to a feast of shellfish, fresh river trout, or salmon.

Though the great wines of Sauternes are produced painstakingly and in minute quantity, there are also large amounts of simple sweet white Bordeaux, which if lacking the elegance, concentration, or balance of the greatest wines, are nevertheless relatively inexpensive and plentiful. They suit many as an after-dinner drink, with dessert or nuts.

On first glance, at least, wine seems to overshadow everything in this famous land of Bacchus. If the vineyards and châteaux dominate, the kitchens are not intimidated; neither are they in competition. Food is straightforward and direct, and, like the simpler table wines of Bordeaux, does its job of satisfying the appetites of hungry men and women without unnecessary embellishment.

Shallots are the distinctive flavouring of the region. Richer and livelier than onions, more subtle than garlic, they add their unique aroma to sauces, stews, or, when chopped raw, to salads and *crudités*. Meals often begin with a grand selection of *crudités*. This might consist of coarsely chopped beetroot served with oil and finely chopped shallots; quartered button mushrooms in a thick herbal tomato sauce; avocado with vinegar and oil; grated carrot and celeriac; sliced tomatoes; tiny shrimps; little black sea snails; and slabs of rich, coarse, home-made pâté. The sauces and dressing are scooped up with crusty fresh bread, fetched twice daily at least, from the local *boulangerie*.

Hearty soups such as *tourin*, onion soup enriched with egg yolks, or, along the Atlantic, smooth rich fish broths, might be served next. Oysters from Arcachon are a perennial favourite, eaten raw by the dozen, or else served chilled with piquant little sausages, *lou kencous*. *Moules à la bassin*, that is, mussels steamed in wine and shallots, then eaten like soup, are equally popular. And both are excellent washed down with bottles of Entre-Deux-Mers or cold, white Graves.

Wine, of course, finds its way into the cooking pot. *Escargots bordelaises* are plump snails stewed in a characteristic sauce of chopped pork, shallots, and red wine. Wine flavours the local *daube*, which is a casserole of beef cooked in goose fat. And in St Emilion a favourite delicacy is lamprey from the Gironde stewed in red wine flavoured with leeks, shallots, and wild mushrooms. It is an expensive speciality, but well worth seeking when in the area.

The great wines of Bordeaux require nothing more to show off their essential quality and character than simple food such as rare roast beef. Even the lesser red wines of Bordeaux taste best with uncomplicated foods. *Entrecôte aux sarments*, for example, is a favourite *bordelais* dish, consisting of no more than a good quality entrecôte steak grilled over a fire made of pruned vine shoots. This imparts a distinctive but delicate flavour to the meat. A simple garnish of chopped shallots and butter is all that is required, although often the steak is served *à la bordelaise*, that is, with a sauce made from shallots, bone marrow, and red wine. Fish such as *alose* (shad) are placed between a moist blanket of vine or laurel leaves then cooked over red-hot embers of a fire made of vine shoots, then served simply with a sauce of oil and tarragon vinegar. Lamb from the salt marshes of the Médoc is another classic, prepared with equal simplicity. Roasted with fresh new vegetables, and served rare, it is ideal with the great wines of Pauillac or St Julien, the subtle and fragrant flavour of the lamb unmasking further delicacies in them.

The nearby forests of the Landes to the west and the Dordogne to the east yield a variety of game. Particularly favoured are small birds such as quail, lark, woodcock, and squab, which are roasted until crisp and crunchy (the smaller varieties can be eaten bones and all), or else made into delectable pâtés, terrines, or casseroles. The breast meat of wild duck is often carved into large, thick slabs, grilled like steak, and eaten just as rare. Fat geese, of course, are also raised throughout this south-west region, prized for their rich liver and fat as well as their succulent meat. *Foie gras d'oie* or *canard* (goose or duck liver) is rich and luscious enough to be served with a really fine sweet Sauterne. The forests of the Landes and Dordogne also yield a valuable harvest of wild mushrooms and truffles. Wild mushrooms such as *cèpes* (a large-capped, strong flavoured variety, known as *boletus edulis*) are an excellent addition to stews and sauces (they can be bought dried to be used as a flavouring), and are also delicious served as *cèpes à la bordelaise*, that is, simmered in butter, shallots, lemon juice, and parsley. Truffles are often used to infuse their pungent aroma into the rich, smoothly-textured liver of duck or geese.

After the main meal, cheese, which goes so well with fine wines, fruit, or a cleansing sorbet (generally fruit-flavoured) is all that is required, although in St Emilion a platter of delicious almond macaroons might be passed with the sweet wine. Indeed, such wines are virtually desserts in themselves. The finest wines of Sauternes and Barsac are made only in certain years when the natural conditions of misty mornings combined with dry, hot afternoons encourage the formation of a rare and desirable fungus known as *botrytis cinerea* (also termed *pourriture noble*, or noble rot) which attacks both the inside and the skin of the Semillon grape, causing it to shrivel and thus concentrate its sugar content. But since this rot does not develop evenly, the vineyards have to be combed over several times during the harvest, so that affected grapes can be harvested literally one by one. As a result, the harvest can last a month, six weeks, or even longer. Naturally these shrivelled grapes have lost a considerable amount of juice, and so make only minute amounts of wine—in fact, each vine in a first-class vineyard is said to produce only a single glass of wine. Yet what wine. Golden, powerful, and mellow, its fine balance of alcohol and residual sweetness (the sugar remaining in the wine) brings a joyous feeling of euphoria, excitement, and awe that such marvellous, compact nectar can be made from plants and by the skill of man.

When such wines come forth, the region of Bordeaux can afford to feel smug and self-important. Secure in the knowledge of her worth, however, she shares without stinting her more accessible riches—abundant table wines and food—nourishing, direct, and without artifice.

RECIPES FROM THE BORDEAUX REGION

Quantities where necessary are given in
Metric, Imperial and US measurements.

Moules à la Bassin

Mussels Steamed in Wine
Serves 4

2.4 l/4 pt mussels
300 ml/ $\frac{1}{2}$ pt/1 $\frac{1}{4}$ cups dry white wine
2 shallots, peeled and finely chopped
1 large onion, peeled and finely chopped
75 g/3 oz/ $\frac{3}{4}$ stick butter
Freshly chopped parsley
Salt
Freshly ground black pepper
1 bay leaf

Scrape and scrub the mussels under running water. Remove the beards. Put into a large bucket of cold water, add a handful of bran, and leave overnight.

Wash mussels well. In a large saucepan add wine, shallots, onion, butter, parsley, and seasonings. Cook briskly for 5–10 min. to reduce liquid. Throw in all the mussels. Cover and cook for 5–10 min. Occasionally shake pan from side to side so mussels cook evenly. (They are cooked when their shells open.) Ladle mussels and the liquid into large soup bowls, discarding any that have not opened.

Serve with plenty of French bread to mop up the cooking liquid.

Suggested wines:
Entre-Deux-Mers, Graves (white)

Tourin

Onion Soup
Serves 6

1 kg/2 lb onions, peeled and finely sliced into rings
1 garlic clove, peeled and chopped
75 g/3 oz/ $\frac{3}{4}$ stick butter
1 tbsp flour
1.8 l/3 pt/7 $\frac{1}{2}$ cups boiling water
Salt
Freshly ground black pepper
3 egg yolks, beaten
French bread, cut into rounds

Melt butter in a large heavy-bottomed saucepan, and sauté garlic and onions until they begin to soften. Season, cover, and cook for 40 min. over a very low heat.

Add flour, and stir in well. Pour on boiling water and simmer for 20 min. Remove a ladleful of liquid and mix with beaten eggs. Return this to the soup, and cook for a further 10 min. without boiling.

Meanwhile bake slices of French bread in the oven. Place one slice in each bowl, and pour on the onion soup.

Suggested wines:
Bordeaux blanc, Entre-Deux-Mers

Escargots Bordelaise

Snails in Bordelaise Sauce
Serves 4–6

4 doz tinned snails
2 tbsp olive oil
1 large onion, peeled and finely chopped
2 garlic cloves, peeled and crushed
250 g/8 oz/$\frac{1}{2}$ lb pork, coarsely minced (ground)
100 g/4 oz/$\frac{1}{4}$ lb smoked bacon or ham, diced
300 ml/$\frac{1}{2}$ pt/1$\frac{1}{4}$ cups dry white wine
3 tbsp tomato purée (paste)
300 ml/$\frac{1}{2}$ pt/1$\frac{1}{4}$ cups water
Salt
Freshly ground black pepper
Freshly chopped parsley

Rinse snails and their shells thoroughly, and set aside. In a large saucepan, sauté onion and garlic until soft and golden. Add minced pork, bacon, and white wine. Add tomato purée and water. Season, cover, and simmer for 1 hr.

Stuff each shell with a snail, and add to saucepan. Cover and simmer for further 1 hr.

Serve hot in a tureen, decorated with parsley.

Suggested wines:
Bordeaux rouge, Médoc, St Emilion

Cèpes à la Bordelaise

Sautéd Mushrooms
Serves 4

350 g/12 oz/$\frac{3}{4}$ lb fresh large mushrooms
1 tbsp olive oil
2 tbsp butter
Salt
Freshly ground black pepper
3 garlic cloves, peeled and finely chopped
3 shallots, peeled and finely chopped
2 tbsp fine white dry breadcrumbs
2 tbsp lemon juice
Freshly chopped parsley

Remove stalks from mushrooms, and chop them coarsely. Melt butter and oil in a frying pan, and sauté mushroom caps until lightly browned. Season. Stir in chopped stalks, garlic, shallots, and breadcrumbs. Toss well, and cook for about 3 min. Add lemon juice, sprinkle with parsley, and serve immediately, as an hors-d'oeuvre.

Suggested wines:
Côtes de Bourg, Canon Fronsac

Rognons à la Bordelaise

Kidneys with Red Wine and Mushrooms
Serves 4

3 veal (or 8 lambs') kidneys, prepared and cleaned
1 tbsp olive oil
2 shallots, peeled and finely chopped
150 ml/$\frac{1}{4}$ pt/$\frac{2}{3}$ cup red wine
Pinch of thyme
Pinch of marjoram
1 bay leaf
Salt
Freshly ground black pepper
100 g/4 oz/$\frac{1}{4}$ lb fresh mushrooms, sliced
4 tbsp butter
2 tbsp tomato purée (paste)
150 ml/$\frac{1}{4}$ pt/$\frac{2}{3}$ cup stock
Freshly chopped parsley

Cut kidneys into 1 cm/$\frac{1}{2}$ in cubes. Drop them into boiling water, and cook for 2 min. Drain and set aside.

In a large saucepan, sauté shallots in oil. Add wine, bring to the boil and reduce by one-third. Add thyme, marjoram, bay leaf, salt and pepper.

Meanwhile sauté mushrooms in one-third of the butter. Add tomato purée and stock. Blend until smooth. Add reduced wine mixture to mushrooms and stock. Simmer to reduce.

In a frying pan, sauté kidneys in remaining butter over a brisk heat for 5 min. Add to sauce, and cook for further 5 min. or until tender. Sprinkle with parsley, and serve immediately, with boiled rice.

Suggested wines:
Bordeaux supérieur, Médoc, Graves (red)

Gigot d'Agneau Médocaine

Roast Leg of Lamb with Spring Vegetables
Serves 6–8

2–2½ kg/4–5 lb leg of lamb
2 garlic cloves, peeled and cut into slivers
1 tbsp goose fat or lard
Salt
Freshly ground black pepper
4 shallots, peeled and finely chopped
3–4 legs of celery, finely chopped
1 glass of red wine
500 g/1 lb baby carrots, peeled and left whole
500 g/1 lb baby onions, peeled and left whole
500 g/1 lb peas
300 ml/½ pt/1¼ cups beef or lamb stock

Make incisions in the lamb and insert garlic slivers. Rub with goose fat or lard, and season well with salt and pepper.

Pre-heat oven to 240°C/Gas Mark 8/450°F. In a large casserole or roasting tin, make a bed of shallots and celery, and place lamb on it. Roast for 15–20 min. to brown. Lower heat to 180°C/Gas Mark 4/350°F. Arrange baby carrots and onions around lamb, and add wine. Continue to to roast for 1–1½ hr. or until juices run pink, not red, when pricked with a fork. Add peas 20 min. before cooking time.

Remove lamb and vegetables to a warmed serving platter, and keep warm. Drain off excess fat from roasting tin. Pour in stock, and bring to boil, stirring with a wooden spoon to scrape up pan juices. Adjust seasoning.

Serve lamb and vegetables hot, with gravy in a separate dish.

Suggested wines:
Haut-Médoc, Pauillac, St Julien, Margaux

Entrecôte à la Bordelaise

Steak with Bordelaise Sauce
Serves 4

4 entrecôtes (rump or fillet), 250 g/8 oz/½ lb each
3 tbsp olive oil
Salt
Freshly ground black pepper
4 shallots, peeled and finely chopped
150 ml/¼ pt/⅔ cup red wine
2 tbsp beef marrow, soaked in water for 2 hr.
Freshly chopped parsley

Marinate entrecôtes in half of the oil, salt, and black pepper for 1 hr. Heat remaining oil in a frying pan, and sauté steaks for 3–5 min. on each side, depending on thickness of steaks and desired degree of rareness. Transfer to a warmed serving dish, and set aside. Add shallots to pan juices, and sauté gently. Add red wine, beef marrow, and parsley. Reduce by half and pour over entrecôtes. Serve immediately.

Suggested wines:
Pomerol, St Emilion

Macarons de St Emilion

Macaroons
Makes about 20

250 g/8 oz/1⅓ cups ground almonds
250 g/8 oz/1⅐ cups sugar
1 tsp vanilla essence
4 egg whites, well beaten

Mix almonds and sugar together in a large bowl. Add vanilla essence, and fold in egg whites.

Line a baking sheet with plain white paper. Drop small balls of mixture from a spoon on to sheet. Bake in a pre-heated moderate oven, 180°C/Gas Mark 4/350°F, for 15–20 min. Remove and set aside to cool (they will harden as they do so). Turn them over, and moisten back of paper with a damp cloth to peel off cleanly.

Suggested wines:
Sauterne, Barsac

Delivering the morning post in Chablis.

BURGUNDY

Nuits-St-Georges, Gevrey-Chambertin, Vosne-Romanée, Meursault, Puligny-Montrachet—the names alone of the towns of Burgundy are enough to send thrills through wine lovers the world over. Likewise, the cuisine of this rich and plentiful land is regarded as one of the finest in Europe, a harmonious partner to her wines. The people celebrate this happy union of riches with gastronomic festivals to rival those of ancient Rome. But despite her grand gastronomic reputation, and the renown of her magnificent wines, Burgundy remains essentially down-to-earth, modest, and approachable.

The region is large and varied, located in eastern France on the crossroads to Switzerland and Italy, between Paris and sun-drenched Provence. Dijon is its largest city and its historical centre, home of the powerful Dukes of Valois, who in the fourteenth and fifteenth centuries oversaw a Burgundian empire that extended as far as Belgium and the Netherlands. Yet beside this bustling, modern city, the rest of Burgundy —from medieval Auxerre to Beaune, capital of the wine trade, from busy little Chablis to the rugged hills of Beaujolais—seems wonderfully, curiously provincial.

Her celebrated cuisine is not sophisticated; its essence, in fact, is simplicity—and it is simply delicious. Like all great regional cooking, it is an outgrowth of practical considerations. *Boeuf bourguignon* is basically peasant fare, meat stewed in red wine, a method of cooking that rejuvenates a rather tough old piece of beef. And *coq au vin* (sometimes pretentiously called *coq au Chambertin*, but who would dare use that great wine for cooking?) was originally created to make use of the old hen that stopped laying eggs. Most wine

districts throughout Europe have a version of this ubiquitous dish, though nowhere is it more delicious than here, served in a dark red wine sauce, garnished with salt pork or bacon, button mushrooms, and baby onions.

The wines of Burgundy, similarly, do not intimidate. Of course, some of the greatest white and red wines in the world are produced here: wines such as Le Montrachet, Chambertin, Romanée-Conti, in short, the richest, warmest, deepest, or most highly scented wines in France—and the most expensive. These greatest wines come from vineyards within the Côte d'Or, that fabled, slender, golden strip of land in which are found Burgundy's most famous wine communes. But Burgundy is a great wine region not only because she produces this élite class of wines, but because she also offers a wide variety to suit every taste, and accessible to all.

Who, for example, has not encountered youthful, fruity Beaujolais? Indeed, when drunk as *primeur* (within just weeks of the Gamay grapes having been harvested) it is the teeth-staining essence of wine at its most basic: purple, grapy, and gulpable. Longer-lasting, deeper examples known as Beaujolais-Villages come from certain communes within the region, such as Brouilly, Chénas, Chiroubles, Fleurie, Morgon, Moulin-à-Vent, and St-Amour. Excellent red and white wines come from the Mâconnais and Chalonnais, such as Pouilly-Fuissé, Pouilly-Vinzelles, St-Véran, Givry, Mercurey, or simple Mâcon *rouge* or *blanc*—wines that share family characteristics of the greater wines of the Côte d'Or, but not their price. North-west of Dijon, apart from the rest of the region, lies the tiny 'wine island' around the town of Chablis. Who would think that this modest, self-contained, and rather unexceptional French provincial town has lent its name to probably the most imitated wine in the world? The real product, of course, is unique, for the Chardonnay, the great white grape of Burgundy, (if it survives the severe frosts that are the hazard of this northern vineyard) produces exceptionally fresh, crisp, racy wine. Though youthful, glinting styles of Chablis are often sought, one should be aware that older, straw-coloured wine from a hot year and a prime vineyard gains a character at once

lusher, deeper, and more mellow. Finally, on a more basic level, there are the warm, bluff, honest wines known simply as Bourgogne and Bourgogne Grand Ordinaire. There is Bourgogne Passe-Tout-Grains, which is red wine made from a mixture of Gamay, favoured grape of Beaujolais, and Pinot Noir, that aristocrat that produces the finest red wines of Burgundy. And there is Bourgogne Aligoté, an inexpensive white wine made from the Aligoté rather than the Chardonnay, which is ideal on picnics, or which, when mixed with Crème de Cassis (a blackcurrant liqueur made in Dijon) becomes the region's favoured *apéritif*, called kir.

When Caesar conquered this region in the first century BC it was absorbed into Transalpine Gaul and became an important link in the trade route between Paris, Autun, Troyes, and Rome. As in so many other great wine regions, it was the Romans who first established the vine

Anticipating lunch at a restaurant in Chablis.

here. A fierce Teutonic tribe, the Burgundii, gave their name to the region when they invaded it in 400 AD. By the ninth century, it had grown in prominence and prosperity and was part of Charlemagne's empire. Today the emperor is well remembered for his holdings in the commune of Aloxe-Corton through the great white wine named Corton-Charlemagne.

Another important wine-related development in the region came with the establishment of the great monastic orders at Cluny, Fontenay, Citeaux, and elsewhere. The monasteries prospered as rich lands were increasingly donated to them. The Cistercians, for example, were once sole owners of the prestigious Clos de Vougeot vineyards, and other valuable plots such as the Clos de Tart at Morey-St-Denis. Can we believe that the monks' spiritual devotion was always in keeping with their high level of devotion to viticulture? Throughout the Dark Ages, the Church not only kept alive wine-making traditions, it also made great advances in viticultural methods and techniques.

Burgundy is modest countryman's country. The point has to be stressed because so rich is this land in great wines, natural produce, and gastronomic traditions that one expects the region itself to be ostentatious, robed in finery like the scarlet and ermine livery of the members of the *Confrérie des Chevaliers du Tastevin*. This brotherhood of Burgundian wine lovers meets regularly at its headquarters in the great Cistercian Clos de Vougeot, an imposing château that stands surrounded by the valuable Pinot Noir vines of the Côte d'Or.

The greatest annual occasion here is the *Trois Glorieuses*, held in the third week in November. Described as the 'largest charity sale in the world', the main event is an auction of wines from vineyards of the Hospices de Beaune, a charitable hospital that also owns some of the finest plots of land in Burgundy. As well as being an important event for lovers of Burgundy the world over (since prices obtained for the wines of the Hospices are taken as an indication of price trends of Burgundy in general for that year), it is also an excuse for a great party which the whole region joins in enthusiastically. The cellars of the great and prestigious *négociant-éleveurs* in Beaune

open their doors to the public, and throughout the town wine flows freely. The *Chevaliers du Tastevin* hold a banquet at the Clos de Vougeot the night before the auction, while the day following it another important Burgundian event, known as *La Paulée*, takes place in Meursault. Originally this was a celebration feast given by the proprietors to the workers who helped during the harvest; today hundreds of proprietors, shippers, workers, and privileged visitors gather together to break bread and drink wine in true Burgundian fashion.

Burgundy is a region of abundant resources. From the Charolles comes what are probably the finest breed of cattle in France, the well-muscled white Charollais; so fine, so tender is its meat that simplicity is the style of its preparation— *entrecôte Charollais marchand du vin* or *maître d'hôtel* (grilled steaks garnished with either wine and shallot butter or parsley butter). Nearby Bresse offers the *poularde de Bresse*, chicken so succulent and tender that it only needs to be split in half and grilled over a fire of vine shoots to be thoroughly enjoyed. These chickens, it is claimed, have an *appellation d'origine contrôlée* as stringent as the finest wines in France.

The wide, lazy Saône river yields pike, perch, tench, and river eel—along with wine, ingredients for a delicious *pochouse*. The rugged forests of the Morvan are stocked with game of every variety, as well as less visible treasures such as truffles and wild mushrooms. The pork butchers of Burgundy are famous for *jambon persillé* (a wonderful terrine of coarsely chopped ham set in a green, wine-flavoured parsley and garlic gelatine), *boudin* (black pudding), *andouillettes* (tripe or chitterling sausage), *cervelas truffé* (pork sausage stuffed with truffles), *rosette* (sausage from Chalon flavoured with pimento and fresh mountain butter), and *jambon de Morvan* (raw dried ham).

In the valley of the Saône, asparagus and cauliflower grow in abundance. Cherries, cheese, and Chablis come from the Yonne, while Dijon has given the world her famous mustard (made from powdered mustard seed mixed with verjuice, which is juice from unripened grapes), Crème de Cassis, and *pain d'épices* (spiced gingerbread).

The gastronomic honours list is virtually endless. And when it comes to richness, how are we to explain why a narrow strip of land called the slope of gold—the Côte d'Or—is able to produce year after year, century after century, wines that have more colour and warmth, deeper and more subtle aroma and bouquet, fuller and more lingering flavour than arguably anywhere else on earth? From within this same narrow strip come not only great, satiny red wines from any number of famous wine communes, such as Gevrey-Chambertin, Morey-St-Denis, Nuits-St-Georges, Vosne-Romanée, Pommard, Volnay, but also from adjoining vineyards come some of the fullest and most compact and profound white wines produced anywhere —the wines of Meursault, Puligny-Montrachet, Chassagne-Montrachet.

The great château of the Clos de Vougeot seen within
the perspective of its surrounding vineyards.

A summer idyll in the town of Fuissé.

The characteristic pungent orange rind of
Epoisses, one of the great cheeses of Burgundy.

In Dijon, mustard (as everything in
Burgundy) comes elegantly dressed.

Many of these famous communes have hyphenated the name of their most famous vineyard to the name of the commune itself. Thus, there is a world of difference between wine from an individual vineyard such as Le Chambertin and wine from the commune of Gevrey-Chambertin. Indeed, wine from the communes (and even wine from individual vineyards) can often be produced by any number of proprietors or shippers, since after the French Revolution large land holdings, including those of the Church, were broken up and auctioned. This is not to imply that the land was then passed on to peasant farmers. Instead, vineyards were divided among many owners—a dominant feature of Burgundian viticulture. The fragmentation into multi-owners was in fact so thorough that few vineyards today are wholly owned or controlled by a single proprietor (those that are are called *monopoles*). The consequence of multi-ownership is important. In Bordeaux, for example, famous wines such as Château Latour or Château d'Yquem are unique, each the product of only one concern. In Burgundy, on the other hand, a well-known growth such as the Clos de Vougeot now has no less than fifty individual plot holders, all producing wine of varying styles and quality, yet all allowed quite legally to sell it under the same name.

Some growers vinify, mature, bottle, and market their own wines, and such *domaine*-bottled Burgundy is both prestigious and a mark of quality. But because many small growers do not have the capital necessary to ensure scrupulous cellar techniques, long maturation, and modern bottling, nor the marketing ability required to sell their product once it is ready to drink, an important role is played in Burgundy by the *négociant-éleveur*. There is no exact translation for the term, because the *négociant* is at once buyer, blender, shipper, and usually grower, too. His role, in the classic sense, is to buy wines from numerous individual producers, and then, in his own cellars (many of which are in Beaune, Nuits-St-Georges, or Mâcon), to nurture them to maturity, blending several of the same *appellation* (either generic, as in simple Burgundy or Mâcon; from a specific commune, as in Gevrey-Chambertin; or from an individual vineyard,

such as the Clos de Vougeot). The aim, ultimately, is to produce end-products that are more uniformly characteristic, of a consistently higher quality, and of a style particular to each house. The wines, in short, are 'elevated'. Thus, growers have been accommodated, and customers who gain familiarity with reliable firms are able to buy in good faith consistently high-quality wine.

As in the *assemblage* of wines, the Burgundian cook, too, can be said to be an *éleveur*. He or she, like the *négociant-éleveur*, begins with raw ingredients that are superior. But it is in the way these ingredients are put together that the essential Burgundian character is revealed.

An amusing story typifies this attitude. Once, long ago, the people of Burgundy found themselves ruled by such overbearing and selfish dukes that they were forced to send the best beef, plumpest Bresse chickens, and all the fish from the Saône, to the regal palace at Dijon. When they had nothing left to eat, they were reduced to gathering the huge snails that feed on the tender vine leaves in the fields. After they had cleaned and boiled the snails, however, they found this paltry diet rather tasteless. But such was the ingenuity of the Burgundian cook that—*voilà*—a sauce was invented, using parsley, shallots, garlic, and fresh butter, which was *formidable*. And so the wily people thrived on this protein-rich diet, rolling with laughter at the thought of what those stingy dukes in Dijon were missing.

Another example of Burgundian ingenuity is the pike *quenelle*. Pike is delicious, but a bony and uncomfortable fish to eat. Thus, the *quenelle* was invented, whereby the flesh of the fish is finely chopped, pounded, sieved, then mixed with *crème fraiche*, and stiffly beaten egg white, and finally poached in a rich stock. The result is ingenious: delicate, light, full of flavour—in short, pike without bones.

In Burgundy, the neat manicured vine seems to come to the very edge of the kitchen window itself. Indeed, food and wine here are in perfect harmony. For wine is not only a drink to accompany food, but also an essential ingredient in the kitchen. *Charollais au poivre* is an entrecôte or sirloin steak marinated in Beaujolais or Mâcon *rouge*, then pounded with coarsely crushed

The Serein river on its way through Chablis.

green, white, and black peppercorns, and pan-fried on a cast-iron griddle. *Jambon à Chablis* is a slab of pink ham cooked in and eaten with that elegant wine. *Jambon à la lie du vin* is another vintager's favourite: thick succulent ham cooked over the wine lees, which are the sediment left over in oak barrels after the wine has been racked (transferred to clean barrels). (The same effect, incidentally, can be achieved by cooking with the sediment thrown in any bottle of old red wine, or vintage or crusted port.) Even oxtail in Burgundy is stewed with grapes, and so becomes *queue de boeuf des vignerons*, a dish fit for a king —or a hungry field worker.

Finally, there are the cheeses and cheese dishes of Burgundy. Even modest wines taste better with cheese; the bigger wines of the Côte d'Or, or mature Beaujolais-Villages are elevated to higher glory. *Fromages des chèvres*, tiny, hard, dry goats' milk cheeses, are beautiful partnered with any full-bodied red Burgundy. Epoisses is an excellent and extremely pungent cheese with a striking shrivelled orange rind (a bacterial growth gives the rind its colour, while rubbing the cheese with marc de Bourgogne helps to draw out moisture, adds flavour—and keeps away the flies). St Florentin is another sharp, strong cheese, while Bleu de Bresse, creamy and blue-veined, is a delicious finish to a Burgundian feast. *Fromage à la crème*, a mixture of fresh curd cheese, sugar, and thick farmhouse cream is another favourite. One other cheese dish encountered everywhere in Burgundy is the *gougère*. There is nothing more delicious than to eat these light, puffy cheese balls straight from the oven with a brimming glass of Beaujolais.

It is this sort of pleasure—simple yet perfect— that epitomizes the character of Burgundy. For with such simplicity is life, like wine and food, 'elevated' to new heights.

RECIPES FROM BURGUNDY

Quantities where necessary are given in
Metric, Imperial and US measurements.

Gougères

Burgundian Cheese Puffs
Makes about 1 doz

300 ml/$\frac{1}{2}$ pt/$1\frac{1}{4}$ cups sterilized milk
50 g/2 oz/$\frac{1}{2}$ stick butter
1 tsp salt
Freshly ground black pepper
Pinch of cayenne pepper
Freshly grated nutmeg (to taste)
100 g/4 oz/1 cup flour
4 eggs
75 g/3 oz/1 cup Gruyère cheese, diced

If not using sterilized milk, bring to boil, and take off skin that forms. Otherwise, add butter in little pieces and bring to boil. Add seasonings, and continue to boil until milk and butter have blended together.

Reduce heat and add sifted flour all at once. Stir energetically with a wooden spatula until the paste comes away from sides of the pan.

Remove from heat, and add eggs, one at a time. Stir well after each addition, and make sure each is thoroughly incorporated before adding the next. Add diced cheese (reserving a few cubes), and mix well.

Butter a baking tray and arrange 1 tbsp of the paste at even intervals. Place reserved cheese on top of each mound, and brush with a little milk. Cook for about 45 min. in a moderate to hot oven, 190°C/Gas Mark 5/375°F, without opening the door.

Serve either piping hot or cold. (If served hot, prick to release steam.)

Suggested wine:
Beaujolais

Jambon Persillé

Ham in Parsleyed Gelatine
Serves 8

2 pigs' trotters, cleaned, split, and soaked for 24 hr.
1.2 l/2 pt/5 cups water or beef stock
300 ml/$\frac{1}{2}$ pt/$1\frac{1}{4}$ cups white Burgundy or other dry white wine
2 carrots, sliced
1 leek, cleaned and sliced
6 shallots, peeled and finely chopped
Salt
Freshly ground black pepper
750 g/$1\frac{1}{2}$ lb cooked ham, cut into uneven chunks
75 g/3 oz parsley, finely chopped
4 garlic cloves, peeled and finely chopped

Place pigs' trotters in a large saucepan. Add water or stock, wine, carrots, leek, 4 shallots, and seasoning. Bring to boil, then simmer for about $2\frac{1}{2}$ to 3 hr., or until meat is very tender. Allow to cool, remove pigs' trotters, and bone meat, making sure to remove tiny bones and gristle. Chop meat coarsely, and set aside with chopped ham.

Strain cooking liquid. There should now be about 600 ml/1 pt/$2\frac{1}{2}$ cups left (if more, then boil to reduce). Add chopped meats, parsley, garlic, and remaining shallots to cooking liquid and simmer for 5 min. Allow to cool for 30 min.

Spoon the mixture into a clean meatloaf or pâté tin. Press down well, and smooth surface. Cover with foil, and place in refrigerator to set. To turn out, place tin in a lukewarm bath for a moment to loosen aspic, and turn out on to a serving dish. Cut into slices, and serve with French bread as an hors-d'oeuvre.

Suggested wines:
Bourgogne Aligoté, Pouilly-Vinzelles, Mâcon blanc

Escargots à la Bourguignonne

Snails in Garlic Butter
Serves 4–6

2 tbsp freshly chopped parsley
3 garlic cloves, peeled and crushed
2 shallots, peeled and finely chopped
250 g/$\frac{1}{2}$ lb/2 sticks butter
Salt
Freshly ground black pepper
4 doz snails (tinned) and cleaned shells

Mix parsley with finely pounded and chopped garlic and chopped shallots. Work this into the

Jambon persillé and other Burgundian *charcuterie*.

butter with a fork, and season with salt and pepper. Chill in refrigerator.

Put a little knob of the seasoned butter in each shell. Add snail to each, then fill with more butter until crammed full. Put stuffed shells, with open ends facing up, in ovenproof dishes (better still, if you can get them, special plates designed for *escargots*). Cook in a fairly hot oven for 7–10 min.

Serve straight from oven, with fresh French bread to mop up the delicious juices.

(Many speciality shops sell snail tongs, forks, and dishes like those used in France.)

Suggested wines:
Bourgogne, Mâcon rouge, Hautes-Côtes de Nuits

Truites à la Dijonnaise

Trout in Dijon Mustard Sauce
Serves 4

25 g/1 oz/2 tbsp butter
2 tbsp oil
4 shallots, peeled and finely chopped
4 medium-sized trout, cleaned, scaled, and washed
150 ml/$\frac{1}{4}$ pt/$\frac{2}{3}$ cup white Burgundy
Salt
Freshly ground black pepper
2 tbsp Dijon mustard
3 tbsp fresh cream
Handful of chopped chives

Heat butter and oil in a large frying pan. Add shallots, and sauté until soft. Lay fish on top of shallots. Season, and add white wine. Slowly bring to boil, and simmer for about 20 min. turning fish once or twice. When they are tender but not soft, transfer them to a hot serving dish, and keep warm.

Stir pan juices over a high heat until they have reduced. Adjust seasoning, and add mustard and cream. Gently heat for a moment (do not boil). Pour over fish, and garnish with chives.

Suggested wines:
Chablis, Pouilly-Fuissé, Meursault

Charollais au Poivre

Peppered Steak
Serves 4

4 medium-sized fillet, rump, or sirloin steaks
2 tbsp mixed green, white, red, and black
peppercorns, crushed coarsely in a mortar
1 glass Beaujolais or other light red wine
50 g/2 oz/$\frac{1}{2}$ stick butter

Place steaks in a glass, earthenware, or enamelled bowl. Mix half of the coarsely crushed peppercorns in the wine, and pour over steaks. Allow to marinate for at least 30 min., preferably longer. Turn occasionally.

Drain steaks, and pat dry with paper towel. Reserve marinade. Rub and press remaining crushed peppercorns into steaks. Leave to stand another 30 min.

Put butter or oil in a large frying pan (use 2 if steaks are large). When butter foam begins to subside, add steaks to pan. Sauté them on both sides for between 3 to 5 min., depending on how you prefer the steaks, and how thick they are. Remove steaks to a hot dish, and keep warm.

Pour out any excess fat from frying pan. Add marinade liquid, and increase heat. Scrape juices with a wooden spoon, and boil liquid until it is almost a syrup. Pour over the steaks, and serve at once.

Suggested wines:
Bourgogne Passe-Tout-Grains, Beaujolais

La Queue de Boeuf des Vignerons

Oxtail cooked with Grapes
Serves 4–6

50 g/2 oz/$\frac{1}{2}$ stick butter
100 g/4 oz/$\frac{1}{4}$ lb bacon, diced
2 large onions, peeled and chopped
2 garlic cloves, peeled and chopped
6 carrots, diced
2 oxtails cut into short lengths
3 bay leaves

Sprig of fresh thyme
Handful freshly chopped parsley
Salt
Freshly ground black pepper
1 kg/2 lb white grapes, seeded and de-stalked

Melt butter in a large casserole. Add bacon, and fry gently. Add onions, garlic, and carrots. Cook over a low heat for 15 min.

Add oxtail and herbs. Season, cover, and cook over a low heat for 20 min.

Lightly crush grapes in a bowl, and add to casserole. Transfer to a very low oven, 140°C/Gas Mark 1/275°F, for 3–4 hr. (until meat almost falls off the bones). Skim fat from surface of sauce, and serve immediately from casserole.

Suggested wines:
Mercurey, Givry, Côte de Beaune

Boeuf Bourguignon

Beef Stewed in Burgundy
Serves 6

1 kg/2 lb topside, rump, or chuck, trimmed and cut into 2$\frac{1}{2}$ cm/1 in cubes
1 large onion, peeled and thinly sliced
2 carrots, sliced
Freshly chopped parsley
Sprig of thyme
2 bay leaves
Salt
Freshly ground black pepper
Half a bottle red Burgundy
2 tbsp olive oil
1 tbsp meat dripping or lard
5 rashers/slices streaky unsmoked bacon, cut into strips
16 small whole onions, peeled
2 tbsp flour
300 ml/$\frac{1}{2}$ pt/1$\frac{1}{4}$ cups beef stock
1 garlic clove, peeled and chopped
1 bouquet garni
250 g/$\frac{1}{2}$ lb button mushrooms

Marinate meat in a large bowl with onions, carrots, herbs, seasoning, red wine, and olive oil. Leave for about 12 hr. (more, if using a tougher cut of meat), turning occasionally.

Heat beef dripping in a large heavy casserole. Add bacon strips and whole onions. Keep heat low, and cook until brown. Remove, and set aside.

Drain meat from marinade, and dry with kitchen towel. Brown meat a few pieces at a time in the hot fat. Remove, and set aside, continuing until all meat is browned.

Add flour to the fat, and cook until it begins to turn colour. (It is essential to cook flour over a low heat for a longer time, because if it burns, it will spoil the stew, and if it is not cooked long enough, it will not add its distinctive flavour.)

Return meat to casserole, and pour over strained marinade. Allow to boil, then add stock, garlic and bouquet garni. Cover, and cook on top of stove for 2–3 hr. (depending on the quality of the meat).

Before the meat has finished cooking, return bacon, onions, and button mushrooms to casserole. Cook for an additional 30 min.

Serve garnished with chopped parsley.

Suggested wines:
Côte de Nuits-Villages, Nuits-St-Georges, Gevrey-Chambertin

Coq au Vin

Chicken in Red Wine
Serves 4

50 g/2 oz/$\frac{1}{2}$ stick butter
100 g/4 oz/$\frac{1}{4}$ lb bacon, chopped
20 baby onions
1–1.5 kg/2–3 lb chicken, cut into 8 pieces
Salt
Freshly ground black pepper
Small glass of brandy
Half a bottle of young red wine (Mâcon or Beaujolais)
300 ml/$\frac{1}{2}$ pt/1$\frac{1}{4}$ cups rich chicken stock
1 bouquet garni
2 garlic cloves, peeled and crushed
2 bay leaves
Sprig of fresh thyme or marjoram
250 g/$\frac{1}{2}$ lb button mushrooms
Knob of butter mixed with flour (beurre manié)
Freshly chopped parsley

Heat butter in a large casserole, and gently fry chopped bacon. Add baby onions, and fry, turning frequently, until golden. Remove, and set aside. Add seasoned chicken pieces, and fry until browned. Return onions and bacon to the pot. Heat brandy in a ladle, and set alight. Pour it flaming over chicken and onions. Shake casserole backwards and forwards until flames subside.

Add red wine and stock, bouquet garni, crushed garlic, bay leaves, and thyme or marjoram. Bring to simmering point, and cover. Cook slowly for about 45 min. Add mushrooms, and cook for another 10 min.

Remove chicken, onions, and mushrooms to a hot dish, and keep warm in oven. Skim off fat from liquid. Raise heat and boil rapidly to reduce liquid to about 600 ml/1 pt/2$\frac{1}{2}$ cups. Remove bay leaves and bouquet garni and correct seasoning. Blend in the *beurre manié* in small pieces, and stir until incorporated for a further few minutes, until sauce thickens (it should be just thick enough to coat a spoon lightly). Pour sauce over chicken, and garnish with parsley.

Suggested wines:
Beaujolais-Villages, Morgon, Moulin-à-Vent

Lentilles

Lentils
Serves 4

250 g/$\frac{1}{2}$ lb brown lentils
1.8 l/3 pt/7$\frac{1}{2}$ cups water
300 ml/$\frac{1}{2}$ pt/1$\frac{1}{4}$ cups good stock
50 g/2 oz/$\frac{1}{2}$ stick butter
Handful freshly chopped parsley
$\frac{1}{2}$ garlic clove, peeled and crushed

Soak lentils for 2 hr. Drain and place in a large saucepan with the water. Bring to boil and allow to simmer for 1$\frac{1}{4}$ hr. The lentils are cooked when they are tender, but not 'mushy'. Strain off any excess water. Add stock, and simmer until liquid is absorbed.

While lentils are cooking, mix garlic and parsley into butter. When lentils are ready, add butter mixture to them, and mix well to coat.

Serve at once, in a hot dish.

Food and wine: the art of Champagne.

CHAMPAGNE

Champagne is unique. No other wine so instantly contributes an air of festivity and gaiety to whatever occasion is celebrated. The wine is special because it makes us feel special.

Yet, though wine has been produced in the Champagne region for nearly two millenia, for the greater part of that time champagne was no more special than wine produced anywhere else. Champagne had its admirers, particularly among royal personages. Henry IV proudly referred to himself as simply 'Lord of Ay' (an important wine town near Epernay). Admittedly, the wines benefited from fortuitous publicity, for, ever since the sixth century, the kings of France came to Reims to be invested. A coronation, after all, is a powerful excuse for a celebration. Nevertheless, until the seventeenth century, champagne was not characterized by the bubbles for which the wine is known and prized today.

Despite the fact that this most special wine is now considered the epitome of luxury, the origins of champagne as we know it were really rather humble. A modest, hardworking Benedictine monk named Dom Pérignon, cellar master of the Abbey of Hautvillers, observed that champagne had a curious tendency to undergo a vigorous secondary fermentation every spring. This was so because the vineyard is a northern one, and in extreme cold weather the wine yeasts that feed on grape sugar during fermentation cannot work. When the temperature rises in the spring, however, they are reactivated. Carbon dioxide is a by-product of fermentation; thus the secondary fermentation in the spring gave the wine a slight sparkle. At that time, however, wine was generally sold in the cask, and the sparkle quickly dissipated as the wine aged.

What if the wine were to be bottled before this secondary fermentation began? Through experimentation, and by introducing the use of cork as a bottle stopper instead of the usual bits of oil-soaked tow, Dom Pérignon found that carbon dioxide could be trapped in the wine. When the corks kept blowing out of the bottles (frightening young cellar apprentices, and losing the precious sparkle in the process) he tied them down with string. The use of bottles, however, was a relatively recent innovation, and many could not withstand the pressure generated by trapped oxygen. The loss of wine through exploding bottles was great, but persistence was rewarded, for those that survived contained a rare wine with a magical succession of tiny, fine bubbles rising from the bottom of the glass. Thus, from humble beginnings, exuberant, vivacious champagne was born.

If champagne has evolved in a period of three hundred years into the sophisticated sparkler that we know today, the Champagne region itself has managed to resist the changes that prosperity and world-wide attention too often bring. Wine villages such as Bouzy, Hautvillers, Verzenay, and Cramant remain modest and quiet. When the people are not working in their vineyards, they tend to live behind doors, not outside them as do people in the south. The harsher northern climate, plus the numbing effects of two world wars that destroyed young men, vineyards, and ways of living, have made them turn inwards. They know that today's prosperity, the result of hard work and good fortune, can be swept away through no fault of their own. Thus, tradition, with its respect for older, more stable values, coexists with the modern realities of a fast-moving twentieth century.

Traditional values guide the *champenois* kitchen, too. For though the wine produced here is refined and elegant, regional cuisine remains straightforward, economical, and nourishing. Meals often begin with hefty bowls of potato, onion, or turnip *potage*. A more elaborate one-pot meal is the *potée champenoise*, a robust brew containing chunks of pork, rabbit, sausage, cabbage, potatoes, and other vegetables. This is food to sit down to after a day spent in the vineyards, when fingers are chafed and numb, and

backs are stiff and creaking. What matter that today a *vigneron* in this exclusive wine region can drive a Mercedes or the newest tractor? Still, it is the land that provides, and its elemental flavours are good enough for him.

The thrifty *champenois* might start a meal with a salad of dandelion leaves from his back garden not for reasons of economy but simply because the spiky, slightly bitter, dark-green leaves have more flavour than anything else available in the village market. They are dressed with bacon strips, hot bacon fat, and a spoonful of wine vinegar, to become *salade aux lardons*. The regional *charcuterie*, which makes full use of the lowly pig in a variety of exciting ways, is full-flavoured and earthy. *Jambonneau de Reims* (small hocks of ham breaded or enclosed in pastry), *boudin* (black pudding), or *fromage de tête* (brawn) all make excellent entrées. A popular main course is the *andouillette de Troyes*, a characteristic sausage made from fatty, succulent chitterlings and tripe, highly seasoned with black pepper. Another down-to-earth speciality is *pieds de porc à la Ste Ménéhould*, nothing other than humble pigs' trotters poached for several hours, then dipped in melted butter, rolled in breadcrumbs, and browned under a red-hot grill (most dishes referred to as '*à la Ste Ménéhould*' are treated in such fashion, including fish, mutton, and lamb).

The nearby Ardennes region also contributes to the robust character of the *champenois* table. In the forests of this still-wild region, home of the poet Rimbaud, wild boar, hare, and game birds such as thrush and quail abound. Equally well known are the smoked ham and coarse pâtés of Ardennes. The Champagne region used to be vast, and extended into what is today the Île de France. Thus, the *champenois* claim Brie, one of the greatest cheeses in the world, as their own. This soft, almost runny, round cheese with a furry white rind is known throughout the world, but there are other fine and distinctive cheeses, such as Chaource, a rich reddish-brown cow's milk cheese, Dauphin, which, flavoured with *fines herbes*, comes in the shape of a fish, creamy Langres, Coulommiers, similar to Brie, or the small, conical Abbaye d'Igny. These cheeses exude strong and assertive odours, but are surprisingly subtle and intriguing in flavour.

While the food of European wine regions usually has an inseparable and natural affinity with the wines produced there, a first impression of the *champenois* table is that it seems at odds with the region's wines. Certainly, it is doubtful that one would drink champagne with *potée champenoise* or *pieds de porc à la Ste Ménéhould*. But the wines of this region go back well before the time when Dom Pérignon added a magical sparkle to otherwise still wines. Robust traditional dishes, therefore, are ideally accompanied by the frank and assertive still wines of the region that today bear the *appellation* Coteaux Champenois. Though these wines can never be inexpensive since they are produced from the same grapes used to make champagne, they are worth seeking, for they add to an understanding of the evolution of champagne, play an important role in the regional kitchen, and, quite simply, are good solid drinking.

Matelote champenoise simmers pike, carp, trout, crayfish, and river eel in the still white wine of the region. Another favourite is *canard au Bouzy*. Bouzy is a well-known red Coteaux Champenois wine, and this speciality consists of rare roast duck served in a rich sauce made from that wine. Simpler everyday *champenois* cooking might include *blanquette de veau*, veal and vegetable stew made elegant with the addition of cream and butter, and ideally accompanied by a

Champagne's humble beginning: the kitchen at the Abbey of Hautvillers.

On the avenue de Champagne, one home of a great wine.

Coteaux Champenoise wine made from Chardonnay grapes. *Civet de lièvre* is also typical *champenois* fare: hare marinated in red wine, stewed slowly, served in a dark winy sauce enriched with hare blood.

Champagne evolved from the earthy, still wines of the region, but simply adding bubbles did not produce that crystal-clear, star-bright wine so loved today. For if carbon dioxide is a desired by-product of secondary fermentation within the bottle, one undesirable result is a fine sediment of dead yeast cells left behind in the bottle. It is extremely difficult to remove this sediment without losing the pressure, and so the wine that Dom Pérignon, Dom Ruinart (a friend and colleague), and the other Benedictine brothers enjoyed was undoubtedly dull and cloudy, albeit sparkling. Madame Clicquot, a remarkable entrepreneur who helped establish the famous house of Veuve Clicquot-Ponsardin, discovered that this sediment could be induced to slide into the neck of the bottle by skilful manipulation, and from there be expelled.

Today such a step is still an essential—and costly—element in the *méthode champenoise*. Once the wine has undergone its secondary fermentation and aged sufficiently, bottles are placed neck first in wooden racks called *pupitres*. Over a period of weeks or months, skilled *remueurs* give each bottle a gentle turn and tilt. Gradually the bottles move from a near horizontal position to an almost vertical one; at the same time the fine sediment is slowly but thoroughly shaken into the neck of the bottle. It is remarkable to watch these silent men with huge hands moving up and down the rows of bottles, deep within the dark, cool chalk caves where the wine is stored, for a skilled operator turns up to 30,000 bottles a day.

Once the sediment has come to rest in the neck of the bottle, the wine can mature in this position (*sur les pointes*) for a considerable period of time. Before the wine can be sold or drunk, however, the sediment must be expelled. The necks of the bottles of wine are therefore placed in an icy solution which freezes solid the small

Fruit-filled *pâtisseries* are elegant partners to elegant wine.

amount of wine containing the sediment. The corks are removed, the bottles given a sharp tap, and the pressure expels the tiny block of ice. This process is known as *dégorgement*. Afterwards, the amount of wine lost is replaced with a *dosage*, that is, a solution of pure cane sugar and wine. The amount of sugar in the *dosage* determines the style of champagne—*brut* (very dry), *extra-sec* (dry), *sec* (slightly sweet), *demi-sec* (sweet), *demi-doux* (very sweet), and *doux* (exceptionally sweet). Though today the overwhelming demand is for *brut* champagne, the sweeter styles have their place and should not be overlooked.

Thus evolved champagne, through the development and perfection of this unique process known as the *méthode champenoise*: still wines were metamorphosed into sparklers. If the typical robust and earthy *champenois* cuisine is a natural partner to those still wines, evolution also has taken place in kitchens of Champagne. For champagne is not only a wine of great delicacy and finesse, it is also a wine of prestige and elegance. Therefore, in the dining-rooms of many of the great champagne houses, renowned for their generous hospitality, and in exclusive restaurants throughout the region, master chefs have evolved an exciting and luxurious repertoire of dishes that are rich yet delicate enough to be accompanied by this most elegant wine, or which use champagne in their preparation. In historic and splendidly furnished mansions in Reims, or along the avenue de Champagne in Epernay, a unique *haute cuisine champenoise* is encountered which is matched in grandeur only by the wine, the surroundings, and the genteel hospitality of the host.

Crayfish, lobsters, and oysters are simmered in champagne, and its lightness and finesse enhance further the delicate and subtle flavours of shellfish. Fish such as sole and turbot are exquisite bathed in a sauce made from fresh cream and champagne, while the pale pink flesh of river trout matches a delicate sauce made from rosé champagne. Traditional favourites such as *coq au vin* and *matelote* (freshwater fish and wine stew) are given new significance when the wine used in their preparation is champagne. *Foie gras*, ham, and little birds such as quail are served cold, set in an amber, trembling champagne aspic.

To keep the trapped carbon dioxide from escaping, Dom Pérignon tied down the corks with string. Today a metal crown cork is generally used at first; after *dégorgement* it is replaced with a second cork held down with a wire muzzle.

A skilled *remueur* induces the sediment into the neck of the bottle by gradually rotating and tilting each bottle from a near horizontal position to an almost vertical one.

After the sediment has collected in the neck, bottles age *sur les pointes*.

Necks of bottles are placed in a freezing solution to trap sediment in a frozen block of ice.

A machine uncorks the bottles, gives them a tap, and the pressure expels the frozen block of ice, and with it the sediment. This process is known as *dégorgement*. Afterwards, the wines are given a *dosage*, a mixture of wine and pure cane sugar, then are recorked and wired.

And desserts such as pears cooked in champagne syrup, or a refreshing *sorbet au champagne* are nothing short of sheer luxury.

To use champagne as a cooking wine might well seem the height of extravagance. For one thing, precious bubbles are lost the moment they touch the pan. Nevertheless, sauces prepared with champagne are finer, lighter, more elegant than those prepared with any other wine, and even if the bubbles are lost, the inimitable bouquet that comes from the unique blend of wines used to produce champagne is evident in the finished dish. True, such distinctions are subtle, but in the realm of *haute cuisine* little is ever obvious.

There are many sparkling wines made throughout France and the world, some of which employ the costly and laborious *méthode champenoise*. Yet champagne remains unique. Like all great wines, it is the happy result of a unique set of natural circumstances, including the chalky sub-soil; climate; the vines themselves and the unique characteristics they acquire in this northern vineyard; even the deep chalk cellars where the wines mature, that extend for miles beneath the modern bustling streets and avenues of Reims and Epernay. As well, perhaps even more than other great wines, champagne is the result of man's skill and ingenuity. Again we return to Dom Pérignon. For not only did he perfect an ingenious method of making still wines sparkling, in addition he experimented with blending wines from varying areas within the Champagne region to produce an end-product with a richer and more distinguished bouquet and flavour than any single vineyard wine would have on its own.

Today the great champagne houses follow the precepts laid down by that knowledgeable monk. In short, the essence of champagne lies in a unique blending of grapes, each of which contributes particular characteristics and balance to the wine. Though many of the champagne houses own vineyards themselves, most must also buy grapes from individual *vignerons* throughout the region. A complex and unique system of grading vineyards has been devised to accommodate both growers and producers, as well as to ensure consumers of quality. Briefly, vine-

The Pinot Noir vineyards of Champagne.

are the prized vineyards of the Montagne de Reims. Here the Pinot Noir is primarily planted, and this rich classic black grape traditionally gives champagne its body and backbone. The Pinot Noir, as well as the sturdier Pinot Meunier, are also grown in the Vallée de la Marne, a stretch of vine-covered hills on either side of the river valley, east and west of Epernay. To the south, on the gentler slopes of the Côte des Blancs, the Chardonnay, a noble white grape, reigns supreme. Chardonnay gives champagne its lightness and finesse.

Each champagne house produces its own style of wine from a unique blend of still wines from vineyards throughout the region. Certain houses, for example, use a higher proportion of black grapes in their blend (*cuvée*) to produce a more robust champagne with strength, body, and aroma, while others seek a lighter, finer, fresher style of wine, and so use a higher proportion of Chardonnay grapes. At its extreme, such champagne is called *blanc de blancs* (literally 'white wine from white grapes'), because it is made entirely from the Chardonnay grape, with no addition of the Pinots in its blend. For the lover of champagne it is a joy to gain familiarity with the differing styles of champagne produced by different houses, for each type and style has its place and occasion.

Most champagne, moreover, is blended from wines of more than one year in order to result in a consistent style and quality that consumers can recognize and depend upon. To achieve such consistency takes not only great skill on the part of the *chef de cave*, who is responsible for the blend, it also requires substantial reserves of older wine that can be drawn upon to improve quality, add character and balance, and achieve consistency. Such non-vintage champagne must age for a minimum of one year in the bottle after secondary fermentation has taken place. Many firms, however, age their non-vintage wine for longer than this legal minimum. Vintage champagne is, of course, produced from wines of a single— and exceptional—year. While consistency is the aim in the production of non-vintage, the aim in the production of vintage is precisely to bring to light individual characteristics of the wine of that particular year. Vintage champagne

yards within the official Champagne region are classified according to an official scale whereby the finest, designated *grand cru*, are assigned 100 per cent value, *premier cru* are given values between 99 per cent and 90 per cent, and lesser vineyards are rated down to 77 per cent.

Each year the *Comité Interprofessionel du Vin de Champagne (CIVC)*, an official body which serves to represent the interests of growers and producers alike, sets a price per kilogram for the finest grapes; *vignerons* who sell to the large houses accordingly receive a percentage of this price depending on the quality rating of their vineyards. Champagne which is subsequently designated *grand cru* must be produced entirely from wines that come from vineyards rated 100 per cent; *premier cru* champagne, likewise, is from wines from 99 per cent to 90 per cent vineyards.

Additionally, different styles of wine come from different areas within the Champagne region. To the west of Reims, extending in a horseshoe around to Verzenay, Bouzy, and Ay,

Poppies grow on former battlefields.

must be aged for a minimum of three years in the bottle, but many firms age such wines for much longer (five or six years is quite normal). Longer ageing on the sediment gives greater flavour, and releases those subtle elements responsible for taste, aroma, and bouquet.

Champagne is so easy to drink, so easy to enjoy, that it brings a sense of euphoria with seeming effortlessness. But as we stare mesmerized at that unending succession of tiny, fine bubbles rising in our glass, we should think for a moment of all the toil and time—the heavy work in the vineyard, the annual harvest traditionally completed with the assistance of coal miners from the north, the skilful blending of dozens of wines to produce the *cuvée*, the manual shake and turn of each and every bottle—taken to produce that crystal-clear, sparkling liquid we down in a moment. And we should think, too, of the people of this essentially rugged land who learned through suffering to live with austerity and prosperity alike.

The 1914 vintage, for example, was harvested by women, children, and old men, because the boys and men of the region were at war. Despite numerous civilian casualties, the vines were tended, and the wine made. Women took over the strenuous work in the cellars; the racking, the bottling, the *dégorgement*; and life continued —in a certain fashion.

How strange to realize that these green and peaceful hills were the scenes of such fierce fighting. Monuments—'*aux enfants morts pour la France*'—are landmarks in every village. Uniform white crosses in military cemeteries are planted in the same chalk soil that gives life to the vines. How strange and admirable that in those horrific days the *champenois* continued to produce this rare and marvellous liquid whose only purpose is to bring joy to man. We are grateful to the people of Champagne for their often stoical dedication to the craft of wine-making in which an effervescent and luminous liquid is bottled for the greater joy of all who drink it.

Quantities where necessary are given in
Metric, Imperial and US measurements.

Salade aux Lardons

Hot Bacon and Dandelion Salad
Serves 4–6

1 large bunch young dandelion leaves (or Webb
lettuce or curly endive)
1 tbsp oil
5–6 rashers/slices lean bacon
$\frac{1}{2}$ tbsp wine vinegar
Freshly ground black pepper

Wash and dry dandelion leaves. Cut bacon into
1 cm/$\frac{1}{2}$ in strips. Heat oil in a frying pan, and
add bacon, frying gently until crisp. Remove
from heat. Put dandelion leaves into a warmed
salad bowl, and add bacon. Mix vinegar with hot
bacon fat and oil. Season with freshly ground
black pepper, and pour over the dandelion leaves.
Toss well, and serve immediately.

Pieds de Porc à la Ste Ménéhould

Grilled Pigs' Trotters
Serves 4

4 large pigs' trotters, cleaned and split lengthwise,
and soaked for 24 hr.
1 large onion, peeled and quartered
2 carrots, thickly sliced
1 bouquet garni
2 sticks celery, coarsely chopped
Salt
10 black peppercorns
50 g/2 oz/$\frac{2}{3}$ cup dried breadcrumbs
2 tbsp butter

Put trotters in a large saucepan with vegetables,
herbs, and seasoning. Cover with cold water,
and bring to boil. Remove scum with a slotted
spoon, cover and allow to simmer for about 3
hr. When tender, remove from the pot, and
allow to cool. Bone carefully. (Strain the cooking
liquid and set aside for soup.) Melt butter gently
in a saucepan. Coat trotters with melted butter,
and roll in breadcrumbs. Place trotters under a
medium grill, and cook gently until golden.
Serve sizzling hot, with French mustard.

Suggested wines:
Coteaux Champenois blanc, rouge

Potée Champenoise

Rabbit and Bean Stew
Serves 6

1 tbsp oil
1 tbsp butter
1 garlic clove, peeled and chopped
1 large onion, peeled and chopped
6 pieces of rabbit
Joint of unsmoked bacon (approx. 750 g/1$\frac{1}{2}$ lb)
250 g/$\frac{1}{2}$ lb dried white haricot beans (soaked in
water overnight)
6 carrots, coarsely chopped
2 leeks, coarsely chopped
2 sticks celery, cut into long lengths
1 bay leaf
1 sprig of fresh thyme (or $\frac{1}{2}$ tsp dried thyme)
Salt
Freshly ground black pepper
Cold water
1 small firm cabbage, cut into chunks
1 kg/2 lb potatoes, peeled and cut into chunks

Melt butter and oil in a large pot, and gently
sauté onion and garlic. When golden, add pieces
of rabbit, and allow to become well coated in

onion mixture. Add bacon, beans, carrots, leeks, celery, and seasonings. Cover with about 2.4 l/ 4 pt/10 cups of cold water, and bring slowly to the boil. Skim off scum, cover, and allow to simmer for 1½ hr. Add cabbage and potatoes, and adjust seasoning. Cook until all ingredients are tender.

Remove bacon and rabbit, and drain liquid (this can be served as soup for a first course). Place vegetables on a large serving platter. Carve bacon, and arrange rabbit on top of vegetables.

Suggested wine:
Coteaux Champenoise blanc

Filets de Sole au Champagne

Fillets of Sole with Champagne
Serves 4

8 fillets of sole
¼ bottle of champagne
Salt
Freshly ground black pepper
1 small onion, peeled and finely chopped
75 g/3 oz/¾ stick butter
150 ml/¼ pt/⅔ cup cream
2 egg yolks
Freshly chopped parsley

Lay the sole fillets in a large pan, and cover with champagne. Add salt, pepper, onion, and knob of butter. Bring slowly to the boil, and simmer for about 8 min.

When fish is cooked (tender but not soft) carefully remove and set aside on a warmed serving platter. Reserve cooking liquid. Melt remaining butter in a saucepan, and add un-beaten egg yolks and cream, beating constantly with a whisk over a very low heat for about 10 min. Gradually add some of cooking liquid until a creamy sauce is produced. Adjust seasoning. Heat sauce, but do not allow to boil.

Pour sauce over the sole fillets, and decorate with parsley.

Suggested wine:
'Blanc de blancs' champagne brut

Blanquette de Veau

Veal Stew
Serves 4–6

1 kg/2 lb breast of veal, cut into 5 cm/2 in pieces
2 large carrots, peeled and cut into chunks
1 onion, peeled and studded with 3 cloves
2 celery stalks, coarsely chopped
1 leek, sliced
Cold water
Salt
Freshly ground black pepper
12 small onions, peeled
50 g/2 oz/½ stick butter
2 tbsp flour
Juice and rind of 1 lemon
Pinch of nutmeg
12 button mushrooms
3 egg yolks, well beaten
150 ml/¼ pt/⅔ cup double cream
Freshly chopped parsley

Place veal, carrots, onion, celery, and leek in a large casserole, and cover with cold water. Season and bring slowly to the boil. Remove grey scum with slotted spoon. Cover and simmer slowly for 2 hr., skimming whenever necessary. After 1½ hr. gently brown the small onions in a saucepan. Add to casserole and continue cooking.

Melt butter in a saucepan, and add flour. Cook for a few minutes. Add about 900 ml/ 1½ pt/3¾ cups of the veal cooking liquid, and whisk vigorously until smooth. Bring slowly to the boil, and simmer for 10 min. Stir in lemon juice and rind, nutmeg, and mushrooms. Season to taste, and simmer for another 10 min.

When veal is tender, drain and remove from pan. Rinse casserole, and return meat and vegetables to it. Pour sauce over, and gently mix together. Bring to the boil, and simmer for 5 min.

Blend egg yolks and cream together with about 300 ml/½ pt/1¼ cups of the hot sauce. Mix well, and pour into casserole, stirring until sauce thickens. Decorate with freshly chopped parsley, and serve with boiled potatoes.

Suggested wine:
Coteaux Champenois blanc

Canard au Bouzy

Duck with Red Wine
Serves 4

3 kg/6 lb duck
150 ml/¼ pt/⅔ cup Bouzy (red wine)
100 g/4 oz/¼ lb mushrooms, chopped
2 shallots, peeled and chopped
Salt
Freshly ground black pepper

Rinse and dry duck inside and out with kitchen towel. Prick skin all over with a skewer to allow fat to escape when cooking. Season well with salt and pepper. Place in a roasting tin on a high shelf in the oven, pre-heated to 220°C/Gas Mark 7/425°F. After 15 min. reduce temperature to 180°C/Gas Mark 4/350°F.

The French prefer their duck pink and, indeed, it is delicious, particularly when served with this rich wine sauce. When pricked with a skewer, the juices should run out slightly pink (about 2 hr.). If you prefer duck cooked a little more, cook until the juices run clear (between 2½–3 hr.).

When ready, remove duck from pan and allow to sit for 20 min. Skim fat, and reserve all pan juices. Deglaze the roasting pan with red wine, and add the juices from the duck. Bring to the boil, and allow to reduce, then add mushrooms and shallots. Season well, and simmer for 5 min. Meanwhile, carve the breast into thin slices. Arrange on a platter, along with legs, wings, thighs, and serve with *sauce au Bouzy* separately.

Suggested wines:
Bouzy (Coteaux Champenoise rouge),
rosé champagne brut

Tarte aux Fraises

Strawberry Tart

1 pâte brisée sucrée (see recipe for pâte brisée, *and add 50 g/2 oz/⅓ cup of granulated sugar to the butter to make* pâte sucrée)
500 g/1 lb ripe strawberries
8 tbsp red currant jelly

Line a 20 cm/8 in flan tin with the rolled *pâte brisée sucrée*. Prick base of pastry case with a fork, and line it with a circle of greaseproof paper. Press the paper well against the pastry, and fill with dried beans. Bake in the middle of a pre-heated oven, 200°C/Gas Mark 6/400°F for 10 min., or until dough is set. Remove paper and beans, prick bottom of pastry case again at frequent intervals, and bake for another 10 min. When cooked, the shell should be light golden in colour. Remove crust from mould, and allow to cool on a rack.

Hull the strawberries, and only wash them if necessary.

Melt the red currant jelly very gently in a saucepan. Then quickly brush it on the inside of the crust, leaving a little of the jelly aside. Arrange strawberries in circles in the jelly-lined crust, and brush remaining jelly on top of the fruit. Allow to set, and serve with whipped cream.

Suggested wine:
Rosé champagne

Sorbet au Champagne

Serves 6

1 bottle brut champagne
600 ml/1 pt/2½ cups sugar syrup (500 g/1 lb sugar dissolved in water)
Juice of 2 lemons

Combine together all ingredients and freeze for 45 min. Remove, beat, and freeze again, for further 3 or 4 hr.

Serve in tall glasses, with sponge fingers.

Suggested wines:
Champagne demi-sec, demi-doux

It is twilight on the Loire. The medieval, renaissance, and classic châteaux that dominate this green and peaceful valley stand mute, save for the occasional footsteps of a caretaker echoing in majestic halls where Catherine de' Medici, Diane de Poitiers, or Charles VII once received privileged guests. Though by day the place is bustling with tourists and visitors, by night a dreamy stillness settles over this historic land whose great moments are long past. The once-deep reds of the fourteenth-century tapestries at Angers have faded to a pale, limpid coral, yet we treasure them all the more for their time-worn colour, a shade duplicated in thousands of glasses of Rosé d'Anjou drunk with vivid enjoyment throughout the world.

The Loire is the longest river in France. It begins life surprisingly close to the Mediterranean, then makes its slow way north and west before spilling into the cold Atlantic in Brittany. Though the social character of the broad valley changes dramatically along the way (people from Sancerre, for example, probably feel little affinity with those from Nantes), nevertheless, the wide river unites diverse provinces and, throughout, one senses a common *joie de vivre*, a way of life that is generous, easygoing, and, above all, positive.

Naturally the character of the wine and food also varies considerably along the Loire. Yet here, too, commonality is more important than regional variations. For the Loire and the rich land she waters provide a generous array of fresh fish, vegetables, and fruit, that are everywhere prepared with classic simplicity and respect for the purity and quality of the ingredients.

A great variety of wine is produced in the

vineyards along the banks of the Loire: the pretty coral wines of Anjou, crisp Muscadet from the region around Nantes, sparkling wines from Saumur, luscious golden dessert wines of the Coteaux du Layon and Vouvray, drier flinty wines from Sancerre and Pouilly-sur-Loire, and grapy reds from Chinon and Bourgueil. But if variety is the keynote, wines from these cool northern vineyards are united by a character at once light, refreshing, and irresistible. Though some wines here have remarkable longevity (La Coulée de Serrant, for example, or some of the great dessert wines of Vouvray) most of the wines of the Loire have a naturally high acidity and a pronounced fruity aroma that make them perfect for drinking while young.

Muscadet, from the Pays Nantais, is a case in point: this popular white wine, at its best, is the epitome of freshness and youth. The vineyards, often tended by horse-drawn machinery, are almost within sight of the Atlantic, and this tangy, inexpensive wine perfectly partners seafood. Some Muscadet is bottled 'sur lie', which means the wine has not yet been racked off its barrel sediment (the wine has not been transferred to clean barrels after sediment has settled in the original barrel). Through longer than normal contact with sediment the wine gains a rounder, fruitier character. The best areas for the production of Muscadet are Sèvre-et-Maine (south-east of Nantes) and Coteaux de la Loire (north-east of the city).

The Muscadet region fringes Brittany, that north-west Celtic province so unlike the rest of France. Crêpe-stands—the Breton equivalent of a fish and chip shop or a hamburger joint—offer an amazingly wide selection of layered pancakes: savoury, sweet, or flambéd in liqueur. Today this quick snack is popular everywhere in France. A more local speciality is the galette. A nutty buckwheat pancake, it makes a satisfying meal when layered with smoked ham and egg, then folded into a neat square packet—delicious with a tart tumbler of Gros Plant, a sharp, crisp VDQS (vin delimité qualité supérieur) wine, not often exported.

Both Gros Plant and Muscadet are natural partners to seafood and freshwater fish, as are so many other Loire wines, including Sauvignon de

The Loire near Savennières.

Touraine, dry Vouvray, Sancerre, sparkling Saumur, and the pink and dry white wines of Anjou. Such a wide selection is matched only by the variety of fish dishes—truite à l'oseille, trout stuffed with a mixture of sautéd shallots and sorrel leaves; quenelles de brochet, a mixture of boned pike, egg whites, and cream, shaped into little 'sausages' and poached; matelote d'anguilles, a smooth white stew of river eel. Fishing, naturally, is a great sport along the Loire, and fish such as pike and the mighty salmon are much-sought prizes. They are usually poached in court-bouillon (a stock flavoured with wine and herbs) then covered in one of the simplest, most exquisite sauces ever invented—beurre blanc, a fusion of whipped sweet butter, reduced wine vinegar, and shallots. Simple though this sauce sounds, it is one of the great triumphs of French cuisine, magically enhancing the fresh delicacy of the fish it accompanies.

Other fish specialities of the Loire include the small fry of the river, which are dipped in a simple flour, water, and egg white batter then fried whole in boiling oil; this friture de la Loire is as delicious as any outsize beauty. Écrevisses are also a favourite—crayfish, often eaten cold at the start of a meal, with home-made mayonnaise and a chilled glass of Rosé de Loire or Rosé d'Anjou,

La Coulée de Serrant, the Chenin Blanc ripens to produce a great, dry white wine with remarkable body, aroma, and assertive elegance that comes from finely balanced acidity. On the other hand, this same grape, only miles away on the south side of the Loire, produces some of the heaviest and richest dessert wines in the world (the great growths at Quarts de Chaume and Bonnezeaux). Elsewhere, in the chalk tufa around Saumur, the Chenin Blanc produces fruity but naturally acidic wines which, blended with Chardonnay and Cabernet to form a *cuvée*, undergo secondary fermentation in the bottle (*méthode champenoise*) to result in excellent (and excellently priced) sparkling wines.

It is not simply varying microclimate and soils that account for such great differences in styles and types of wine, it is also a matter of priority. At La Coulée de Serrant, for example, the vineyard is harvested several times in succession by hand (it is too steep to allow the use of machines; thus the grapes are loaded on to horse-drawn sledges). Combing the vineyards by hand is a costly business, but it ensures not only that ripe bunches of grapes are selected, but that bunches that are over-ripe or have been attacked by 'noble rot' are excluded.

On the other hand, *vignerons* south of the river pray for the exceptional fungus known as *botrytis cinerea*, for when it attacks Chenin Blanc grapes, leaving them shrivelled and covered with a fine white fur, natural sugar is concentrated and the wines take on a rich scent of honey and fruit that is unmistakable. In the great growths of Quarts de Chaume and Bonnezeaux, therefore, bunches of grapes are also selected individually, but the priority is exactly the opposite to that at La Coulée de Serrant: only bunches of over-ripe grapes are gathered. In Saumur, to confuse matters further, a high acidity is sought to give 'zip' to the sparkling wines, and so grapes are often harvested before they are yet fully ripe.

Though La Coulée de Serrant, Bonnezeaux, and Quarts de Chaume bear their own *appellations*, the larger area for the production of sweet wines is the Coteaux du Layon, while Savennières is a general *appellation* for other dry white wines produced around that commune. Nearby areas known as Coteaux de l'Aubance

the colour of the wine mirroring the faded pink of the shellfish.

Rosé d'Anjou is one of the best known and most popular of all Loire valley wines, for this medium-dry thirst-quencher, produced in vineyards around and between Angers and Saumur, is at once inexpensive, uncomplicated, and pretty to look at. Vinified traditionally by pressing the grapes intact (Cabernet Franc, Gamay, Groslot, and Cot are all used), the must ferments on the skins for only a few hours until the desired colour has been drawn out. Another pink wine produced here is the distinguished Cabernet d'Anjou (slightly sweeter, softer, and more mellow), while pink wine known as Rosé de Loire is always dry, paler than its cousins, with a clean, flinty freshness that goes well with the sound country cooking of this region.

The pink wines of Anjou may be the best known (they account for well over half the total production here), but the most distinguished undoubtedly are the great white wines, both dry and lusciously sweet, from Savennières and the Coteaux du Layon. The Chenin Blanc, known locally as the Pineau de la Loire, is the most important vine of this region, and it is remarkably versatile. At Savennières, for example, and in particular on the steep, sunbaked spur known as

Saumur, one of many magnificent Loire châteaux.

The delicate tints of the Loire:
crayfish tails and Rosé d'Anjou.

and Coteaux de la Loire produce dry and medium-dry white and rosé wines.

Within this overwhelming flood of white and pink wine we find, between Angers and Tours, a rare enclave of red wine-producing communes. Chinon, Bourgueil, St Nicolas-de-Bourgueil, and Saumur-Champigny all produce distinctive light wines with remarkable and intense fruity scents—deep raspberry and strawberry rather than grape—a reminder perhaps that this area is known as the Garden of France.

We are in sweet Touraine, a fertile valley where a rustic countryside is paid tribute with a stretch of magnificent and grandiose châteaux such as Azay-le-Rideau, Chenonceau, Loches, Amboise, and Chambord. Chambord, standing within a 14,000-acre forest, was a royal hunting estate, and, indeed, this pastoral land is still paradise for sportsmen. Deer, wild boar, pheasant, partridge, and quail are all plentiful in autumn and winter.

If the chase was a prerogative of royalty and the wealthy, common folk were satisfied with raising the culinary status of the lowly pig. And raise it they did—to imaginative new heights. One magnificent speciality of this region combines prunes from Touraine (said to be the fattest and juiciest in France) with pork, *porc aux pruneaux*, bound together in a rich cream sauce. Other favourite pork dishes include *rillons* (pork riblets cooked until 'caramelized') and *rillettes* (potted paste of belly pork bound in its own fat). Both are delicious with a chunk of crusty French bread and a brimming glass of Sauvignon de Touraine.

The *cuisine tourangelle*, like the French language spoken in Touraine, is classically pure. Vegetables such as broad beans, asparagus, leeks, lettuce, or even cabbage arrive on the table simply prepared, pure, crisp, and beautifully green. Some of the best cultivated mushrooms (*champignons de Paris*) are raised in damp, dark chalk caves near Saumur and Vouvray, the same caves in which the sparkling Loire wines are produced and aged (many of these caves, curiously, have been turned into 'troglodyte houses', cool and half-hidden in the cream-coloured hills). The creamy or brown mushrooms are either tinned, or eaten fresh, raw with

A farmyard in the upper Loire.

vinaigrette dressing, or simply grilled then seasoned with fresh sweet butter, salt, and pepper. Wild mushrooms such as broad-capped *cèpes*, or smaller yellow *girolles*, are gathered in deep woods, and lend their distinctive flavours to such hearty dishes as rabbit stewed in Chinon wine, or braised saddle of venison.

Probably the best known and best wine of Touraine comes from Vouvray, a remarkable commune located on the north bank of the Loire, not far from Tours itself. Dry, semi-sweet, and very sweet, as well as fine, light sparkling wines are all produced from the versatile Chenin Blanc. The best, rarest, and most expensive wines, as always, are the great sweet wines, which have extremely rich texture and scent, and also remarkable longevity (the greatest can be kept for a hundred years). Wine from Montlouis, on the south side of the Loire, offers a similar range in style, character, and quality, and though it is the sweeter wines that connoisseurs seek, the other styles should not be overlooked.

While Vouvray and Montlouis are familiar to many, there has at the same time been a quiet,

steady increase in the production of fresh, un-complicated, dry white, rosé, and red wines that are known by the larger *appellation* Touraine. In particular, the Gamay (the grape of Beaujolais) is used to produce enticing, light, young wines, such as Touraine Gamay *primeur*, meant to be consumed weeks or months from the vintage.

White wine that matches the Gamay in freshness and youth is produced from the Sauvignon, a grape originally from Bordeaux that thrives so well on the upper reaches of the Loire, where it produces good and even great wines at Quincy, Menetou-Salon, Reuilly, and the twin communes of Sancerre and Pouilly-sur-Loire. Firm, fruity, and with that grape's dis-tinctive character, Sauvignon de Touraine, though perhaps lacking the depth of such wines from farther up-river, is deliciously drinkable, especially on a balmy, undisturbed evening along the river, with no more than a handful of fresh oily walnuts, or a dollop of soft, creamy cheese.

Farther east, the Loire river loops up towards Paris and the city of Orléans. The wines of the

Orléannais are not well known outside the region (a certain amount of VDQS white, rosé, and red is produced here), but the wine vinegars from Orléans are famous throughout the world —if not as famous as its patron saint, Joan of Arc. Though all wines will turn sour if exposed to air, a good wine vinegar is produced by introducing a 'mother vinegar' (a bacterial fungus) to the wine in order to induce an acetic fermentation. The best wine vinegars are aged in wood, while many destined for table use are flavoured with condiments such as mustard, shallots, garlic, tarragon, or onions. True, vinegar is the product of wine, but it can also be its nemesis, over-powering delicate flavours and bouquet when used in excess. An excellent salad dressing typical of the Loire makes use of the distinctive *huile de noix* (walnut oil) combined with just a drop of good wine vinegar, salt, and freshly ground black pepper.

Up-river, the Loire bends south once more towards its source high in the rugged Auvergne. The character of the land, on these upper reaches near the two famous wine communes of

Crottin de Chavignol, the dry, hard traditional goat's milk cheese, is produced in the Sancerre region and delicious with that wine.

Sancerre and Pouilly-sur-Loire, is somewhat more vigorous and robust. The landscape, certainly, is stunningly beautiful. Herds of brown-furred goats nibble sweet grass and wild flowers on majestic, high meadows, while the wind whispers over waving, swaying fields of grass and wheat. The faded sophistication that so colours the lower stretches of the Loire is here lacking; we sense that winters are colder, the people more hard-working. Indeed, these two communes are closer to Beaune than they are to Angers, and the Burgundian influence is apparent in lively folk dancing and hearty, unassuming country cooking. A slice of rabbit and pork pâté; *veau au vin*, veal sautéed in vegetables and red or white wine; *pâté de pommes de terre*, a simple potato-spread eaten at the start of a meal; or *poulet rôti*, spit-roasted spring chicken, are typical foods of this region.

If the food seems slightly heavier and more down-to-earth, so does the wine of Sancerre and Pouilly-sur-Loire. Indeed, the Sauvignon grape here takes on a pronounced fresh yet decidedly earthy aroma that is extremely appealing. The name of the commune, Pouilly-sur-Loire ap-plies to wine made from the lesser Chasselas grape, while wine produced from the Sauvignon is called Pouilly Blanc Fumé, a name that derives not from some imagined 'smoky' taste, but rather from the bloom on the grapes before the harvest. Across the river in Sancerre, excel-lent wine is produced in tiny hamlets such as Sury-en-Vaux, La Côte, Bué, and Chavignol (where the great goat cheese Crottin de Chavig-nol is made).

The mighty Loire continues upstream for another 300 miles or so, but for our purpose the journey is over. Night is falling quickly, and vermilion shades colour the still water from Pouilly-sur-Loire down through Touraine to Angers and Nantes. The châteaux-lined Loire seems unreal in this dreamy, fairy-tale twilight, and we allow ourselves to sink into reverie, imagining grander days of chanson and chivalry while sipping pretty pink wine the colour of crayfish tails and tapestries, drifting towards that small paradise that uncomplicated wine and food and the beauty of a perfect pastoral land-scape so effortlessly create.

Quantities where necessary are given in
Metric, Imperial and US measurements.

Crêpes
Pancakes
Makes about 12 *crêpes*

100 g/4 oz/1 cup plain flour
2 eggs
Pinch of salt
150 ml/ $\frac{1}{4}$ pt/ $\frac{2}{3}$ cup milk
150 ml/ $\frac{1}{4}$ pt/ $\frac{2}{3}$ cup water
2 tbsp melted butter

Sieve flour into a large mixing bowl. Make a well in the centre, and break eggs into it. Add a pinch of salt, and mix thoroughly with a wooden spoon. Gradually add milk and water, and beat with a wire whisk until mixture is smooth, the consistency of light cream. Stir in melted butter, and put in the refrigerator for at least 2 hr., preferably overnight.

Stir batter well. Butter a small frying pan, and allow it to get hot. Then turn heat down, and pour about 1–2 tbsp of batter into middle of pan. Quickly tilt pan from side to side so the batter covers the base evenly and thinly. Cook for about 1 min., shaking pan to loosen *crêpe*. Lift edge with a spatula, and if it is golden, turn it over, and cook the other side. This second side will need less cooking time. Slide *crêpe* on to a warm plate. Grease pan, and continue in the same manner. *Crêpes* can be kept warm by covering the plate they are on with another and setting it over a pan of simmering water.

With this basic recipe one is able to make countless dishes, sweet or savoury.

A *crêpe* stand in Nantes.

Crêpes aux Fruits de Mer

Seafood Pancakes
To stuff 6 *crêpes*

6 crêpes *(see basic recipe)*
25 g/1 oz/2 tbsp butter
1 shallot, peeled and finely chopped
$1\frac{1}{2}$ tbsp flour
300 ml/$\frac{1}{2}$ pt/$1\frac{1}{4}$ cups hot milk
Salt
Freshly ground black pepper
Pinch of nutmeg
250 g/$\frac{1}{2}$ lb shredded or diced shellfish (crab,
scallops, prawns)
50 g/2 oz/$\frac{2}{3}$ cup grated cheese

Melt butter in a saucepan, and gently sauté shallot. Add flour, and cook for 2 min. Slowly add milk, a little at a time, stirring constantly. When all milk has been added, bring slowly to the boil, and allow to simmer for 5 min. Fold in seafood, and mix well. Season.

Place a large spoonful of filling on each cooked *crêpe*, and roll up. Reserve about a quarter of the sauce, and thin with a little milk. Arrange stuffed *crêpes* in a shallow baking dish, and cover with remaining sauce. Decorate with prawns, and sprinkle with grated cheese. Heat in a pre-heated oven, 180°C/Gas Mark 4/350°F, for 10 min., until cheese has turned golden. Serve immediately.

Suggested wines:
Muscadet de Sèvre-et-Maine, Muscadet 'sur lie', Rosé de Loire

Galettes

Buckwheat Pancakes
Makes about 12 *galettes*

50 g/2 oz/$\frac{1}{2}$ cup plain flour
50 g/2 oz/$\frac{1}{2}$ cup buckwheat flour
2 eggs
Pinch of salt
300 ml/$\frac{1}{2}$ pt/$1\frac{1}{4}$ cups milk
2 tbsp melted butter

Use same method as in basic *crêpe* recipe.

A *galette* is layered and folded rather than stuffed. The *pave nantais* is filled with smoked ham, fried egg, and cheese. Other fillings could be fried onions, mushrooms, sausage, or cooked chicken.

Place the fillings in layers, on top of each other, then fold the galette in half and in half again, to make a triangle. Serve immediately.

Suggested wine:
Gros Plant, Rosé d'Anjou

Rillettes

Potted Pork
For 6–8 small terrines

1 kg/2 lb belly pork
500 g/1 lb shoulder or butt of pork
2 garlic cloves
Water
Salt
Freshly ground black pepper

Cut belly and shoulder (or butt) of pork into $2\frac{1}{2}$ cm/1 in pieces. Sprinkle liberally with salt, and place in a large saucepan with garlic cloves. Add sufficient water barely to cover the meat. Cover the pan and cook over very low heat for 4 hr. (if water evaporates, add a little more to ensure pork does not fry in its own fat).

After 4 hr., remove lid, and continue to cook until water has evaporated. Allow to cool overnight.

Shred pork into individual fibres (it is easier to do this with the hands) and place in a large mixing bowl. When all the meat is shredded, mix it well with its own fat with a wooden spoon. Season with plenty of salt and black pepper (it should be highly seasoned). Pack into individual crocks, chill, and serve with French bread. (Seal with pork fat if not eaten right away.)

Suggested wines:
Sauvignon de Touraine, Quincy, Reuilly

Porc aux Pruneaux

Pork with Prunes
Serves 6

500 g/1 lb large dried prunes
300 ml/ $\frac{1}{2}$ pt/1 $\frac{1}{4}$ cups Vouvray (dry)
6 slices pork fillet
Salt
Freshly ground black pepper
Flour
50 g/2 oz/ $\frac{1}{2}$ stick butter
1 tbsp red currant jelly
150 ml/ $\frac{1}{4}$ pt/ $\frac{2}{3}$ cup double cream

Soak prunes overnight with about three-quarters of the wine. Season pork fillets, and lightly dredge with flour. Heat butter in a large frying pan, and brown fillets on each side. Pour in the prunes and their liquid, and remaining wine. Bring slowly to the boil, cover, and simmer over a low heat for 40–45 min.

When fillets are cooked, remove them and the prunes to a hot serving dish, and keep hot in the oven. Bring juices to the boil and allow to reduce. Stir in red currant jelly until it is dissolved. Slowly pour in cream, stirring constantly until sauce is smooth, thick, and shiny. (Make sure the sauce does not boil, or the cream may curdle.) Check seasoning, then pour over the pork fillets and prunes. Serve immediately.

Suggested wines:
Vouvray, Sauvignon de Touraine, St Nicolas-de-Bourgueil

Truite au Muscadet

Trout in Muscadet
Serves 4

50 g/2 oz/ $\frac{1}{2}$ stick butter
2 tbsp shallots, peeled and finely chopped
1 carrot
2 celery stalks
1 leek (only white and light green part)
100 g/ $\frac{1}{4}$ lb mushrooms
Salt
Freshly ground black pepper
4 freshwater trout, cleaned and gutted
$\frac{1}{2}$ bottle Muscadet
300 ml/ $\frac{1}{2}$ pt/1 $\frac{1}{4}$ cups stock
Bouquet garni
2 tbsp flour blended to form a paste with
25 g/1 oz/ $\frac{1}{4}$ stick butter (beurre manié)
150 ml/ $\frac{1}{4}$ pt/ $\frac{2}{3}$ cup single cream
Juice of $\frac{1}{2}$ lemon
Freshly chopped parsley

Melt butter in a saucepan, and gently sauté shallots. Julienne the carrot, celery, and leek, and add them to the pan. Cover, and cook gently for 15 min. Add mushrooms, and cook for 2 min. Season with salt and pepper.

Line a large baking dish with tin foil. Season fish and arrange on foil. Spread vegetables over fish and pour on wine and stock. Add bouquet garni and season. Bring almost to simmering point, then put in a pre-heated oven, 180°C/ Gas Mark 4/350°F. Baste fish frequently, and cook for about 20 min., or until just tender. Do not overcook. Transfer fish and vegetables to a serving dish and keep warm. Pour cooking liquid into a saucepan, and boil down until it has reduced by one-third. Remove from heat, and beat in the *beurre manié* (flour and butter paste). Add half of the cream, return to heat, and slowly heat through (but do not boil). Gradually add rest of cream. Correct seasoning, and add lemon juice to taste. Pour sauce over trout and vegetables, and garnish with freshly chopped parsley.

Suggested wine:
Muscadet de Sèvre-et-Maine

Saumon au Beurre Blanc

Salmon with Butter Sauce
Serves 4

4 salmon steaks
150 ml/ $\frac{1}{4}$ pt/ $\frac{2}{3}$ cup Sauvignon de Touraine
$\frac{1}{2}$ onion, peeled and sliced into rings
6 black peppercorns
Sprig of parsley

Beurre Blanc
3 shallots, peeled and finely chopped
3 tbsp white wine vinegar
2 tbsp cold water
Salt
Freshly ground white pepper
250 g/8 oz/2 sticks unsalted butter

Place salmon steaks in a shallow ovenproof dish, with white wine, onion, and seasonings. Cook for about 15 min. in a moderate oven, 180°C/ Gas Mark 4/350°F. When cooked, strain, and keep fish warm while preparing sauce.

Put shallots, vinegar, cold water, salt, and pepper in a small saucepan. Bring to the boil and allow to reduce to about 1 tbsp of liquid. Remove from heat, and start to beat in butter, a little at a time. Replace pan over very low heat, and continue to add butter, beating constantly. (Be sure the heat is even, since the butter will separate if the heat is too high.) The sauce should be smooth and as thick as cream.

Serve warm, poured over the salmon. (This is also delicious over any white fish, shellfish, or vegetables.)

Suggested wines:
Sancerre, Pouilly Blanc Fumé, Chinon

Crêpes au Crème de Noix

Almond and Walnut Pancakes
Stuffing enough for 6 crêpes

6 crêpes (see basic recipe)
4 egg yolks
4 tbsp sugar
50 g/2 oz/ $\frac{1}{2}$ cup flour
450 ml/ $\frac{3}{4}$ pt/2 cups boiling milk

1 tbsp vanilla essence
25 g/2 oz/ $\frac{1}{3}$ cup ground almonds
25 g/2 oz/ $\frac{1}{3}$ cup ground walnuts

Beat egg yolks and sugar in a large bowl, until mixture turns pale yellow. Beat in flour until smooth. Gradually add boiling milk, beating constantly. Transfer to a small saucepan, and stir over a medium heat until sauce thickens and becomes smooth. Bring slowly to the boil, then simmer gently, stirring all the while.

Remove from heat, and stir in vanilla essence and ground nuts.

When mixture has cooled, spread it on the less good side of each cooked *crêpe*, and roll up. Arrange in a baking dish, and sprinkle with sugar. Place in a pre-heated oven, 200°C/Gas Mark 6/ 400°F, for 10–15 min. Serve immediately.

Suggested wines:
Coteaux du Layon, Bonnezeaux, Quarts de Chaume

Crêpes Suzette

Sauce enough for 8 crêpes

8 crêpes (see basic recipe)
100 g/4 oz/1 stick unsalted butter
1 tbsp sugar
4 tbsp Cointreau
150 ml/ $\frac{1}{4}$ pt/ $\frac{2}{3}$ cup orange juice
Grated rind and juice of 1 lemon
Grated rind of 2 oranges
Orange slices to garnish

Melt butter in a large frying pan, and add all other ingredients. Heat gently. Place a *crêpe* in the pan, and soak both sides in sauce. Fold it in half and in half again, to make a triangle. Push it to one side of the pan, and continue in this way with all the *crêpes*. Sprinkle with sugar, and garnish with orange slices.

Just before serving, heat a little more Cointreau in a ladle. Set it alight, and pour over the *crêpes*. Serve immediately.

Suggested wines:
Coteaux du Layon, Bonnezeaux, Vouvray

The temperamental mistral, in winter savagely cold, but now, in summer, like a blast-furnace, has finally dropped. Tall rows of cypress, planted to break its unremitting force, bow in perpetual obeisance, but people stand straight once more, relieved, tempers visibly cooled. At outdoor tables, under the shade of dappled plane trees, they linger over beaded glasses of cloudy anise-flavoured *pastis*, and look forward dreamily to the midday meal.

It is Friday. Those who live by the azure coast, or near Marseilles, anticipate a bubbling, saffron-scented cauldron of *bouillabaisse*, fishy festival of the colours, smells and freshness of the south of France. To some, though, Friday would not be complete without *brandade de morue*, a Provençal dish of pounded salt cod mixed to a thick paste with olive oil, garlic, and milk. Still others rub their hands in glee at the thought of *le grand aïoli*, a feast of poached whiting, salt cod, red mullet, and other fish, hard-boiled eggs, boiled potatoes, carrots, artichokes, and beans. The broth in which the fish has cooked is served first, with slices of fried bread and a dollop of *aïoli* in each bowl. Afterwards the *aïoli*—that pungent garlic mayonnaise that in its concentrated potency and unashamed egg-yolk-yellow sheen seems the very essence of this sun-baked land—is eaten in great quantity with the poached fish, egg, and boiled vegetables.

Deep, long swallows of powerful Côtes du Rhône slake thirsts worked up by this garlicky feast, and afterwards a drowsy, sleepy state of contentment descends over the entire region, from two until four, five, or even six o'clock in the afternoon. Try at those times to buy your *baguette*, pâté, or yellow-skinned chicken and

you will have no luck, for shops and stalls close their faded green or peeling pink shutters to keep out the world. They open again when it is cooler—only slightly cooler—and men emerge to congregate in the shade of plane trees, on dirt-covered promenades with benches that face each other. Time now for other serious business —the evening session of *boule* begins.

The serious business of playing *boule*.

How we love the south of France. Below Lyons, the mighty Rhône descends through the steep, roasted, vine-terraced gorge known as the Côte Rôtie, then glides slowly past the rearing hill at Hermitage. Honey-and-nut scented Montélimar comes next, then Orange, the impressive ruins of Châteauneuf-du-Pape, and the papal residence that dominates walled Avignon. To the west lies the rugged Massif Central; to the east, the Alps, from where this great river springs. Finally, below Avignon, it branches into myriad arteries that trickle slowly towards the warmth of the Mediterranean.

The Roman ruins in towns such as Nîmes and Arles remind us that Provence is so named because it was once a province of the Roman Empire. Farther south still, we reach' the swampy river-delta lands known as the Cam-

argue. Wild horses, pink flamingos, and gypsy 'cowboys' roam this remote land. And to the east, past industrial Marseilles, the fabled beaches and resorts of the Côte d'Azur glisten in the clear blue light. Over all hangs the heavy inviting scent of juniper, wild thyme, rosemary, and lavender.

In this dark-skinned land, people and flavours are direct, forthright, assertive, as colourful as scarlet tomatoes, as lively and peppery as the braided strings of tight-cloved Provençal garlic that hang in every kitchen.

Though the wines of the Côtes du Rhône vary tremendously, both in style and quality, they too share the character of this sunny southern land. They are at once robust and full-bodied, and have a power that comes from grapes that have ripened in intense heat to produce a concentration of sugar, and thus a high degree of alcohol (sugar is converted into alcohol during fermentation). Châteauneuf-du-Pape, one of the best known wines of the Rhône, boasts the highest minimum alcohol content in France: 12.5 per cent. In the nearby wine communes of Gigondas and Vacqueyras, it is not uncommon for huge red wines to attain a natural alcohol level of up to 16 per cent. In Beaumes-de-Venise, Muscat grapes ripen to a luscious, druggingly sweet, intensely fragrant, and (since it is slightly fortified) powerful state to produce Muscat de Beaumes-de-Venise. Even the pink wines of the region have a body and assertiveness that is remarkable. In the case of Tavel and Lirac rosé, the southern climate, plus a delicate blending of different varieties of black and white grapes, result in dry, forceful, sur-prisingly full-bodied wines with up to 13 per cent alcohol. These, certainly, are 'wines of the sun'.

Châteauneuf-du-Pape has a name that is both easily remembered and evocative, for the vineyards extend through wine communes that surround the ruined fourteenth-century summer residence of popes when they were seated at Avignon. The wine, once savoured by popes (and anti-popes) today is still acclaimed. The vineyards are some of the most bizarre in Europe, for stumpy, lush, free-standing vines spring from fields of huge smooth pebbles.

The ruins of
Châteauneuf-
du-Pape.

The 'soil' at Châteauneuf-du-Pape.

fieriness, while the Grenache contributes finesse). There are, however, no firm rules on the exact proportions of grapes needed to produce this wine, which means that styles vary among producers (some make deeper, darker wine which needs longer ageing; others blend a higher proportion of white grapes to produce a younger, fresher style). Traditionally Châteauneuf-du-Pape needed at least five to ten years ageing before it was ready to drink; today, however, the prevailing taste is for younger, lighter wines.

Châteauneuf-du-Pape is a big, powerful wine by any standard. Similar wine is produced at Gigondas, at the foot of the Montmirail hills, and in various other wine communes in this southern sector of the Rhône valley. An even bigger and fuller wine, however, comes from the north: Hermitage. Dark, rich in tannin, and with a harsh, deep fieriness that comes from the Syrah grape, Hermitage, a generation or two ago, was as well known and popular as the wines of Bordeaux and Burgundy. In those days, however, people who drank wine had both the time and money necessary to 'lay down' such wines for the decade or so needed to allow them to mellow, lose some of their fire, and develop a subtle and complex bouquet that only comes from bottle-ageing. Today, most of us are less patient; or perhaps we seek more immediate, if less complex pleasure from our wine. Hermitage, nevertheless, is a great classic, and the red and white wines from the surrounding area known as Crozes-Hermitage are worth seeking, too.

Opposite the town of Tain l'Hermitage, on the west side of the Rhône, the vines that flourish on the granite hills produce both deep, rich red, and full-bodied white wines that bear the *appellation* St Joseph. The sun-baked vineyards of Cornas (the name means 'burnt ground' in Celtic) also produce powerful, heady red wine from the Syrah grape. Curiously, to the south and east, still white and full-bodied sparkling wines are produced in the wine communes of St Péray and Die. Clairette de Die is a luminous sparkler with a fresh and intense bouquet that comes from a high proportion of the Muscat grape. These *méthode champenoise* wines in particular are powerfully refreshing.

There is no earth in sight. Despite problems (imagine trying to plough such a field), these huge pebbles store heat by day then warm the vines on summer nights that are sometimes quite brisk, allowing the grapes to reach a rich state of ripeness. But heat and ripeness alone are not sufficient to produce great wine. For Châteauneuf-du-Pape and other great wines of the Rhône—those from the Côte Rôtie, Condrieu, and Hermitage, for example—have a richness, depth of flavour, and complexity that raise them well above less distinguished 'hot country wines' generally produced in southern climes.

In the case of Châteauneuf-du-Pape, a rare combination of strength, aroma, and delicacy is generated in part through a traditional blending of up to thirteen permitted varieties of both black and white grapes to gain a desired balance (the Clairette and to a lesser extent the Syrah, for example, give strength and a certain gutsy

The wine commune of Gigondas on the slopes of the Mont Ventoux range.

Slowly, we are making our way up-river, away from the Mediterranean, the herbs, and olive groves of Provence. Indeed, this path north was the natural trade route in Roman days (today it is the natural route for holiday-makers heading for the south of France). Yet though the vineyards near Vienne are closer to gastronomic Lyons and Burgundy than to Avignon, the wines produced on these upper stretches have a decidedly sunny, southern style as well.

The Côte Rôtie, meaning 'roasted hill', is a fit name for these ancient terraced vineyards that are scorched in mid-summer and treacherous to till. The large area divides naturally into the Côte Blonde and the Côte Brune—legend has it that a nobleman willed his lands to be shared between his two daughters, one fair, the other dark. The character of wines from each of these areas corresponds with the legend, and through blending wines from the lighter Côte Blonde with the heavier wines of the Côte Brune, a balance of strength and smoothness, and a complex yet delicate bouquet is achieved.

The vineyards of Condrieu, below the Côte Rôtie, produce dry and medium-dry white wine exclusively from the Viognier grape. Its crisp assertive freshness acquires a deeper, more compact, and profound character with age, but always the wines retain delicate fruity and floral scents. (The greatest wine of Condrieu is known as Château Grillet, a minute estate that is entitled to its own *appellation* because it produces some of the finest, most fragrant white wine in France.)

These wines are the great and prestigious products of the Rhône valley, quality wines, produced, by necessity, in small, defined areas. Equally important, from our point of view, are the relatively plentiful red, rosé, and, to a lesser extent, white wines that bear the more common *appellation* Côtes du Rhône or Côtes du Rhône-Villages. Honest, full-bodied wines of the sun, they are produced primarily in co-operatives, the *vignerons* of this sleepy southern land presumably content to leave the making and marketing of wine to others.

While the rosé and white wines are attractively fresh, and relatively powerful, the red wines of the Côtes du Rhône vary considerably in style. Many wines, for example, are made to be drunk while young and fruity. A type of fermentation known as *macération carbonique* is employed, which retains freshness and fruit above all, to produce wines that are extremely attractive when drunk young. Some Côtes du Rhône is sold as *primeur*, and, like the popular, youthful wines from Beaujolais to the north, is meant to be imbibed within weeks of the vintage. By six months, its fresh fruitiness is lost. On the other hand, Côtes du Rhône red can also be dark, rich, full-bodied, and in need of bottle-ageing to gain character.

In particular, wines from sixteen superior communes that conform to stricter regulations (limited production, restricted yield, compulsory tasting, for example), called Côtes du Rhône-Villages, generally produce fuller, darker wines meant to be laid down to improve for perhaps two or three years, and maybe more, depending on the vintage. Such wines approach the character of greater wines—Châteauneuf-du-Pape and Gigondas.

The Côtes du Rhône are about the 'biggest' of all quality French wines—that is, the wines are made from grapes that have received more sun, have more sugar, are a darker colour, and have higher alcohol levels than many others. Yet the finest wines, undoubtedly, have an underlying delicacy. Other wines make up for lack of finesse with increased body, guts, and strength. Though neither fine, delicate, nor particularly complex, they competently hold their own—and there are times when, of course, that is all we ask.

Here in the south of France, a carafe of plummy *vin rouge* or *vin rosé* goes down quite easily when accompanied by such typically strong-flavoured foods as *anchoïade*. This is a sauce made from pounded anchovies, garlic, and olive oil. A bowl of it is often served at the start of a meal, to be spooned over salad, used as a dip for raw legs of celery, fennel, or carrots, or spread on to rounds of coarse, country bread that has been toasted over an open fire.

Indeed, if the Côtes du Rhône produces 'wines of the sun', the cuisine of the south of France likewise gains its character from that flaming, angry ball that captivated Van Gogh with its brilliance and unrelenting intensity during the painter's stay in Arles.

The markets of Provence are a riot of colour, as bright, as varied, as sensuous as the bikini bottoms that dot the sandy southern beaches. Huge pregnant aubergines (eggplant) swell to magnificent size here, while ripe, red tomatoes grow beyond their conventional form into weird irregular shapes. Deep-green courgettes (zucchini), strings of thin-skinned pungent onions, piles of fine, rounded *haricots verts* (green beans), long, dimpled cucumbers, and at least a dozen different types of lettuce are laid out in the morning light that slants through the canopy of plane trees lining the broad avenues. Tiny, green-fleshed melons from Cavaillon scent the air with their particular perfume, while oozing, splitting figs attract both shoppers and honey bees. Apricots, small and dry, with an intense, concentrated flavour, are displayed beside bulging watermelons that are often split in half and

Basil has a permanent place in the cuisine of Provence.

Pont du Gard near Nîmes, a Roman aqueduct.

onions, olives, anchovies, and olive oil is baking over a *feu de bois*. Let's take home slices of this tasty Provençal 'pizza' to begin our meal.

Whatever else we decide to prepare, we had better pick up some more fresh herbs. The basil, of course, sits on the windowsill, soaking up the sun. But that stall over there is selling bunches of flat-leaved parsley, tarragon, chervil, thyme, sorrel, and rosemary. Fresh, bitter, oily, sweet or pungent, these herbs of Provence fill us with pleasure. Along with olive oil and garlic, they are the most distinctive elements in the cuisine of the south.

Rosemary is massaged into lamb or kid along with olive oil and coarse salt, which is then spit-roasted over glowing coals until crisp and brown. Sea bass and red mullet are delicious stuffed with sprigs of fresh fennel, grilled over a fire of dried fennel stalks and branches. The *bourride*, a favourite fish soup, is flavoured with saffron, garlic, and parsley. Up in the scrubby hills, hare or rabbit is caught, skinned, and stewed with bacon, parsley, juniper berries, and wine. And in upland *mas*, those whitewashed ranches that seem to sprout from the hills, a well-worn *daube* bubbles slowly on top of every stove. In the *daube* (both the name of the cooking vessel and this classic country stew) wild thyme and bitter orange-peel flavour tough old meat that has marinated in red wine until it is as tender and fragrant as the best steak.

Tiny-leaved deep green basil lends its warm and peppery scent to salads and sauces. When pounded in a mortar with crushed garlic, olive oil, and pine nuts, it becomes one of the most delicious of all sauces: *pistou*. *Pistou* is similar to Italian *pesto*, found down the coast in Genoa, and is the star ingredient of *soupe au pistou*, a rich vegetable brew, brimming with all the scents of a sunlit Provençal garden.

Ultimately, this is the gift of the south of France: days that dawn with a cloudless azure sky, boundless, holding on to day, making it last longer than anywhere else, before relinquishing it imperceptibly into deep, starry night; clean fresh air smelling of herbs, honey, and heat; tangy salt wind that makes our faces and skin feel tight and good; and wine and food of the sun. How we love them.

filled with local wine. Pears, oranges, lemons, pomegranates ripen to perfection under constant, clear blue skies.

What shall we have for lunch today? An aubergine, a few of those courgettes, some onions, garlic, tomatoes, and peppers will make a delicious *ratatouille* when stewed together slowly in thick, green, virgin olive oil. On the other hand, we can slice some carrots and courgettes and layer them in an earthenware dish together with the boiled potatoes left over from yester-day's *grand aïoli*. Pour over a beaten egg or two, sprinkle with chopped herbs, and this *tian de Provence* makes a fragrant and filling meal. Can we pass that pile of tomatoes, the lettuce, and tubs of pointed black, green, or rich brown olives swimming in brine and herbs, or the salted anchovy fillets? Together they will make that classic favourite, *salade niçoise*. But what's that burnt, dusty, spicy smell coming from up the street? An old Citroën van has propped open its side, and inside, in a portable oven, *pissaladière*, thin bread dough covered with sliced sweet

Quantities where necessary are given in
Metric, Imperial and US measurements

Salade Niçoise

Serves 4

1 lettuce, washed and dried
250 g/$\frac{1}{2}$ lb cold blanched French beans
3 firm tomatoes, quartered
1 green pepper, coarsely sliced
2 hard-boiled eggs, peeled and quartered
4 anchovy fillets
10 small black olives
1 small tin tuna, drained and flaked
1 garlic clove, peeled and crushed
3 tbsp olive oil
1 tbsp wine vinegar
Salt
Freshly ground black pepper
Freshly chopped chives

Arrange lettuce in a large salad bowl. Place
French beans over lettuce, then add tomatoes,
pepper, and eggs. Decorate with anchovy fillets
and olives. Lay flaked tuna on the top. Garnish
with freshly chopped chives. Make dressing with
garlic, olive oil, vinegar, and seasoning. Serve
dressing in a bowl separately.

Suggested wine:
Côtes de Provence rosé

Anchoïade

Anchovy Sauce
Serves 4

2 garlic cloves, peeled
50 g/2 oz tin anchovy fillets in olive oil
6 black olives, pitted and chopped
4 tbsp olive oil
Few drops wine vinegar
Freshly ground black pepper

Pound garlic in a mortar. Add anchovy fillets
and olives, and pound well. Add olive oil, a drop

at a time. Mix in a little vinegar, and season to
taste with pepper.

This sauce can be served as a dip for fresh raw
vegetables such as fennel, whole radishes, sticks
of celery, carrots, cucumbers, and others in
season, along with rounds of coarse, thickly
sliced bread, preferably toasted over an open fire.

Suggested wines:
Costières du Gard, St Joseph, Cornas

Soupe au Pistou

Provençal Vegetable Soup
Serves 6

250 g/$\frac{1}{2}$ lb French beans, cut into 2$\frac{1}{2}$ cm/1 in lengths
1 large onion, peeled and diced
250 g/$\frac{1}{2}$ lb carrots, diced
100 g/4 oz dried haricot beans (soaked overnight)
250 g/$\frac{1}{2}$ lb courgettes (zucchini), sliced
3 tomatoes, peeled and chopped
2 potatoes, peeled and diced
50 g/2 oz vermicelli, broken into short lengths
3 garlic cloves, peeled
Large handful fresh basil, chopped
2 tbsp olive oil
Grated Parmesan or Gruyère cheese

Put all vegetables into 1.8 l/3 pt/7 cups of
boiling salted water. Simmer for 1 hr. Just before
vegetables are cooked, add the vermicelli.

Meanwhile, crush garlic and fresh basil, using a mortar and pestle. When a paste has formed,
add olive oil, drop by drop, stirring constantly.

When the pasta is cooked, add a ladleful of
soup liquid to basil mixture, and mix well. Stir
this into the soup.

Sprinkle with grated cheese, and serve with
French bread.

Suggested wine:
Tavel rosé

Ratatouille
Vegetable Stew
Serves 6

*2 large aubergines (eggplants), peeled and
cut into rough cubes
3 medium courgettes (zucchini), sliced
5 tbsp olive oil
2 garlic cloves, peeled and crushed
2 large onions, peeled and thinly sliced
3 red or green peppers, chopped
4 large tomatoes, peeled and chopped (or 1 large tin
of Italian plum tomatoes)
Salt
Freshly ground black pepper
Handful freshly chopped basil (or 1 tsp dried basil)*

Sprinkle aubergines and courgettes with salt, and
put in a colander. Place a weighted plate on top,
so excess moisture and bitterness will be pressed
out. Leave for 1 hr. Pat dry.

Heat olive oil in a large saucepan. Gently fry
garlic and onions until soft and golden. Add
aubergines, courgettes, and peppers. Cover and
simmer for 35 min. Then add tomatoes and basil.
Season, and cook uncovered for further 20 min.

Serve hot or cold as an hors-d'oeuvre, or as
an accompaniment to grilled or boiled meats.

Suggested wines:
*Côtes du Rhône (white) or Côtes de Provence
rosé*

Tian des Legumes avec Sauce Diable
Egg and Vegetable Casserole
Serves 4–6

*1 small aubergine (eggplant), cut into slices
3 small courgettes (zucchini), sliced
4 tbsp olive oil
1 garlic clove, peeled and finely chopped
1 large onion, peeled and sliced
3 medium potatoes, semi-boiled, peeled, and sliced
2 carrots, sliced*

*5 eggs
Salt
Freshly ground black pepper
1 tbsp mixed fresh herbs (or 1 heaped tsp dried
herbs)*

Place aubergine and courgette slices in a colander.
Sprinkle with salt, and cover with a weighted
plate. Allow to stand for 1 hr., until moisture and
bitterness is drawn out. Pat each slice dry on both
sides.

Grease a large earthenware baking dish.

Heat 1 tbsp olive oil in a large frying pan.
Gently sauté garlic and onion until soft and
golden. Transfer to baking dish. Place sliced
semi-boiled potatoes on top of onions. Season,
and lightly sprinkle with herbs.

Pour another spoonful of olive oil into frying
pan, and gently sauté the carrot. After a few
minutes, again transfer to baking dish, and lay on
top of potatoes. Season, and do same with
aubergines and finally courgettes.

Beat eggs, and pour over vegetable mixture.
Pour remaining olive oil over top. Cover and
bake in a moderate oven, 180°C/Gas Mark 4/
350°F, for about 20–25 min. until egg is set.

Serve immediately, cut into wedges, with
sauce diable, French bread, and green salad.

Sauce Diable

*4 shallots, peeled and finely chopped
150 ml/$\frac{1}{4}$ pt/$\frac{2}{3}$ cup white wine
Sprig of fresh thyme
1 bay leaf
Salt
Freshly ground black pepper
75 g/3 oz/$\frac{3}{4}$ stick butter
Pinch of cayenne pepper*

Put shallots, white wine, thyme, bay leaf, and
seasoning together in a small saucepan. Bring
slowly to the boil, and allow liquid to reduce a
little. Remove thyme and bay leaf. Beat in
butter, a little at a time, until mixture is thick and
smooth. Season to taste with cayenne pepper.

Suggested wines:
Tavel or Lirac rosé

Aïoli

Garlic Mayonnaise
Serves about 4

4 garlic cloves, peeled
Salt
1 egg yolk (at room temperature)
150 ml/¼ pt/⅔ cup olive oil
Freshly ground black pepper
1 tbsp lemon juice

Mash garlic and salt in a mortar and pestle until almost liquid. Transfer to a mixing bowl. Add egg yolk, and mix in well with a fork. Add a few drops of olive oil, and beat well. Continue to do this, beating in the oil a drop at a time, until half of the oil has been mixed in and the sauce is thick and smooth. Add remaining oil in a steady trickle, beating constantly. Season with salt and pepper and lemon juice to taste. (This amount of garlic produces a fairly strongly flavoured mayonnaise. Fewer—or even more—cloves can, of course, be used.)

Serve with fish, boiled meats, raw vegetables, boiled eggs, and even snails.

Suggested wine:
Côtes du Rhône

La Daube de Boeuf Provençal

Provençal Braised Beef
Serves 6

1.5 kg/3 lb braising beef, cut into about 6 cm/2½ in
squares, and 1 cm/½ in thick
300 ml/½ pt/1¼ cups Côtes du Rhône
Sprig of fresh thyme
1 bay leaf
2 garlic cloves, peeled and crushed
Salt
Freshly ground black pepper
2 onions, peeled and thinly sliced
6 carrots, thinly sliced
5 tbsp olive oil
4 rashers/slices of bacon, cut into short lengths
500 g/1 lb tomatoes, peeled and chopped
1 strip of orange peel

6 anchovy fillets
1 tbsp capers
2 tbsp wine vinegar
1 garlic clove, peeled
1 tbsp freshly chopped parsley

Place pieces of beef in a large bowl with wine, thyme, bay leaf, garlic, salt, pepper, onions, and half of the carrots. Cover and leave to marinate for at least 3 hr., preferably overnight, basting occasionally.

Remove meat and vegetables from marinade, and set liquid aside. Pour half of the olive oil into a large casserole. Make alternate layers of bacon, beef, vegetables, and tomatoes, ending on a layer of tomatoes. Pour in marinade liquid and, if necessary, some extra stock, to cover meat and vegetables. Bury the orange peel in the middle. Gradually bring to the boil, cover, and simmer for 4 hr.

Crush anchovy fillets and capers in a bowl to make a paste. Beat in olive oil, vinegar, garlic, and parsley. Add this anchovy paste to casserole, 1½ hr. before *daube* is ready. At the same time add remaining sliced carrots. Cover and continue to cook until beef is tender.

Remove meat and lay on a warmed serving dish. Pour liquid and vegetables over beef slices, and serve with buttered noodles, rice, or boiled potatoes.

Suggested wines:
Côtes du Rhône-Villages, Hermitage,
Côte Rôtie

Civet de Lapin

Stewed Rabbit
Serves 4

2 tbsp olive oil
1 large onion, peeled and chopped
4 rashers/slices of fatty bacon or ham, chopped
1 rabbit, cut into pieces
Handful freshly chopped parsley
6–8 juniper berries, coarsely crushed
Sprig of fresh thyme
Salt
Freshly ground black pepper
300 ml/½ pt/1¼ cups Côtes du Rhône
150 ml/¼ pt/⅔ cup stock

Heat oil in a large casserole, and gently fry onions and bacon until soft. Add rabbit pieces, and sauté until browned on all sides. Add parsley, juniper berries, thyme, salt, and pepper. Add wine and stock. Bring to the boil, cover, and simmer until tender, about 2 hr. Arrange rabbit pieces on warmed serving platter. Reduce sauce, and pour over rabbit.

Suggested wines:
Gigondas, Côtes du Rhône-Villages,
Châteauneuf-du-Pape

Pissaladière

Makes 1 large *pissaladière*

25 g/1 oz dried yeast
150 ml/¼ pt/⅔ cup tepid water
500 g/1 lb/3½ cups flour
1 tsp salt
3 tbsp olive oil
3 large onions, peeled and sliced
12 small black olives, stoned
12 anchovy fillets
Salt
Freshly ground black pepper

Dissolve yeast in tepid water, and pour into a large mixing bowl. Add enough flour to make a soft dough. Cover with a damp cloth, and leave in a warm place to rise, about 30 min.

Put remaining flour into another mixing bowl with salt, and add the risen yeast and flour dough. Mix well until firm enough to be shaped into a ball. Turn dough out on to a floured board, and knead well for 10 min. until smooth and elastic. Roll dough into a ball. Place in a bowl, cover with damp cloth, and leave in a warm place until it has doubled its volume (this will take about 1 hr.).

Meanwhile, heat oil in a large frying pan. Add onions, cover, and cook until they are very soft and golden, about 30–40 min.

When dough has risen, knead again. Grease a large rectangular baking sheet. Stretch and pull the dough until it fits the baking sheet. It should not be more than 1 cm/¼ in thick. Spread onions over dough. Arrange anchovy fillets in criss-cross pattern, then dot with olives. Season. Bake in a moderate oven, 180°C/Gas Mark 4/ 350°F, for 30 min.

Serve cut into slices sprinkled with olive oil.

Suggested wine:
Côtes du Rhône primeur

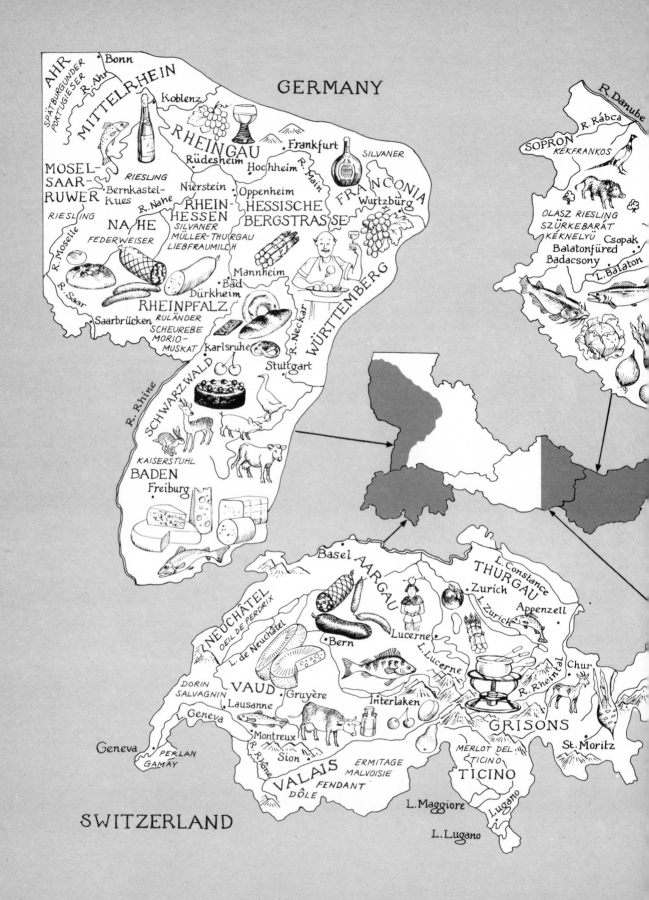

GERMANY

AHR
SPÄTBURGUNDER
PORTUGIESER
R. Ahr
• Bonn

MITTELRHEIN
• Koblenz

RHEINGAU
Rüdesheim
Hochheim
• Frankfurt
R. Main
SILVANER

MOSEL-
SAAR-
RUWER
RIESLING
Bernkastel-
Kues
Nierstein
Oppenheim
FRANCONIA
Wurtzbürg

R. Nahe
RHEIN-
HESSEN
HESSISCHE
BERGSTRASSE

RIESLING
NAHE
FEDERWEISER
SILVANER
MÜLLER-THURGAU
LIEBFRAUMILCH

R. Moselle

R. Saar

Mannheim
Bad
Dürkheim
RHEINPFALZ
Saarbrücken
RULÄNDER
SCHEUREBE
MORIO-
MUSKAT
Karlsruhe

WÜRTTEMBERG
R. Neckar

Stuttgart

R. Rhine

SCHWARZWALD

KAISERSTUHL
BADEN
Freiburg

SOPRON
R. Rábca
R. Danube
KÉKFRANKOS

OLASZ RIESLING
SZÜRKEBARÁT
KÉKNELYÜ Csopak
Balatonfüred
Badacsony
L. Balaton

Basel AARGAU
NEUCHÂTEL
OEIL DE PERDRIX
L. de Neuchâtel
• Bern
Lucerne •
L. Lucerne
L. Constance
THURGAU
Zurich
L. Zurich
Appenzell

DORIN
SALVAGNIN
VAUD
Lausanne •
Gruyère
Interlaken
R. Rheintal
Chur

Geneva
PERLAN
GAMAY
L. Geneva
Montreux •
R. Rhône
Sion
VALAIS
DÔLE
ERMITAGE
MALVOISIE
FENDANT

MERLOT DEL
TICINO
GRISONS
St. Moritz
TICINO

L. Maggiore
Lugano
L. Lugano

SWITZERLAND

CENTRAL EUROPE

TOKAJ-HEGYALJA

TOKAY ESSENCIA
TOKAY ASZU
Tokay •

MÁTRA MTNS
KADARKA
KÉKFRANKOS
DEBRÖI HÁRSLEVELÜ

R. Tisza

• Eger
EGRI BIKAVER
EGRI LÉANYKA

• Budapest

• Debrecen

R. Danube

R. Sárviz

• Pécs

R. Körös

R. Berettyó

Csongrád •

• Szeged

Villány •

HUNGARY

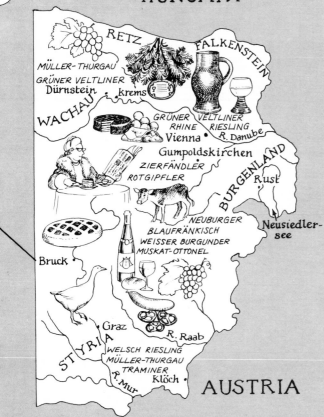

RETZ

FALKENSTEIN

MÜLLER-THURGAU
GRÜNER VELTLINER
Dürnstein • Krems •

WACHAU

GRÜNER VELTLINER
RHINE RIESLING
• Vienna R. Danube

Gumpoldskirchen
ZIERFÄNDLER
ROTGIPFLER

BURGENLAND

Rust

Neusiedler-see

NEUBURGER
BLAUFRÄNKISCH
WEISSER BURGUNDER
MUSKAT-OTTONEL

Bruck

• Graz
R. Raab

STYRIA

WELSCH RIESLING
MÜLLER-THURGAU
TRAMINER
R. Mur Klöch •

AUSTRIA

A pretzel seller in Salzburg.

AUSTRIA

A century ago, Austria formed the core of a vast 600-year-old empire that extended through much of modern Czechoslovakia, Hungary, parts of Yugoslavia, Romania, and northern Italy; today she is a small neutral country with a total population less than London's. Vienna, capital of the then Austro-Hungarian Empire and home of the Habsburgs, was the glamour centre of Europe, if not the world; today this old-fashioned and faded central European capital exists on the fringe, perched precariously between east and west. The city was fragmented by the Allied powers after World War II, and administered by them until 1955; Bratislava, on the Czech border, is only some thirty-five miles to the east, while Budapest is just a few hours away. The empire is dead. Yet Mozart and Haydn, Schubert and Strauss, *Strudel* and *Schlagobers, Wiener Schnitzel* and wine (*Wien und Wein*)—in short, a natural passion and zest for cultured good living—remain, as unconquerable, as sentimental as the Danube itself.

Nowhere is this cultivated way of life more apparent than in the coffee houses of Vienna, which offer up to fifty varieties of that brew left behind by the Turks. In addition, they are a place in which to read the daily papers (thoughtfully supplied on cane holders), meet old friends, catch up on gossip, see and be seen, or doze in the waning afternoon. To *habitués*, such places as Demel, on the Kohlmarkt, the Hotel Sacher, across from the Opera House, or Prückel, on the Stubenring, are no less than a second home. Regulars have tables reserved, and the black-coated waiters know exactly what type of coffee and which newspapers each client requires. Some go so far as to receive telephone calls and have

A beer garden in Salzburg makes a popular
meeting-place.

An habitué enjoys coffee and the news
in the afternoon sun
of the Prückel café in Vienna.

their post delivered to their café. It is almost incidental that the *Einspänner* (hot coffee served in a glass topped with *Schlagobers*—whipped cream), *Strudel*, or *Sachertorte* (chocolate cake layered with apricot jam then covered in chocolate icing) are so irresistibly delicious.

If cafés are integral to the Viennese way of life, the *Heurigen* found throughout the wine districts of this country also demonstrate a uniquely Austrian attitude to wine, food, and good living. The word '*heurig*' means literally 'this year's', and signifies both a wine tavern and the wine itself, which is always young, fruity, fresh—this year's wine. The symbol of such taverns is a cluster of fir branches or a straw wheel that is hung out to announce that the *Heurige* is open (many *Heurigen* are seasonal, staying open only for as long as this year's wine lasts). Some, like those found on the outskirts of Vienna, in villages such as Grinzing, Sievering, and Heiligenstadt, are immense (the Beethoven-haus, for example, where the composer wrote

A faithful regular in a *Heurige*
in the Wachau.

Playing cards in Vienna's Stadtpark.

Fidelio is a favourite and large gathering place for smart Viennese); on the other hand, in wine districts such as Niederösterreich and the Burgenland, a *Heurige* can simply be a couple of crude picnic tables set up in the back garden or front drive of a wine producer's house, under a trellis of vines or in the shade of a linden tree. The wine and food are probably served by his wife or children through an open kitchen window, and most of the people who gather are friends or neighbours.

The fresh wine comes in stout quarter-litre glass mugs, smelling of grapes and youth, and is usually accompanied by simple foods such as salty pretzels, rolls sprinkled with caraway and dill seeds, Liptauer cheese (a pungent, paprika-flavoured spread that helps work up a thirst—if such help is needed), slices of smoked pork, pickled vegetables, home-made sausages, and hard-boiled eggs. One can sit for ever (as in Viennese cafés) at any of numerous unpretentious spots along the banks of the Danube, drinking

Heurige, nibbling a piece of meat, and listening to the sound of water and the sentimental singing that always begins before long when old friends and relatives gather in the country.

Austria is perhaps not well known internationally as a major wine-producing country. During the nineteenth century, the Austro-Hungarian Empire was so vast that its vineyards included those of Hungary, the Alto Adige region of north-west Italy (an area that still produces wines much closer in style to Austrian than to Italian), and Slovenia, in northern Yugoslavia. Today, of course, her wine country is considerably smaller, yet a remarkable variety of wine continues to be produced. It is perhaps surprising to discover that Austria, known primarily for dry-to-medium-dry light wines, also produces full-bodied fruity red wines, as well as rich, spicy, and naturally sweet dessert wines.

One imagines Austria to be a land of alps and mountain streams, but this is only one aspect of a varied landscape that reflects its character in the tints and flavours of the wine it produces.

Niederösterreich (Lower Austria) is a vast province that extends both south of Vienna and north to the Czechoslovak border. It is the country's largest and most important wine-producing area, and a source of both high-quality wines produced in limited quantity and also plentiful light table wines. Such easy-drinking wines are generally produced from grapes grown by the so-called 'high culture' system pioneered by the Austrian viticulturist, Dr Lenz Moser. By this method rows of vines are planted wide distances apart, thus allowing the widescale use of machinery; moreover, the vines are pruned and trained in such a manner as to yield substantially more crop. The Austrian Quality-Wine Seal, incidentally, is a guarantee of quality and authenticity awarded to wines that have undergone a strict official examination to ensure, among other things, that each is exclusively of Austrian origin, reaches a minimum must weight, and is typical of the region in which it is produced. The wine district known as the Wachau is probably the best known within Niederösterreich, a craggy, brown, austere stretch of land along the banks of the Danube, between the two baroque monasteries of Melk and Stift Gottweig. Since the natural banks of the river here are so steep, they have had to be terraced and separated by walls to prevent erosion. The best wines are produced from grapes grown on these upper slopes. The Grüner Veltliner, Austria's most important, versatile, and distinctive grape, gives wine that is fruity, assertive, yet pleasantly sharp, the result of a balanced acidity. As well as the Grüner Veltliner, the most widely planted grape varieties in Niederösterreich are the Rhine Riesling, Welsch Riesling, Müller-Thurgau, and Weisser Burgunder.

One of the best known Austrian wines comes from Niederösterreich—a light, gulpable table wine called Schluck (the word, after all, means 'gulp'). Other light, delicate white wines come from Falkenstein and Retz, while connoisseurs seek the individual characteristics of single vineyard wines from communes such as Loiben, Dürnstein, Krems, and Stein. Gumpoldskirchen is famous for its rich late-gathered wines made from the unique local grape varieties known as Zierfändler and Rotgipfler.

The Burgenland is another important wine region south of Vienna, centred around the steamy Neusiedlersee, a weird marshy lake twenty miles long but never more than six feet deep. The vineyards here once formed part of the important Hungarian wine region centred around Sopron. After World War I, the residents voted to become a part of Austria, but Hungarian influence is still apparent in the lively gypsy *csárdás* (both the name of the tavern and the folk dances performed there), the vivid food, and character of the people. Here the vines grow on gentle, mineral-rich slopes in a humid, hot-house atmosphere that is due to a high level of evaporation from the lake. Steamy autumn mists and long slow Indian summers produce the perfect conditions for over-ripening of grapes. *Botrytis cinerea* sets in with remarkable regularity. Though elsewhere in Europe such wine made from over-ripe grapes is a rare and prized marvel, producers in the Burgenland are able to produce in quantity luscious, naturally sweet dessert wines that bear the quality designations *auslese*, *beerenauslese*, and *trockenbeerenauslese*, terms which signify increasingly higher degrees of

The Danube at Dürnstein, an important wine town in
the Wachau, and one of the most beautiful.

ripeness and sweetness—higher, in fact, than their German counterparts. Such wines are naturally popular in Germany, providing Austria with a reliable export market. But they are also increasingly exported elsewhere now, as many more appreciate the beauty of a well-made, golden, naturally sweet wine.

Additionally, the Burgenland produces a variety of pungent, full-bodied, but often dry wines. The Grüner Veltliner, for example, here takes on an entirely different character—at once peppery, rich, full, and rather soft, not sharp. As well as the Grüner Veltliner, wine is made from the Welsch Riesling, Weisser Burgunder, Muskat-Ottonel, and Neuburger, while the Blaufränkisch produces a fruity, full-bodied red wine (similar mellow red wine comes from vineyards around Sopron, across in Hungary, where the same grape is known as the Kékfrankos).

Styria, to the south, has vineyards on the hills south of Graz that continue through to Yugoslavia's famed Ljutomer vineyards just fifty miles away. The wines produced from the Welsch Riesling and Müller-Thurgau are fruity and pleasant, and at least one district, that of Klöch, produces notable, pungent wine from Traminer grapes which have ripened on hot volcanic slopes to a sultry, spicy state.

The smallest wine region in Austria is found within Vienna itself: there are actually some 700 hectares of vines cultivated within the city limits. Vineyards to the west and north used to be extensive and important, and today even celebrated wine suburbs such as Grinzing, Nussdorf, and Stammersdorf feel the great city encroaching their borders. Yet these towns, and the wines produced on the slopes that rise above the Danube, will always be important both from a traditional and cultural point of view. Composers such as Beethoven, Mozart, and Schubert often came to them to drink wine and work (the two activities, it seems, could not be separated), and today these towns remain just as important in the lives of many Viennese. Most of the Grüner Veltliner, Rhine Riesling, or Weisser Burgunder produced here never reaches the bottle; it is drunk while young and frothy as *Heurige* in those delightful taverns, with a plate of Liptauer cheese and a stick of celery or pretzels, or with those deceptively simple Viennese dishes that have been handed down for generations.

Every Viennese housewife has her favourite way of preparing *Tafelspitz*, a popular national dish of succulent, tender boiled beef, served with mashed potatoes and a piquant horse-radish sauce. Such is the subtlety of the Viennese, however, that there are no less than twenty-four different cuts of meat that can be used in its preparation, each with its own set of devotees who swear that nothing else will suffice. They all

An inviting *Heurige*, a welcome resting-place in the Wachau.

however, agree that the meat must be of excellent quality, preferably cut from the leg or back. The broth in which the meat cooks is served as a clear soup, *Rindsuppe*, garnished perhaps with *Leberknödeln* (large liver dumplings), *Speckknödeln* (bacon dumplings), *Fritatten* (strips of pancake), or simply *mit Ei*, (with an egg poached in the simmering broth).

The preparation of Vienna's most famous dish, *Wiener Schnitzel*, takes no less care, for, simple though this breaded escalope appears, there are certain steps necessary to achieve perfection. A true *Wiener Schnitzel* is made of veal pounded to the thickness of an eighth of an inch; it should actually be just bigger than the plate on which it is served. The meat is coated lightly in flour, dipped in beaten egg, and rolled in fine dry breadcrumbs before being quickly fried in smoking lard. It should never be oily, and is served with a wedge of lemon—nothing more.

Almost as typical and popular is the Viennese version of fried chicken known as *Backhendl*. Spring chickens are split in half and flattened with a cleaver. Then they are coated with flour, dipped in egg, rolled in breadcrumbs, and fried in lard in exactly the same manner as *Wiener Schnitzel*. They are delicious served with a hot potato salad garnished with fried onions and bacon, and with a dish of sliced cucumbers marinated in lemon juice and sugar. A mug or two of young Grüner Veltliner doesn't hurt, either.

Other Austrian favourites are those from beyond present-day borders, for culinary alliances die harder than political ones. Goulash, for example, is eaten often here, but it is a refined, milder version of the famous *Magyar gulyás* of Hungary. Pork and sauerkraut, roast goose, and steamed bread dumplings and gravy are favourite carry-overs from Bohemia (and probably easier to come by today in Vienna than in Prague). And Venetian dishes such as *risotto* and fried fish are reminders of the time when Austria had an outlet to the Adriatic via Italy.

Even in the one realm the Viennese claim as purely their own—the art of pastry-making— echoes from the Empire are heard. But what matter if the Hungarians claim they invented *Strudel*? Or that the Czechs contributed the secret of making sweet steamed dumplings like *Marillenknödeln*, filled with fresh apricots, or *Zwetschkenknödeln*, stuffed with juicy plums that have been pitted and themselves filled with sugar and ground nuts? If the Empire is dead, in the realm of pastries, the Viennese today continue to reign supreme. No one can stretch out *Strudel* as finely, as transparently, nor fill it with a more delicious mixture of apples, butter, raisins, and sugar. Who but the Viennese would watch anxiously the result of a seven-year court case between Demel and the Hotel Sacher for the right to attach the epithet 'genuine' to the famous *Sachertorte*? And what of the *Linzertorte*, a raspberry jam pie covered with a lattice of buttery pastry, or the light, airy soufflé known as the *Salzburger Nockerl*, the varieties of *Kuchen* (cakes), or any of those numerous small biscuits (cookies) that are so delicious with a glass of sweet wine, such as *Zimtsterne* (cinnamon stars) or *Vanillekipfeln* (vanilla crescents), served with a generous dollop of *Schlagobers* on the side?

One could go on and on, listing creations as elaborate as the many baroque monasteries and churches found throughout this country. But our favourite is somewhat simpler: *Kaiserschmarrn*, the favourite dessert of Franz Joseph I, as its name commemorates. Just a pancake of flour, eggs, butter, sugar, and raisins, cooked in the pan, then torn vigorously (fanatically is not too strong a word) into small pieces with two forks. Yet the very arguments that rage over how small or large the pieces should be, or whether *Kaiserschmarrn* should be covered with jam or powdered sugar, testify that it is something much more—something indefinably, curiously linked with the old men who play Hungarian cardgames in the Stadtpark, wear medals on their chests on national holidays, or read newspapers and doze for hours in the Prückel café; with the young musicians playing Mozart in the exclusive Kärntnerstrasse as though the composer himself were conducting them; with the fragrance of steamed dumplings and gravy on a bitter January morning when steam and mist rise from the Danube as they did when the river symbolized the glory of a nation.

The Empire may be dead, but Austria is very much alive.

RECIPES FROM AUSTRIA

Quantities where necessary are given in
Metric, Imperial and US measurements.

Liptauer Käse

Paprika Cheese Spread
Serves 6

250 g/8 oz/$\frac{1}{2}$ lb curd cheese
100 g/4 oz/1 stick butter at room temperature
2 tbsp sour cream
Salt
1 tbsp caraway seed
1 tbsp sweet Hungarian paprika
$\frac{1}{2}$ small onion, peeled and grated

Cream butter in a mixing bowl, add curd cheese
and sour cream, stirring well. Add salt, caraway
seed, paprika, and grated onion. Mix well.
Arrange on a plate, and smooth out with a knife.
Serve as an appetizer, with carrot sticks and
bread rolls.

Suggested wines:
Grüner Veltliner, Welsch Riesling

Leberknödeln

Liver Dumplings
Serves 6

250 g/$\frac{1}{2}$ lb calf's liver
4 small bread rolls
25 g/1 oz/$\frac{1}{4}$ stick butter
1 onion, peeled and chopped
1 tbsp freshly chopped parsley
2 eggs, beaten
Salt
Freshly ground black pepper
Pinch of nutmeg
$\frac{1}{2}$ tsp marjoram
50 g/2 oz/$\frac{2}{3}$ cup dried breadcrumbs
2 tbsp flour

Grind the calf's liver, or finely chop with a sharp
knife. Break up the rolls. Soak them in water,
squeeze dry, and pluck apart.

Melt butter in a frying pan, and sauté onions
and parsley until golden.
Combine all ingredients, and shape into small
balls about 2$\frac{1}{2}$ cm/1 in in diameter. Drop into
boiling soup or stock. Boil uncovered for about
10 min., or until dumplings rise to surface.
Serve in bowls, with soup or broth.

Suggested wines:
*Weisser Burgunder, Welsch or Rhine
Riesling from Lower Austria*

Tafelspitz

Boiled Beef
Serves 4–6

1 kg/2 lb beef (rolled rump or sirloin)
2 carrots, sliced
2 sticks celery, cut into short lengths
1 medium onion, peeled and quartered
1 small parsnip, peeled and cut into rounds
4 tomatoes, halved
1.8 l/3 pt/7$\frac{1}{2}$ cups water
Salt
Freshly chopped chives

Put all vegetables into a large pot, add water,
salt, and bring to the boil. Add beef, and bring to
boil again. Cover, and simmer very slowly for 3
hr., or until meat is tender.
Remove meat from pot, and carve into
medium-thick slices. Arrange on a warmed
serving platter, and sprinkle with chives, surrounded by the cooked vegetables. Strain stock,
skim off fat, and serve first, as a soup, with
Leberknödel, or other dumpling.
Tafelspitz can be served hot, with horse-
radish sauce, sautéd potatoes, and boiled cabbage,
or cold, with chive sauce or creamed apple sauce,
cabbage salad, and pickles.

Suggested wines:
Blaufränkisch, Grüner Veltliner

Wiener Schnitzel

Breaded Veal Fillet
Serves 4

4 veal fillets (100–150 g/4–6 oz each)
Salt
Freshly ground black pepper
Flour for dredging
2 eggs, well beaten
Fine breadcrumbs
250 g/8 oz/1 cup lard
Lemon wedges

Pound veal fillets to about 6 mm/¼ in thickness (thinner, if possible). Make a few cuts around the edges, so they will not curl up when fried. Season with salt and pepper on each side. Dip the fillets in flour, then in beaten eggs, then in breadcrumbs. Shake off excess crumbs. Heat lard in a large frying pan. Add fillets, and fry quickly until golden brown. Turn and cook the other side. Remove, and drain on kitchen towel.

Serve immediately, with wedges of lemon, sautéed potatoes, and green salad.

Suggested wine:
Grüner Veltliner kabinett from Lower Austria

Backhendl

Fried Chicken

Backhendl is cooked in exactly the same way as *Wiener Schnitzel*. Large, meaty chicken quarters, dipped in flour, eggs, and breadcrumbs, are fried in lard. Cooking time, which depends on the size of the chicken quarters, is longer than for veal (about 15 min. each side). Keep cooked chicken pieces in oven on rack to warm and drain while remaining chicken pieces are being fried.

Serve garnished with parsley and lemon wedges, accompanied by a tart cucumber salad.

Suggested wines:
Styrian Traminer, Welsch Riesling from Burgenland

Linzertorte

Almond and Jam Tart

100 g/4 oz/1 cup flour
3 tbsp sugar
150 g/6 oz/1½ sticks butter
150 g/6 oz/1¾ cups ground almonds
½ tsp cinnamon
½ tsp powdered mace
½ tsp ground cloves
Juice and grated rind of 1 lemon
2 egg yolks
250 g/8 oz/1 cup good quality raspberry jam
1 egg white
Sugar to sprinkle

Sift flour into a large mixing bowl. Add sugar, butter, almonds, cinnamon, cloves, mace, lemon juice and rind, and egg yolks. Beat until mixture is smooth. Form into a round dough, and allow to stand in the refrigerator for 1 hr.

Roll out about two-thirds of the dough, about 6 mm/¼ in thick, to fit a 25 cm/10 in flan tin. Lightly butter tin, and line bottom and sides with dough. Spoon in raspberry jam, spreading it evenly over dough.

Roll out remaining dough, and cut into thin strips. Form a criss-cross lattice over top of dough. Brush with egg white, and bake in a moderate oven, 180°C/Gas Mark 4/350°F, for 50–60 min. or until golden. Sprinkle with sugar and serve cold.

Suggested drink:
Ruster beerenauslese or coffee

Kaiserschmarrn

Emperor's Pancake
Serves 4–6

4 egg yolks
3 tbsp sugar
$\frac{1}{2}$ tsp lemon juice
Pinch of salt
450 ml/ $\frac{3}{4}$ pt/2 cups milk
100 g/4 oz/1 cup flour
75 g/3 oz/ $\frac{3}{4}$ stick butter, melted
4 egg whites, stiffly beaten
3 tbsp raisins soaked in kirsch
Icing (powdered) sugar

In a large mixing bowl, beat egg yolks with sugar, lemon juice, and salt, until thick and yellow. Slowly add milk and flour. Beat until mixture is smooth. Add half of the melted butter. Fold in egg whites.

Heat remaining butter in a large frying pan (or cook in two batches). Pour in the batter (which should be fairly thick). Sprinkle on raisins, and cook over a moderate heat until under-side is golden brown. Turn over and cook other side similarly. With two forks, tear the pancake into small pieces, and cook for a further 1 or 2 min.

Remove to a warmed plate, and dust with icing sugar. Serve with a fruit *compote* if desired.

Suggested wines:
Auslese or beerenauslese from Burgenland

Salzburger Nockerl

Salzburg Omelette
Serves 4

25 g/1 oz/ $\frac{1}{4}$ stick butter
75 g/3 oz/ $\frac{1}{2}$ cup sugar
6 egg yolks
6 egg whites, whipped
$\frac{1}{3}$ tbsp flour
150 ml/ $\frac{1}{4}$ pt/ $\frac{2}{3}$ cup milk
Castor sugar to sprinkle

Cream butter and sugar together until smooth. Add egg yolks, whites, and flour, and mix well. In a small saucepan, bring milk to the boil. Pour into a large baking dish. Fold in egg mixture, and bake in a hot oven, 240°C/Gas Mark 8/450°F, until a pale biscuit-colour, about 5 min.

Scoop out large pieces of the omelette, and place on a warmed dish. Sprinkle with sugar, and serve immediately.

Suggested wines:
Gumpoldskirchner, Ruster auslese

In the town of Bernkastel-Kues, along the banks of the Moselle, the wine festival of the Mittelmosel is in full swing. Hikers in half-legged trousers who have made their way here over hills or through the valley reap the fruit of their thirsty efforts, and down glass after glass of Bernkasteler Kurfürstlay, Wehlener Sonnenuhr, *kabinett* and *spätlese*, while tucking into great platters of juicy pork steaks charred over spitting wood fires. Elsewhere, in the square by the *Rathaus* (town hall), a local brass band entertains an appreciative audience, while from half-timbered *Weinstuben* throughout this medieval town an occasional Teutonic howl sounds over the joyous strains of the electric accordion.

To gain a perspective of this frantic, raucous communal party, and of hundreds of others like it that take place throughout Germany's wine regions, it is necessary literally to rise above the dancing, drinking, singing, and eating that goes on every year until the small hours of the morning. And so we wind our way through the town square, past booming tubas and trombones, up cobbled lanes and narrow alleys. The road begins to climb, the music fades, and we find ourselves on the fringes of vine-covered slopes. We climb higher and higher (resting now and then, because it is remarkably steep) until finally a magnificent vista spreads before us. The slopes of this green valley are so steep that it hardly seems anything could grow on them, the soil nothing but a cover of slippery, scraggy, grey slate. And yet here, and on nearly every slope that rises from the winding Moselle river as far as the eye can see, row upon row of towering vines spread themselves to the sun, basking in its lingering warmth. By night, the very slate soil that looks so mean

A vista of the Moselle valley from the Doktor vineyard
above Bernkastel-Kues.

and inhospitable radiates warmth and helps the firm, tiny Riesling grapes to ripen slowly. It is this annual miracle—the creation of firm, fruity, elegant wines, the most elegant in the world, say some, from a cold, steep northern vineyard— that is the cause of such merriment below.

Germany's Rhineland (those lands watered by the Rhine and Moselle, their tributaries, and tributaries of their tributaries) is virtually a continuous vineyard, for this remarkably compact western region of the German Federal Republic has no less than eleven designated quality-wine regions. And yet, though in close proximity, the nature of the regions themselves varies considerably, and different climatic and soil conditions result in wines with distinct and recognizable characteristics.

The Mosel-Saar-Ruwer (the designated area for quality wines embraces the smaller tributaries of the Saar and Ruwer, since wine produced from grapes grown on their slopes shares the characteristics of wine from the Moselle) is an area of steep, winding, grey-green valleys devoted almost entirely to viticulture. The well-draining

slate slopes must almost always be tended by hand, for no machine can possibly make its way over these terraced and sometimes precipitous vineyards. Yet here the aristocratic but temperamental Riesling is in its element, for when nature blesses the land with a dry June, necessary for the flowering of the vines, and a long, hot autumn, then marvellous, exciting, and racy wines are produced that maintain an essential balance of fruit, scent, and acidity. But winemaking here is a chancy and delicate occupation, for when nature has been ungenerous, and not fully ripened the fruit, then the wine can be rather thin and sharp. Fortunately, however, a lucrative industry has developed that transforms thin, acidic wine into excellent sparkling Sekt.

The Rheingau, on the other hand, is a stretch of distinguished vineyards between Rüdesheim and Hochheim, on the gentler, richer, south-facing slopes of the Taunus mountains. The sun beats down on the fertile loam and loess and is reflected on to the vines off the shimmering surface of the wide Rhine, so that Riesling wines produced in communes such as Rüdesheim,

Deinhard's cross-arched cellars in Koblenz; traditionally, the oval-shaped wooden *Fuder* is used for Moselle wine, while the round *Stück* contains wine from the Rhine.

German wineries are models of efficiency and utilize the latest technologies alongside traditional methods, as seen in this cellar in Deidesheim, an important wine town in the Mittelhaardt of the Rheinpfalz.

Geisenheim, Winkel, Oestrich, Johannisberg, and Hochheim (which is actually located on a stretch of the Main) have a magnificent depth of flavour and fruit, and a complex, intriguing elegance. When mists rise from the Rhine during warm autumn weather, they provide the conditions for the production of some of Germany's greatest wines. For during one such autumn, in 1775, a miraculous method of making wine was discovered quite by accident. The monks at Schloss Johannisberg could never begin harvesting their grapes until they had received permission from their sovereign prince. This year permission was late in coming, and as a result the fragile Riesling grapes began to wither and rot. When the courier eventually arrived, the despondent monks still harvested the grapes. The wine they produced from the furry, shrivelled, useless-looking grapes, however, was magnificent. The rot, more elegantly called *Edelfäule*, had concentrated the sugar in the fruit, thus giving sweeter, heavier, and more beautiful wine than ever before. Even the sweetest, most luscious wines of the Rheingau have an essential underlying acidity that both allows them to age and develop subtle nuances and complexity, and ensures that their high natural sweetness rarely cloys.

Across the river in the fertile, flatter wine lands of the Rheinhessen, rich soils and a milder climate produce an abundance of gentle and pleasant easy-drinking wines. Grapes such as the Silvaner (which yields nearly twice as much crop as the Riesling) and the Müller-Thurgau (a hybrid grape variety produced from a cross between Riesling and Silvaner) flourish easily. In a sense they are Germany's most important grape varieties, not because they produce the greatest wine, but because they produce a great quantity of consistent quality. Both are used to produce the popular blended wine known as Liebfraumilch, a generic name that can legally only be applied to 'mild' sweetish *Qualitätswein* produced in the Rheinhessen, Rheinpfalz, Nahe, or Rheingau. (Liebfraumilch, incidentally, was originally wine made by monks in the Liebfrauenstift monastery near the town of Worms: *Minch* means monk, and this word gradually changed to *Milch*.) Among important wine

communes of the Rheinhessen are Nierstein, Oppenheim, Bingen, and Nackenheim. Niersteiner Gutes Domtal is one soft, easy-drinking wine recognized and enjoyed by many. It is important to note, however, that this easy-to-remember name is applied to vast amounts of wine of differing standards—and the same is true of wines sold under such popular and recognizable names as Liebfraumilch, Bereich Bernkastel, or Piesporter Michelsberg. The great classics of Germany, on the other hand, are estate-bottled wines that bear the name of a precise and single vineyard, such as Bernkasteler Doktor, Winkeler Hasensprung, or Forster Ungeheuer, to name but a few.

Farther south still, in the upper Rhenish lowlands, tremendous flat plains lead away from the

The Liebfrauenkirche in Worms whose vineyards and those of the Liebfrauenstift monastery gave the name to the popular Liebfraumilch.

Rhine to the slopes of the Haardt mountains. This is the Rheinpfalz (also known as the Palatinate), a hot, bright land that seems, unbelievably, almost Mediterranean in character. The people are darker, the villages seem hot and sleepy, and fig and palm trees as well as field after field of healthy vines abound along the *Deutsche Weinstrasse*, a sunny wine road that winds through vineyards and villages. Not surprisingly, wines made from distinctive grape varieties such as the Ruländer, Scheurebe, and Morio-Muskat are sensuous, full-bosomed, and spicy, while in the finest vineyards located in the Mittelhaardt —the heart of the Haardt—in communes such as Deidesheim, Forst, and Ruppertsberg, the classic Riesling ripens to a deep and rich state, at once fiery and exceedingly fine.

Each of the remaining German wine areas, though perhaps less well known outside the country, produces wines that are congenital expressions of the land. The elegant golden-tinged wines of the Nahe Valley, for example, seem almost to match the colour of the golden sunbaked sandstone terraces where the vines thrive. The Kaiserstuhl wines of Baden gain their pithy, fierce character from grapes grown on an outcrop of rich volcanic tufa alongside Germany's Schwarzwald (Black Forest). Dry, piquant Silvaner from Franconia, bottled in the distinctive flagon-shaped *Bocksbeutel*, has a unique taste and aroma unlike wine made from this grape elsewhere; it is not difficult to understand why it was Goethe's favourite. And indeed, red wine from the Ahr (pale, light, fragrant, produced from the Spätburgunder and Portugieser grapes), the fruity, mild wines of the castle-lined Mittelrhein, fragrant Riesling from tiny Hessische Bergstrasse, or the red and white wines made from grapes grown near industrial Stuttgart, in the Württemberg region, all have their groups of devotees who swear that nothing tastes better— and make their opinions known through their enthusiastic participation in celebrations of the fruit of the land.

German wine is certainly cause for celebration, and down below, in Bernkastel, in Hochheim (the town that gives us the word 'hock'), at Bad Dürkheim's annual *Wurstmarkt* (sausage festival), or in any of hundreds of other wine towns, the singing and drinking continue.

No other people in Europe, it seems, enjoy themselves with quite the same wholehearted and vigorous energy as the Germans. The sometimes uncontrollable wailing of electric accordions and unrestrained singing sound constantly from the depths of subterranean dens, and *Pokale*—stubby green- or gold-stemmed goblets—of cool wine are downed in an endless succession. On Rhine cruises, on the great Köln-Düsseldorfer ships that make their way between those two cities, tables are kicked back and the singing and drinking begin long before the Lorelei rock is sighted. And even in the smallest, most modest *Weingarten*—just a few tables or chairs along the road in some wine producer's front garden—there is inevitably a welcoming sense of warmth, enjoyment, and hearty good cheer.

Germans are great trenchermen, and attack their food with the same energy and gusto with which they drink their wine. At the annual *Wurstmarkt* in Bad Dürkheim, wine of the previous vintage is served in *Schoppen*—straight, no-nonsense glasses that hold no less than a half-litre—to be drunk like water while consuming huge platters of *Wurst* and sauerkraut.

There are about 1,500 different varieties of German *Wurst*, most of them, it seems, represented at this incredible sausage gathering. Basically they divide into three types which vary according to the way they are made.

Brühwurst are scalded sausages made of finely minced pork or beef, and include (the original) *Frankfurter*, *Bratwurst* (a juicy, well-seasoned pork sausage that is generally fried or grilled), and *Weisswurst* (small, pale veal sausages, delicious for breakfast), as well as larger sausages, that form part of a cold meat platter, such as *Bierwurst* (reddish-brown, oval-shaped pork and beef sausage), and *Fleischwurst* (a fine, smooth sausage made from chopped pork, beef, and garlic).

Kochwurst is a family of boiled sausages made from liver, tongue, or blood. The most familiar member is *Leberwurst*, here a coarser, more highly spiced liver sausage than the version we know, and often eaten hot with sauerkraut, or used to make dumplings that are served in clear

Quality produce in the *Hauptmarkt* of Trier.

A cool moment on a warm afternoon – a *Weingarten* in
the Rheingau.

beef broth. *Blutwurst* is a sort of black pudding that is a Rhineland favourite, especially when sliced and fried with onions and bacon until crisp, then garnished over a purée of apples and potatoes appropriately called *Himmel und Erde*— heaven and earth. *Sülzwurst* is a type of brawn, containing large pieces of pork in aspic, while *Pfälzer Saumagen*, a great favourite at the Dürkheim *Wurstmarkt*, is a sow's stomach stuffed with meat and seasonings, boiled, and cut into thick slices.

The third group of German sausages are *Rohwurst*, and includes those which have been preserved either by smoking or air-drying, such as German salami, *Cervelat* (finely minced beef and pork sausage smoked until golden brown), and *Teewurst*, a popular spicy little sausage, ideal for spreading on pumpernickel, *Landbrot* (flat, round rye loaf), *Vollkornbrot* (whole-grain rye

bread), or any of the other fine and numerous German breads.

The food of the Rhineland is obviously much more than just *Wurst*, important though that food is. Much more, too, than the sort of fare that is generally plentiful at wine festivals and other celebrations. Nevertheless, wine festival fare demonstrates an essential German concern for simple and pure foods of the highest quality served in generous amounts. Open wood fires blaze, and huge pork steaks, chops, slabs of beef, and half-chickens are roasted quickly and simply. *Schweinshaxen* and *Kalbshaxen* (knuckles of pork and veal) are roasted until their fatty skins are crisp and brown, while *Eisbein* (pickled pig's knuckle) is stewed for hours until the meat virtually falls from the bones. These are foods you rip into with bare hands and wash down with long swallows of fresh young wine.

Fishing on the banks of the Moselle below the vineyards of Graach.

Another Rhenish favourite, served in homes, restaurants, at wine festivals—everywhere—is *Sauerbraten*, a classic German pot roast in which a large piece of beef is marinated in vinegar, wine, and spices for up to a week, cooked slowly on top of the stove, and served with sauerkraut, potatoes, or dumplings. Game from the Schwarzwald and other forests is popular, and venison and hare are marinated in vinegar, wine, raisins, and juniper berries, and stewed slowly in the marinade until the liquid becomes a thick, dark, rich gravy. In Swabia, a gastronomic paradise that embraces the Baden-Württemberg wine region, this gravy is spooned over *Spätzle*, tiny, delicate flour and egg dumplings, cut from a board into boiling stock, then fried quickly in butter or lard. In this region, any meat dish served with gravy provides an excuse to indulge in these wonderful light dumplings, whose name affectionately translates as 'little sparrows'.

Dumplings, in fact, are indispensable to the German diet, and can metamorphose at any time and in any course. Soups are a favourite start to the main, midday affair, and range from cold fruit and wine soups to hearty winter brews such as *Kartoffelsuppe* (potato soup) and *Frankfurter Linsensuppe* (brown lentil and sausage soup). But quite often a meal begins simply with a bowl of clear beef broth garnished with flour and egg dumplings, *Leberknödeln* (liver dumplings), *Markklösschen* (button-sized marrow balls), or perhaps with *Maultaschen*, 'mouth pockets' of dough stuffed with meat and spinach and poached in broth. As well as *Spätzle*, larger and heavier cousins such as *Semmelklössen* (bread dumplings) and *Kartoffelklössen* (potato dumplings) mop up tasty gravy and pan juices from such dishes as *Rinderrouladen* (beef olives stuffed with mustard, bacon, and onions), or *Spiessbraten* (a rolled piece of beef stuffed with onions and herbs and roasted on a spit). Finally, sweet dumplings such as *Marillenknödeln*, filled with apricots, or *Dampfknödeln*, steamed yeast dumplings, and other dessert dumplings fill any still-empty spaces at the end of a meal. They are delicious with *Weincreme*, a concoction of wine, sugar, and eggs cooked together gently until thick, then poured over dumplings, cakes, or eaten on its own.

The food of Germany's wine lands is robust and filling, simple and pure, though perhaps to some a little heavy and bland. In a sense, however, variety, spice, and seasonings are provided amply in the great selection of German wines that naturally accompany the foods. For not only are there distinct and subtle nuances among wines from the eleven quality-wine regions, there are also great varieties in flavour and aroma among the principal grapes. So important are these to the enjoyment of German wine that the name (or names) of the grape variety (or varieties) can usually be found on the bottle. Indeed, it is a pleasant task to learn to recognize and differentiate characteristics of the classic and elegant Riesling, and the Silvaner and Müller-Thurgau, as well as to encounter varieties perhaps less well known, such as the warm, full-bodied Ruländer, sultry, intriguing Morio-Muskat, intensely scented Scheurebe, spicy Gewürztraminer, and easy-ripening, mild Kerner.

As well as the region and grape variety used to produce a particular wine, it is also important to recognize its quality level, which is based on the degree of ripeness of the grapes used. This is important because ripeness of grapes determines the sweetness, and thus the style of a wine, which can range from dry to lusciously sweet. Ripeness is measured by the use of a scale, developed by a chemist and physicist named Oechsle, which measures the sugar content in the grape must (unfermented grape juice). The higher the sugar content, the riper the grapes, and, in the German priority of wine-making, the better the wine. Must weight is measured in Oechsle degrees, and a scale of levels is used to determine the quality levels of German wine.

A wine, first of all, must reach a certain must weight in order to be given the designation *Qualitätswein*. If the wine under examination falls below this level then it can only be sold as *Deutscher Tafelwein*, provided it has been approved by the authorities and comes from one of the five designated German table-wine regions. German wine reaching a level of between 60 to 72 degrees Oechsle (depending on the area) is designated *Qualitätswein bestimmter Anbaugebiete*, (usually abbreviated *QbA*) which means that it is a quality wine from one of the eleven wine regions. Wines with higher degrees of ripeness are allowed to carry a distinctive designation, *Qualitätswein mit Prädikat* ('quality wine with distinction'). This is classified further. The term *kabinett* designates wine that is better than average—made from grapes which are riper than average. *Spätlese* (the word actually means 'late-picked') refers to grapes that have been allowed to remain on the vine longer than normal—wine produced from such grapes therefore has a higher degree of ripeness and richness. *Auslese* is even more special, for it is made from bunches of grapes that have been selected individually. *Beerenauslese*, the next step up, is made from extremely ripe and over-ripe berries that have actually been individually selected. And finally, *trockenbeerenauslese*, the triumph of German wine, is rare and exquisite, made from individually selected grapes that have been affected by *Edelfäule*, and shrivelled and dried to an intensely concentrated state. This unbelievable hierarchy of ripeness is correspondingly a hierarchy of sweetness, and the higher quality levels represent some of the finest, richest, and rarest wines in the world.

It should be pointed out that the reason many of the lower quality level German wines are relatively sweet is not because of a high degree of ripeness or natural residual sugar, but rather due to the German method of wine-making, which, in order to reach a balance of fruit and acidity, allows the addition of a certain amount of unfermented grape juice to wines up to *spätlese* level. This practice is known as *Süssreserve*, and the amount that can be added is determined by law.

Wines that reach the highest quality levels —*auslese, beerenauslese, trockenbeerenauslese*, and the rare *Eiswein*, made from grapes that have actually been harvested while frozen, then quickly pressed and fermented—are so rich and full of flavour and complexity that they are best enjoyed on their own, without the distraction of food. Wine up to *spätlese* level, though, can be superb with meals, provided the food is a balance to the wines. Delicately flavoured trout from the Moselle or Rhine, for example, poached in wine until its skin turns a striking shade of blue, is partnered beautifully by a delicate yet firm Riesling from the Mosel-Saar-Ruwer. On the other hand, the large pure-white spears of *Spargel* (asparagus) that are grown in mounds of earth around Schweigen and are served hot with hollandaise sauce, boiled potatoes, and shavings of air-dried *Schinken* (ham) probably demand a richer, heavier wine, such as a Ruländer *spätlese* from Dürkheim, or Maikammer in the Rheinpfalz. In the Nahe, an onion tart is an autumn favourite, since it is a perfect accompaniment to Federweisser, a milky sort of wine drunk soon after the harvest, tasting of yeast and known for its restorative powers. Cheese is adored throughout Germany, much of it of the strong-scented variety. *Handkäse mit Musik* is the whimsical name for a potent, hand-moulded, sour curd cheese that is eaten in the Rhineland, garnished with chopped onions and capers; its intensive taste requires a wine of similar character, such as a distinctive, spicy-scented Gewürztraminer *kabinett*. Rich goose liver, much loved by Germans, is one of the few foods best accompanied by wines of *auslese* level or higher. Delicate and subtly flavoured food such as river salmon, however, sometimes requires wine with little or no residual sweetness—and here a *trocken* (dry) wine from Franconia, or a *halbtrocken* (semi-dry) Silvaner might be the choice.

Trocken and *halbtrocken* are relatively new styles of wine that are increasingly available. The terms, however, have no bearing on the quality level of a wine. Just as *Süssreserve* is often added up to *spätlese* level, *trocken* and *halbtrocken* wines have correspondingly lower amounts of the unfermented juice added to them to result in dry and semi-dry wines. They can usually be recognized by yellow (dry) and green (semi-dry) seals around the neck of the bottle. Many think that these styles of wine are best suited for drinking with meals, but, as always, it is simply a matter of taste.

German wine can at first seem over-complicated and scientific. In reality, like the robust, uncomplicated, and pure foods of the Rhineland, it is not that difficult to appreciate. The revellers at the festivals that take place annually throughout Germany's wine regions know it is there, ultimately, to drink and to enjoy—and who are we to disagree?

Quantities where necessary are given in
Metric, Imperial and US measurements.

Rollmops mit Sauersahne

Rollmops with Sour Cream
Serves 4

1 medium onion, peeled and thinly sliced
350 g/12 oz jar of good quality pickled herring
150 ml/¼ pt/⅔ cup sour cream

Soak onion in salt water for 30 min. Rinse, wring out, and mix with sour cream and herring cut into large pieces.

Serve chilled, as an appetizer.

Suggested wines:
Ruländer from Kaiserstuhl vineyards of Baden, Gewürztraminer from Rheinpfalz

Frankfurter Linsensuppe

Lentil Soup with Frankfurters
Serves 4

250 g/½ lb brown lentils, soaked for 1–2 hr.
1.8 l/3 pt/7½ cups beef stock
2 tbsp butter
1 onion, peeled and chopped
2 carrots, chopped
2 legs of celery, chopped
4 frankfurters, cut into rings
Salt
Freshly ground black pepper

Heat butter in a saucepan, and gently fry vegetables until soft. Add lentils and stock, and

Frankfurter Linsensuppe: lentils and sausages combine in this Rhineland favourite.

simmer for $1\frac{1}{2}$–2 hr, or until lentils are cooked. Add frankfurters 30 min. before serving. Season with salt and pepper.

Suggested wines:
Halbtrocken (semi-dry) Ruländer, Müller-Thurgau from Rheinpfalz

Himmel und Erde

Heaven and Earth
Serves 4

3 large potatoes, peeled and sliced
3 tart cooking apples, peeled, cored, and sliced
1 tbsp lemon juice
1 piece lemon rind
Pinch of cinnamon
1 tbsp sugar
3 tbsp butter
1 large onion, peeled and finely chopped
2 rashers/slices bacon, chopped
Salt
Freshly ground black pepper

Cook potatoes in boiling salted water for about 15 min., or until tender.

Meanwhile, place apples in another pan, together with lemon juice, rind, cinnamon, sugar, and a little water. Cover, and cook until they have formed a purée.

Strain potatoes, and mash with butter. Mix with the apple purée, seasoning to taste.

Fry bacon and onions until soft. Garnish potatoes and apples with fried onions and bacon.

Serve with sausages, liver, kidney, or black pudding.

Suggested wines:
Halbtrocken (semi-dry) Müller-Thurgau from Rheinpfalz, Silvaner from Rheinhessen

Blaue Forelle

Blue Trout
Serves 4

In order to turn a prominent blue, the fish must be extremely fresh, and handled as little as possible.

Court-Bouillon
150 ml/$\frac{1}{4}$ pt/$\frac{2}{3}$ cup dry white wine
3 tbsp wine vinegar
1 l/1$\frac{3}{4}$ pt/4$\frac{1}{2}$ cups water
1 carrot, sliced
1 onion, peeled and thinly sliced
1 bouquet garni
1 bay leaf
Salt
6 black peppercorns

1 kg/2 lb trout
Freshly chopped parsley

Put all ingredients for *court-bouillon* into a large pan, and bring to the boil. Simmer for 30 min. Put freshly caught and cleaned trout into a large pot, and add enough *court-bouillon* to cover the fish. Bring to the boil, and simmer for about 10–15 min., until it turns blue and fish is fully cooked. Strain, and arrange on a platter. Decorate with parsley and wedges of lemon.

Serve with boiled potatoes.

Suggested wines:
Riesling kabinett from Mosel-Saar-Ruwer, trocken (dry) Silvaner from Franconia

Sauerbraten

Braised Spiced Beef
Serves 4

150 ml/$\frac{1}{4}$ pt/$\frac{2}{3}$ cup vinegar
150 ml/$\frac{1}{4}$ pt/$\frac{2}{3}$ cup water
2 medium onions, peeled and thinly sliced
Salt
Freshly ground black pepper
1 bay leaf
3 cloves
10 juniper berries, coarsely crushed

750 g/1½ lb beef joint (shoulder or round)
2 tbsp beef fat
1 tomato, quartered
1 tbsp flour
Pinch of sugar
1 tbsp cream or wine

Cook vinegar, water, half the sliced onions, and seasoning together for 10 min. Pour this over the beef, and marinate, covered, for 3–5 days in the refrigerator, turning occasionally.

Remove beef, and pat dry with kitchen towel. Melt lard in a large casserole, and brown meat on all sides. Add remaining onion, tomato, and half of the marinade. Bring slowly to the boil, cover, and simmer for 1 hr. or until done, turning meat over once during cooking.

When ready, remove beef, and carve into medium-thick slices. Arrange on a warm serving platter.

Mix flour with pan liquid until smooth. Add remaining marinade, and stir until smooth and thick. Add sugar, and adjust seasoning. Add cream or wine, if desired, and continue to cook until sauce thickens.

Serve sauce separately or poured over meat, with potatoes, dumplings, or *Spätzle*.

Suggested wine:
Riesling spätlese from Rheingau

Spätzle

Little Dumplings
Serves 4

4 eggs, well beaten
Flour
Salt

Add as much flour to the eggs as needed to form a soft but pliable dough. Then add a pinch of salt.

With a sharp knife, cut small pieces of dough from edge of a chopping board into boiling salted water. Cook for about 2–3 min.

Remove with a slotted spoon, and plunge into cold water. Drain and put on a platter. Fry in a little butter immediately before serving.

Serve with *Sauerbraten*.

Rinderrouladen

Beef Rolls
Serves 4

4 thin slices of beef (preferably rump steak)
Salt
Freshly ground black pepper
4 rashers/slices bacon, cut up into small pieces
1 onion, peeled and finely chopped
1 tbsp freshly chopped parsley
1 tbsp German mustard
1 tbsp flour
2 tbsp butter
150 ml/¼ pt/⅔ cup water
150 ml/¼ pt/⅔ cup beef stock or wine
2 tbsp cream (optional)

Pound beef slices until fairly thin, then rub with salt and pepper. Mix bacon, onion, parsley, and mustard together. Spread this on to one side of each beef slice. Roll up tightly, and secure with string.

Dip rolls lightly in flour, and fry in butter to brown all sides. Add water, and bring to simmering point. Cover and cook for 25 min. Remove lid, and cook until water has evaporated, about 5 min. Remove rolls, and place on a warmed serving dish. Add beef stock or wine to pan juices, to make gravy, scraping bottom of the pan. Adjust seasoning and, if desired, add cream. Pour over meat rolls, and serve with *Kartoffelsalat* (German potato salad) and a cucumber salad.

Suggested wines:
*Scheurebe or Kerner from Rheinpfalz or
Riesling from Nahe*

Kartoffelsalat

Warm Potato Salad
Serves 4

4 medium potatoes
4 rashers/slices bacon, cut into small pieces
1 medium onion, peeled and finely chopped
4 tbsp oil
2 tbsp vinegar
Salt
Freshly ground black pepper
1 tsp celery salt

Cook potatoes in their jackets until tender, and allow to cool.

Peel and slice potatoes. Mix with oil, vinegar, salt, pepper, and celery salt, and allow to marinate for at least 1 hr.

Fry bacon and onion together until onion is soft and golden.

Just before serving, pour warm bacon and onion mixture over potatoes.

Lauck Gemuse

Leeks with Bacon and Onion
Serves 4

1 tbsp oil
3 rashers/slices bacon, finely chopped
1 medium onion, peeled and finely chopped
6 medium leeks, cut into rounds
300 ml/$\frac{1}{2}$ pt/1$\frac{1}{4}$ cups beef stock
Salt
Freshly ground black pepper
Pinch of nutmeg
1 tbsp freshly chopped parsley
3 tbsp cream

Fry bacon and onion together in a saucepan until golden. Add beef stock and leeks. Cover, and simmer for about 20 min. Season, and add a pinch of nutmeg and parsley. Just before serving, add cream.

Rumtopf

Rum Pot

To be started in May as fruits come into season.

1 bottle of black rum
Brown sugar
Soft fruit, such as strawberries, raspberries, sour cherries, red currants, apricots, peaches, (but no black fruit), all peeled

Place 2 or 3 peach stones and 2 cherry stones in a large, tall ceramic container. Add 500 g/1 lb fruit, and 500 g/1 lb brown sugar. Pour on bottle of rum. From now on add 500 g/1 lb each fruit to 250 g/$\frac{1}{2}$ lb brown sugar. Continue to add fruit in layers, and do not mix. Make sure fruit is all the time covered with rum.

Place a weighted plate on top to keep down the fruit. Cover well, and set aside. Never mix the fruit until December—just keep adding layers, whenever a different fruit is in season.

Let stand until mid-December. Then mix well, and serve with whipped cream.

Weincreme

Wine Cream
Serves 6

450 ml/$\frac{3}{4}$ pt/2 cups QbA wine
5 tbsp sugar
150 ml/$\frac{1}{4}$ pt/$\frac{2}{3}$ cup water
5 eggs
Pinch of cinnamon
Juice of $\frac{1}{2}$ lemon
Grated rind of $\frac{1}{2}$ lemon

In a double boiler over a low heat, stir all ingredients to a thick froth. Pour into sherbet glasses, and chill before serving.

Serve over slices of sponge cake, dumplings, or on its own.

Overshadowed by her produce, a woman selling
paprikas in Budapest.

The Magyars rode out from the Urals to a land where the soil was rich and the water clear and plentiful. They stayed to create a civilization that remains the basis of modern Hungary. This is a Hungary rich in tradition and heritage even though its roots are not always traceable to any definite source. The Hungarian language, for example, is mysterious; related to neither Romance, Germanic, nor Slavic tongues, it finds its closest link with Finnish. The musical heritage of this small country is rich and distinctive, though, again, it is difficult to pinpoint the exact source of the infectious Magyar melodies so praised by St Gellért, the first bishop of Hungary, over 1,000 years ago. What is clear is that music and the Hungarian spirit are inseparable—from Bartók and Kodály to the gypsy fiddler (of fact and fantasy), music is as indispensable in this country as a bowl of *gulyás* or the paprika that flavours it.

Culinary traditions and eating habits date back to the days of those wandering horsemen. The national fondness for sour cream probably developed from the Magyar taste for fermented mare's milk, which, among other things, made a heady alcoholic beverage. *Magyar gulyás* (known as Hungarian goulash everywhere but here) originated centuries ago, when roving horsemen reconstituted sun-dried pieces of meat in broth. The Magyars also dried pellets of flour and eggs to take on mounted forays into the Carpathian mountains, or on raids that took them as far as present-day Germany, Italy, Switzerland, and France. These portable pellets were called *tarhonya* and could be added to a bubbling cauldron of *gulyás*, cooked over an open fire. Though the dough is no longer dried until hard, a similar favourite staple is the small flour and egg

dumpling known as *galuska*, which is either dropped into boiling soups or stews, or else boiled then fried in lard with onions and paprika.

One of the best-known wines of Hungary owes its name to a Magyar legend. In the sixteenth century, the Turkish army of the mighty Ali pasha attacked the beautiful walled town of Eger. The men of Eger fought valiantly, without cease. They kept the Turks at bay by pouring boiling oil or pitch over them, and as they kept a sleepless vigil, their wives shuttled back and forth with food and flagons of wine. The pungent, fiery, local brew not only fortified the men, it also routed the enemy. For when the Turks saw the sleepless, red-eyed men of Eger, with dark wild beards stained red from gulping wine in haste, they fled in horror, believing the Magyars were fired with demonic energy through drinking the blood of bulls. Thus, Egri Bikavér (Bull's Blood) saved the town and became a legend.

The most typical and customary eating houses of Hungary are called *csárdás*, and they, too, originally were inns that served the needs of Magyar herdsmen or highwaymen alike. Though today the *csárdás* that line the shores of Lake Balaton, or those found in the hills outside Eger, are frequented more by city folk from Budapest than by wandering nomads, these unique inns are lively and exciting. The food is generally simple—a selection of Hungarian sausages and salami (believed by many to be the best in the world) accompanied by long, mild radishes, onions, or pickled vegetables; a variety of grilled meats, liver, and paprika sausages served on a thick wooden platter. The wine is good—and cheap. And the gypsy music, as essential as either wine or food, is vibrant, emotional, and spontaneous. Indeed, a candle-lit table in a *csárdás*, a pitcher of glinting, golden Badacsonyi Kéknyelü, and the heart's blood melody of a gypsy fiddler is as romantic as romantic should be.

Badacsonyi Kéknyelü is only one of many sound wines produced on the ridge of volcanic hills that rise along the north shore of Lake Balaton, and possesses characteristics inherent in

In Badacsony, on Lake Balaton, outdoor stalls sell wine by the pitcher, along with fried *fogas*, to eat and drink while listening to lively music.

the best white wines from this steamy region: a beautiful golden tinge and a fragrant aroma that comes from mineral-rich soil, heat, and the humid air that rises from the largest freshwater lake in Europe. A certain strength and fieriness make it ideal not only for the food of Balaton, but also for drinking on sultry, sweaty summer nights out of doors, singing, talking, flirting.

As well as Kéknyelü, a variety of other interesting wines are produced on this fertile northern shore, including full-bodied and pungent Badacsonyi Zöldszilváni, and a powerful, spicy Olasz Riesling. This useful grape, which is grown in many other parts of Hungary, is also known as the Welsch Riesling (a cousin to the Rhine Riesling of Germany), which here and in Balatonfüred and Csopak takes on a marked, assertive character and a certain round, fullness that is very attractive. Finally, one of the best-known and most popular wines of this region is Badacsonyi Szürkebarát. The name means 'grey friar', and the grape used to produce it, the Pinot Gris, gives wine of surprisingly rich and luscious texture—golden, fragrant, at once a touch sweet yet decidedly tangy.

Lake Balaton is the 'Hungarian Sea' to the people of this land-locked nation, a place for recreation and relaxation, and a source of much-loved fish. The favourite here is undoubtedly the *fogas*, or pike-perch, prized for its lean, white, and tender flesh. This angry, sneering fish is usually bent into a curled shape for frying or grilling; or else it is served cold with a salad of sliced cucumber marinated in a vinegar and sugar dressing. The great fish of the Danube, of course, is the carp, which has a smooth, densely textured flesh, delicious when cut across the wide body into steaks and fried in breadcrumbs, or served in a paprika and sour cream sauce. Other favourites from lake and river include catfish and river bleak. They are often dipped in batter, fried whole, dusted with paprika, and served simply on a piece of paper at outdoor *csárdás*. In unison, eager hands attack the food, and pitchers of green-gold wine remedy the inevitable swallowing of a bone or two.

Halászlé is another Magyar favourite not only along the shore of Lake Balaton, but in Budapest, Szeged, Tokay—anywhere a river or lake yields fish at all, for it combines available freshwater fish in a thin, red, hot broth seasoned liberally with both sweet and fiery round cherry *paprikas*. In *halászcsárdás* (inns specializing in fish) this fiercely flavoured soup is served in little tin pots, and the sound of satisfied spoons clanking away provides an excellent accompaniment to the gypsy fiddle.

Hungarians love their soup. In summer, light, bright-red sour cherries (morellos) are displayed in colourful abundance on market stalls throughout the country, shouting for attention over darker, more sombre shades of dried sweet or hot *paprikas*. They are used to make an excitingly different, deliciously refreshing summer soup called *meggyleves*. Cold, sweet, sour, and spicy, this pretty pink soup is sheer joy to drink on blistering days when searing city heat almost takes the appetite away. Other delicious cold fruit soups are made from stewed plums, pears, and apples.

In winter, hearty root vegetables such as potatoes, beetroot, and kohlrabi are made into filling, rib-sticking brews enriched with sour cream. A meal might simply begin with a bowl of broth in which a chicken has boiled, together with a handful of *galuskas*, those ever-ready flour and egg dumplings. Or soup can be the highlight of an evening. We should remember that Hungary's most famous dish, *Magyar gulyás*, is a soup, when authentically prepared. It is almost always made of beef and potatoes, and, though it is seasoned liberally with paprika, is rarely hot. Caraway seeds are a more characteristic flavouring than chilli peppers, and *galuskas* are usually added to the boiling broth before it is served.

The thick, red, rich stews we perhaps think of as goulash are in fact stews known as either *pörkölt, tokány,* or *paprikás*. The name varies with the type of meat used, the way it is cut, or the amount of liquid in which it is braised. *Pörkölt*, for example, can be made from veal, beef, pork, tripe, or even fish, cooked with copious amounts of onion, paprika, and very little liquid, so that a thick, highly seasoned sauce results. *Tokány* is similar, but the meat is generally cut into strips rather than cubes, and less onion and paprika are used. The *paprikás* is chicken, veal, lamb, or mutton stew in which the onion

Sunflowers,
an important crop for
Hungary, producing
both seed and oil.

Buda and Pest face each other, divided – and united – by the Danube.

and paprika sauce is thickened with sour cream. *Csirke paprikás* (paprika chicken) is perhaps the best known of such dishes. In each, the authentic Hungarian flavour comes from slowly stewing sliced or chopped onions in pure pork lard until they are soft and golden (neither butter nor oil give the right taste or colour). Then, off the stove, a generous spoonful of Hungarian paprika is stirred in. The pan must be removed from the heat to ensure that the paprika does not burn and thus become bitter.

Hungarian paprika is so characteristic and essential to this lively cuisine that it is perhaps surprising to learn that the pepper only made its way into the country in the seventeenth century. Today, in the vicinity of towns such as Szeged and Kalocsa on the Great Plain, brightly coloured strings of peppers are seen drying in the sun, or else draped in huge piles in market stalls. There are many varieties, most of which are not nearly as fierce as their bright colour suggests. The most highly prized (such as 'noblesweet' paprika) are valued for their rich red colour, and deep, pungent aroma, not their sharpness—though of course there are also varieties that will take the roof off your mouth, if that is what you want. It is important, incidentally, to use authentic Hungarian paprika in order to gain the richness of colour and unique fragrance that are the hallmark of Hungarian dishes. So important is this seasoning that in most Hungarian homes a little bowl of paprika is always on the table beside the salt cellar.

The rich and paprika-flavoured cuisine of Hungary naturally calls for full-bodied and robust wines. Wines that exactly match the exciting character of the food come from vineyards around Eger. Beneath the streets of this historic town where people once took refuge from invading Turks lies a maze of deep, cool caves, hollowed out of the mineral-rich volcanic tufa that feeds the vines. These vast cellar-galleries are covered in a furry, grey-black fungus, and provide the perfect atmosphere for mellowing and maturing a variety of excellent table wines.

Bikavér (Bull's Blood) is certainly the best-known wine from Eger, and its character is indeed perfectly matched to Hungarian food:

deep, rich, full-bodied, with a touch of fire lurking within. Kadarka, Kékfrankos, Médoc Noir, and Cabernet Franc are grapes that grow on the volcanic slopes of the Mátra mountains and blend together to produce the dark, powerful wine. Egri Bikavér is hard and tannic when young, but ageing in black oak casks in cellars below the town allows it to develop a mellow and vigorous harmony.

Egri Leányka is a popular white wine from this district, ranging from dry to medium sweet (depending upon the state of ripeness of the grapes at harvest). It has a rich warmth that combines well with various Hungarian soups. Another historic and traditional wine also produced at Eger is Debröi Hárslevelü. The Hárslevelü (lime leaf) is a distinctive native grape variety that is also grown in the Tokay district. Here, in the favourable climate of the Mátra mountains, the grapes ripen to produce wine that is rich, spicy, even fiery, but with a natural acidity that balances its sugar content. Such dry-to-sweetish white wines, incidentally, are here enjoyed with breaded pork or chicken, liver paste, or veal in a sour cream sauce. Richness, to the Hungarian way of thinking, offsets richness.

There is a Hungarian saying that 'wine needs a bed'. Rarely do people drink wine without at least a little nibble. A bottle of wine is opened; a plate of Debrecen sausage appears. One glass leads to another, and as more plates and dishes are brought in, a spontaneous feast is spread. The process is reciprocal, for Hungarian food, in turn, works up a healthy thirst that can only be quenched by long swallows of heady local wine.

Töltött káposzta, cabbage leaves stuffed with minced pork, cooked over a bed of sauerkraut, then served with a sour cream and paprika sauce is an example of such 'wine-thirsty' fare. So is the *fatányéros*, an enormous Transylvanian mixed-grill consisting of pork chops, bacon, steak, sausage, and liver, served together on a huge wooden platter. These greasy, juicy meats, streaked with grill marks, cry for jugs of Kékfrankos or Cabernet, plummy, alcoholic 'jug' wines produced on the baked Hungarian plain. The Kékfrankos (Blue French) grape also produces excellent wine in vineyards around Sopron, near the border of Austrian Burgenland (where similar wine is produced). This fairly light, mellow red wine, with a hint of sweetness, is excellent with paprika chicken or with any of the great variety of pork dishes, boiled and served with dumplings, braised with onions and peppers, or cooked or served with *lecsó*, a characteristic green pepper, tomato, and paprika mixture that is the Hungarian equivalent of *ratatouille*.

Hungary, of course, was once a partner in the dual monarchy of the immense Austro-Hungarian Empire, which extended through much of Czechoslovakia, Romania, Yugoslavia, and parts of northern Italy. Today, it seems, little remains from those splendid, if anachronistic, imperial days. One thing, at least, still links Hungary with the old empire: a love bordering on passion for all things sweet. The pastry and coffee shops of Budapest, after all, used to be almost as famous as those of Vienna. The *dobostorta*, a masterpiece of layers of thin sponge and chocolate cream which was the speciality at Gerbeaud's at the turn of the century, was no less highly regarded than the *Sachertorte* of Austria, created by the master baker to Prince Metternich. And if you ask a Hungarian, he will tell you that *Strudel*, the flaky whimsical creation which, in its lightness and perfection, is the quintessence of Vienna, originated—where else? —in Hungary. Indeed, the art of making this wonderful elastic paper-thin dough (in Hungary it is called *rétes*) is an art still handed from mother to daughter (or son) in both countries. Another Hungarian favourite is the *palacsinta*, a thin pancake spread with both savoury and sweet fillings, or sometimes layered into a rich and elaborate creation. The *rakott palacsinta*, for example, consists of several layers of pancake, spread with apricot jam, ground walnuts, cream, and raisins. It is cut into thick wedges, like a cake.

A small glass of *barack pálinka*, a clear, fiery apricot brandy, might be downed with such sweets, though it is usually taken as an aperitif— or even for a breakfast pick-me-up (to get the day started on the right foot). A special Hungarian meal, on the other hand, should end with the country's greatest and most famous wine, Tokay Aszu.

Tokay is legendary. Peter the Great bought a

plantation in this remote corner of Hungary, which today borders both Czechoslovakia and the Soviet Union. Indeed, the Czars loved the wine, and every year, after the vintage, large casks were shipped from Sárospatak to St Petersburg. Catherine the Great is supposed to have murmured, 'My empire would be complete if I owned the Tokay hills'. Louis XIV called Tokay 'the wine of kings, the king of wines'—a rare compliment indeed, considering the great wines that came from his own country. The composer Schubert, it is said, only composed with a glass of Tokay on the piano.

The vines that produce this magnificent and unique wine flourish on the hills of the Tokaj-Hegyalja district, sheltered by the great range of the Carpathians. During the long, slow, misty autumns, the Furmint, Hárslevelü, and Muskotaly grapes ripen fully and slowly. In the best years, the fungus *botrytis cinerea* attacks the grapes, causing them to shrivel by evaporation, and concentrating grape sugar and aroma to produce a rare, haunting fragrance that is unique to wines made from such grapes. Selected bunches of grapes with a high proportion of shrivelled *aszu* berries are gathered in *puttonys*—wooden hods strapped to the workers' backs.

The *aszu* berries are next treaded or crushed by machine into a sort of pulpy homogeneous dough. It is this *aszu* dough that is added to a new base wine in varying proportions. The number of *puttonys* of dough added to 136 litres of base wine determines the eventual grade of sweetness of the final product. For example, Tokay Aszu is sold as either three, four, five or, very rarely, six *puttonys*. Sometimes an even higher grade is made: Tokay Aszu Essencia, so concentrated that the degree of sweetness is too high to be measured by *puttonys*.

Once the *puttonys* of *aszu* dough have been added, the wine is transferred to traditional barrels, called *gönci*, in which it ages in the dark, deep, fungus-covered cellars under towns such as Tolcsva, Sárospatak, Sátoraljaújhely, or Tokay itself. The barrels are only loosely stopped with glass, and as the wine evaporates a unique bouquet and flavour results through the wine's contact with the oxygen of these ancient caves, which

Breakfast in Tokay.

are up to 800 years old. So dank and moist are they that the cellar fungus, *cladisporium*, which lives on alcohol fumes, grows over virtually everything within a matter of months.

Tokay Szamorodni is not made from selected bunches of *aszu* grapes. Szamorodni is a Polish word meaning 'as it is grown' (many of the original Tokay merchants came from Poland, where the wine is still very popular today) and, not surprisingly, both grapes that have been affected by *botrytis* as well as those that have not are harvested together and vinified in a normal manner. Since the percentage of affected grapes is variable, the wine ranges in style from dry to fairly sweet. It is sold in the traditional clear-glass Tokay half-litre bottle, and its full bouquet and fine and distinctive aftertaste reveal its aristocratic pedigree.

One other wine should be mentioned: Tokay Essencia, which is even more rare and exclusive than Tokay Aszu Essencia, for it is made only in the smallest quantity from the pure juice that has trickled down from the weight of the *aszu* berries after they have been harvested. It is so concentrated that it is actually gritty in texture, a rare and amazing nectar that will last well over a hundred years. In imperial days, the wines of Tokay were a privilege of kings and emperors. Tokay Essencia, however, was so special that it was reserved only for Czars—on their deathbed. So magnificent was this enormous honeyed wine that it was credited with life-prolonging properties.

Though Essencia is today so scarce as to be virtually non-existent (those small amounts that are made being used primarily to enrich Aszu), it is a tribute to a modern Socialist Republic that the great wines of Tokay are available to all. Even outside their own country, Tokay and other Hungarian wines are remarkably inexpensive. Together with a culinary heritage based on Magyar traditions, they are a source of rich everyday pleasure that is unquestionable; no mystery shrouds their goodness.

Quantities where necessary are given in
Metric, Imperial and US measurements.

Halászlé

Fish Soup
Serves 4–6

1.5 kg/3 lb different kinds of freshwater fish,
cut into pieces
4 onions, peeled and sliced into rings
1 tbsp Hungarian sweet paprika
Salt
1 green pepper, sliced
1 fresh chilli pepper, seeded and cut into rings (or
1 tsp crushed chilli or cayenne pepper)

Boil heads, tails, and fins of fish in a large pot of
salted water. Add onions, paprika, and salt.
Allow to simmer for 1 hr.

Strain stock and pour over pieces of fish.
Bring to the boil. Add green pepper and chilli.
Allow to simmer for about 30 min. Do not stir,
but shake occasionally, in order not to break up
the fish.

Serve hot or cold.

Suggested wines:
Egri Leányka, Badacsonyi Kéknyelü

Meggyleves

Sour Cherry Soup
Serves 4

500 g/1 lb sour cherries (or tinned morello cherries)
1.8 l/3 pt/7 $\frac{1}{2}$ cups cold water
250 g/8 oz/1 $\frac{1}{7}$ cups sugar
$\frac{1}{2}$ tsp cinnamon
4 cloves
1 egg, beaten
1 tbsp lemon juice
2 tbsp sugar
150 ml/$\frac{1}{4}$ pt/$\frac{2}{3}$ cup sour cream

Combine cherries, water, sugar, cinnamon, and
cloves in a large saucepan. Bring slowly to the

boil, and allow to simmer until soft, 30–40 min.
Then set aside to cool.

Combine egg and sugar in a large mixing
bowl, beating well. Add sour cream, and mix
well. Slowly add the cherry *compote* to this
mixture, then lemon juice to taste.

Pour into bowls, and serve chilled.

(Try also with plums, apples, pears, or rhubarb.)

Suggested wines:
Olasz Riesling (Rizling), Badacsonyi
Szürkebarát

Galuska

Dumplings
Serves 4–6

500 g/1 lb flour
Pinch of salt
2 eggs
6–8 tbsp water
25 g/2 oz/$\frac{1}{4}$ cup lard

Sift flour into a large mixing bowl with a pinch
of salt. Make a well in the centre, and add eggs.
Beat vigorously, adding enough water to make
a thick paste.

Place dough on a chopping board, and, with
a sharp knife, cut off small pieces into boiling
salted water. Boil *galuskas* until they rise to the
surface. (Do not try to boil too many at once, or
they will stick together.) Drain, and rinse in cold
water to prevent sticking.

Heat lard in a large saucepan, and add *galuskas*.
Stir well, so all are coated in hot fat.

Serve with *gulyás* or *pörkölt*, or as a separate
dish, tossed in sour cream.

Csirke Paprikás

Paprika Chicken
Serves 4

1.5 kg/3 lb chicken, cut into 8 pieces
25 g/1 oz/2 tbsp lard
1 garlic clove, peeled and finely chopped
2 large onions, peeled and finely chopped
1 tbsp Hungarian sweet paprika
Salt
Freshly ground black pepper
150 ml/$\frac{1}{4}$ pt/$\frac{2}{3}$ cup chicken stock
150 ml/$\frac{1}{4}$ pt/$\frac{2}{3}$ cup sour cream

Lightly brown chicken pieces in lard. Remove, and set aside. Drain off most of the fat, add onions and garlic, and sauté for 10 min. Remove pan from heat, add paprika, and stir well. Return to heat, cover, and continue to cook for 30 min. (Be careful not to scorch the paprika, or it will turn bitter.) Add chicken pieces, salt, and pepper to the soft mixture, then a little stock, to moisten. Cover, and cook for 30–40 min., or until chicken is cooked through. Add more stock occasionally, if chicken becomes too dry.

When cooked, adjust seasoning. Transfer to a warmed platter, and spoon on the sour cream.

Serve immediately, with rice, and cucumber salad.

Suggested wines:
Soproni Kékfrankos, Egri Bikavér

Töltött Káposzta

Stuffed Cabbage
Serves 4

1 large Savoy cabbage
25 g/1 oz/2 tbsp lard
1 medium onion, peeled and finely chopped
1 garlic clove, peeled and chopped
100 g/4 oz/$\frac{1}{2}$ cup rice
500 g/1 lb minced (ground) lean pork
Salt
Freshly ground black pepper
2 tbsp Hungarian sweet paprika
Pinch of marjoram

1 egg, beaten
1 kg/2 lb sauerkraut
2 tbsp flour
300 ml/$\frac{1}{2}$ pt/$1\frac{1}{4}$ cups sour cream

Boil about 8 of the cabbage leaves in a large pan of salted water, until almost tender. Drain, and set aside to cool. Rinse sauerkraut several times in cold water.

Melt lard in a frying pan, and gently fry onion and garlic until golden. Add rice, and mix well. Then add minced pork, and season with salt, pepper, and marjoram. Remove pan from heat, and add half of the paprika, then beaten egg, and mix well.

In the middle of each softened cabbage leaf place a heaped spoonful of meat mixture. Roll leaf up tightly, making sure sides are tucked in, and secure with a toothpick. Repeat until all the mixture has been used up.

Put half of sauerkraut into the bottom of a large casserole. Arrange cabbage rolls on top, followed by remainder of sauerkraut. Cover with water. Bring slowly to the boil, cover, and simmer for 2 hr.

When cooked, transfer the rolls to a warmed serving dish. Mix flour with sour cream, and add to sauerkraut and cooking liquid in casserole. Add rest of paprika, and stir until sauce is smooth and thick. Bring slowly to the boil, and simmer for 5–10 min. Pour over the stuffed cabbage, and serve immediately, sprinkled with sour cream.

Suggested wines:
Debröi Hárslevelü, Badacsonyi Szürkebarát

Gulyás

Goulash
Serves 4–6

50 g/2 oz/¼ cup lard
2 large onions, peeled and finely chopped
1 garlic clove, peeled and finely chopped
1 tbsp Hungarian sweet paprika
1 kg/2 lb shin of beef, cut into 2½ cm/1 in cubes
1 tsp caraway seeds
Salt
400 g/14 oz tin of tomatoes
2 large potatoes, peeled and cut into small cubes
2 green peppers, cut into strips

Melt lard in a large casserole, and add onions and garlic. Fry gently, until soft and golden. Remove pan from heat, and stir in paprika. Return to heat, and add a little water. Then add meat, caraway seeds, salt, and tomatoes. Mix thoroughly, cover, and cook for 1½ hr., or until meat is almost tender.

Add potatoes and peppers. Pour in sufficient water to cover meat. Bring to the boil, simmer, cook until potatoes are tender.

Serve in bowls, with *galuskas*.

Suggested wine:
Egri Bikavér

Pörkölt

Pork and Paprika Stew
Serves 4–6

25 g/1 oz/2 tbsp lard
2 medium onions, peeled and finely chopped
1 garlic clove, peeled and finely chopped
1 tbsp Hungarian sweet paprika
1 kg/2 lb stewing pork, cut into 2½ cm/1 in cubes
Salt
250 g/½ lb tomatoes, peeled and chopped (or 1 large tin, drained)
1 large green pepper, sliced

Melt lard in a large heavy-bottomed casserole. Add onions and garlic, and fry gently until soft and golden. Remove pan from heat, and add

paprika, mixing well. Return to heat, and add a little water. Add pork, and a pinch of salt. Cover, and simmer for 40 min.

Add tomatoes and pepper, and cook until meat is tender, about a further 1 hr.

Serve with *galuskas*.

Suggested wines:
Tokay Szamorodni, Debrői Hárslevelü

Uborkasaláta

Cucumber Salad
Serves 4–6

1 medium to large cucumber
Salt
4 tbsp wine vinegar
2 tbsp water
1 tbsp sugar
Freshly ground black pepper
Crushed chilli peppers to taste

Peel cucumber, and slice as thinly as possible (a mandoline is useful for this purpose). The slices should be almost transparent. Place slices in a bowl, cover with plenty of salt, and fill with water. Set aside for about 30 min.

Turn them into a colander, and squeeze slices hard to remove liquid. Place in the rinsed bowl. Add vinegar, water, sugar, pepper, and chillies. Mix well, and allow to chill for about 30 min.

Serve with *csirke paprikás* (paprika chicken).

Rakott Palacsinta

Layered Pancakes
Serves 6

12 thin pancakes (see recipe for crêpe*)*
175 g/6 oz/¾ cup apricot jam
50 g/2 oz/2 squares chocolate, grated
100 g/4 oz/1 stick butter, melted
100 g/4 oz/1 cup ground walnuts
250 g/8 oz/½ lb cottage cheese
2 egg yolks
50 g/2 oz/⅓ cup raisins
3 egg whites, well beaten

250 g/8 oz/1 ⅐ cups sugar
Vanilla sugar for dusting

Butter an ovenproof dish. Place one pancake in the bottom, and spread with apricot jam. Cover with another pancake, spread with some of the grated chocolate, and baste with a little melted butter. Add a third pancake, and spread with walnuts mixed with a little sugar. Mix cottage cheese, egg yolks, some sugar, and raisins together. Add another pancake, and spread with the cottage cheese mixture. Repeat layering of pancakes in this way until all ingredients are used up. But leave top pancake plain. Bake in a moderate oven, 200°C/Gas Mark 6/400°F, for 10 min.

Meanwhile, make a meringue with beaten egg whites and about 100 g/4 oz/⅔ cup sugar. Take pancakes from the oven, and spread the meringue mixture over top. Bake for 10 min., or until top becomes brown. Dust with vanilla sugar.

Serve warm, cut into wedges like cake.

Suggested wine:
Tokay Aszu

Familiar-shaped bottles of Tokay ageing in the State cellars in Tolcsva.

Grilling ribs of beef at the annual wine festival in Lugano.

SWITZERLAND

Up here in the lower Alps near the medieval town of Gruyère, the grass is greener and the air fresher than perhaps anywhere else on earth.

Harebells, edelweiss, and honey-scented clover decorate the undulating meadows and pastures, and gentle cows wearing leather straps around their necks from which hang enormous metal bells meander slowly through the fields. As they nibble the sweet grass their large heads wag to and fro, filling the still day with a symphony of bells that sounds and resounds through the valleys and crags.

Twice a day the rich milk is gathered from these cows and taken to village cheese manufacturers who produce the distinctive Swiss cheeses known throughout the world. Alpine herdsmen used to perform the strenuous cheese-making tasks, but today cheese factories are models of Swiss efficiency. Tradition, however, dies hard in the mountains, and simple foods that once sustained herdsmen on long winter nights are still national favourites.

Fondue, for example, is no more than cheese melted in an earthenware crock. Cubes of crusty bread are speared with long forks and twisted into the bubbling mixture. The Valaisan speciality known as *raclette* is even simpler. Best enjoyed out-of-doors, this is no more than a wheel of the local cheese (also called Raclette) heated in front of an open fire, or under a grill. The crusty melted cheese is then scraped on to a plate and eaten with boiled potatoes, raw onion, and pickles. In many homes and restaurants, ritual and elegant equipment accompany these meals, but they are really only variations of the herdsman's daily diet of cheese.

Delightful Swiss wines known as Fendant

The steep upper Rhône valley of the Valais at Sion.

and Dorin perfectly accompany the simple cheese specialities, and indeed the Swiss drink both in great quantities. In fact, it often comes as a surprise to discover that in this idyllic mountainous land the vine is cultivated extensively and wine-making is an important industry. Vineyards grace the shores of Lakes Geneva and Neuchâtel, the warm area of the upper Rhône valley known as the Valais, in Ticino (the Italian section of Switzerland), and to a lesser degree in eastern and central Switzerland, too.

Swiss wine is varied and distinctive, and, like most other Swiss products, made efficiently and with care. But it is not well known abroad, simply because the Swiss are great wine drinkers, and consume most of the home wine produced, as well as a good deal that is imported. Swiss wine is, however, exported in small quantities, and should be sought. Its delicate, fruity, sometimes semi-sparkling character adds a certain light-hearted authenticity to a *fondue* party with friends.

Swiss wine and food both reflect the uniquely various culture of this tiny country. Four languages are spoken: French, German, Italian, and Romansh (an Illyrian language with Latin roots). The Swiss Confederation is made up of twenty-three fiercely independent cantons (states). Each has its own character, culture, and local government within a central government. The country has been inhabited by Celts, Romans, Germanic tribes, and Burgundians. And yet these varying influences and cultures fused peacefully into a national entity as long ago as 1291. Regional contrast remains extreme, but the common bonds that unite the people are stronger than any differences.

Two of the most important wine regions in Switzerland are the French-speaking cantons of Vaud and Valais. In the Vaud, vines hug the sunny, south-facing slopes of Lake Geneva to the east and west of Lausanne, while in the lush upper Rhône valley of the Valais, vines thrive on virtually every protected slope up to an altitude

Cows grazing in sweet alpine meadows; their milk is the essence of Switzerland's famous cheeses.

of over 900 metres (3,000 feet). It is a spectacular sight: the vines stretch towards the afternoon sun, while the bare-faced rocks of the Alps glisten majestically across the river.

Most of the wines produced in these two regions are white, and undoubtedly the great grape here is the Chasselas. Originally brought to Switzerland by soldiers who were in service to the French, the Chasselas has adapted favourably to local conditions, soil, and climate, and produces wine with an unique bouquet and character that is more attractive than the equivalent produced elsewhere, in France or Germany, for example. In the Vaud, white wine made from the Chasselas is called Dorin, while in the Valais it is Fendant (and, to confuse matters further, wine made from the same grape around Geneva is called Perlan). Such wines differ considerably between each region, and there are naturally subtle and qualitative differences among wines produced within each. Dorin is generally lighter and more delicate, at once lively and refreshing.

As we move east, however, wine becomes stronger and fuller, reflecting the difference in climate of the sheltered, hot upper Rhône valley, which leads to the Valais.

Indeed, as we follow the Rhône towards its glacial source high in the Swiss Alps, the rich and fertile valley is uncommonly lush. The Valais is the driest section of Switzerland, and it is blessed with hot summers and long mild autumns. The vineyards and orchards are watered by clear springs that cascade from melting alpine glaciers. The vine clings to the sunny slopes upon terraces that are at times treacherously steep, while below, on the flatter land along the banks of the river, there is a variety of apple and pear orchards, beside fields of rich-smelling onions, cabbages, cauliflower, and tomato plants that look strangely like vines, with large, green, unripe fruit.

The Fendant of the Valais is strong and heady white wine, with an appetizing and clean bouquet. Particularly delicious with cheese dishes such as *fondue* or *raclette*, it is a popular and useful wine that can be drunk on its own, or with a variety of other foods such as fried freshwater fish, cold meats, or stewed veal. There are numerous small wine producers within this region who can be relied upon for individual and distinctive wine, while nearly 5,000 growers and producers belong to a co-operative association called Provins Valais that produces a variety of reliable and excellent wine.

Red wine is produced in both the Vaudois and Valais, mostly from a blend of Pinot Noir and Gamay grapes. The Dôle of the Valais is fragrant and full-bodied, surprisingly so from these northern vineyards, and can accompany steak, roast meat, and game. The Salvagnin of the Vaudois is also blended from Pinot Noir and Gamay, and it too is good; lighter and attractively fruity.

Other important Swiss wine regions centre around Neuchâtel and Ticino. The wine of Neuchâtel is mostly white, and is often slightly sparkling (since much of it is bottled early, resulting in a secondary fermentation that takes place in the bottle). As in the Vaud and Valais, much of the white wine of Neuchâtel is produced from the Chasselas, and generally sold under the regional name Neuchâtel. Additionally, a distinctive and celebrated rosé comes from this region. It is made from the Pinot Noir grape and is called colloquially 'Oeil de Perdrix', or 'partridge's eye', referring to the wine's pale and distinctive colour. Unlike much rosé that is lightweight or sweetish, this wine is strong and dry, and delicious taken with an outdoor lunch, a picnic in the mountains, or a light supper.

The red wine of Ticino is unlike any other in Switzerland. The best is produced from the Merlot, a grape that originally came from Bordeaux, where it is blended to soften the harsh and tannic Cabernet Sauvignon. Here, it makes a soft, deep, and powerful red wine similar to Italian red wines from the Veneto, not far across the border. Wine is produced under strict official control, and what has been inspected and approved receives a VITI seal. Merlot del Ticino partners pasta, roasts, the veal dishes of the region, or the characteristic *busecca*, a vegetable and tripe soup that is consumed with zest—particularly during the annual *Sagra del Vino*, a

Lilies guard a Swiss chalet in Marthalen.

wine festival that explodes with excitement in dreamy Lugano after the harvest.

The food of Switzerland mirrors cultural divisions between its regions that correspond approximately with the language divisions. The cuisine of French-speaking Switzerland has, not surprisingly, much in common with that of France. This is seen not only in cooking methods but also in sauces and classic dishes that have been adopted by Swiss cooks. In German-speaking Switzerland, food resembles that found on the other side of the Rhine. The *Berner Platte* is typical, a trencherman's platter of piping hot sauerkraut served with a variety of ham, *Wurst*, and beans. If, in the south, the *charcuterie* resembles that of France, here one finds a great variety of German-style *Wurst*. In the Italian canton of Ticino, on the other hand, the *cucina* is similar to that found across the border in Lombardy. Veal is cooked to perfection in such typical dishes as *ossobuco*, stewed shin of veal served with *risotto*. Many inventive pasta dishes are enjoyed, while such desserts as *zabaione* (a creamy mixture of Marsala, sugar, and egg white) replace either French *pâtisserie* or German *Kuchen* (cakes).

Finally, in the Grisons, where Romansh is spoken, one finds unique mountain specialities such as *Bündnerfleisch*, beef, mutton, or goat's flesh dried in pure, clean mountain air. The flesh becomes as hard as leather, yet remains surprisingly sweet and aromatic. It is eaten raw, shaved into thin slivers. (Menus here often reflect this curious cultural *mélange* by offering such unique Swiss specialities as *risotto mit champignons*.)

Though the Swiss have borrowed much from bordering countries, there are also foods that are unique to this alpine land. Cheese obviously plays an important role in the diet. Creamy, sober Emmenthal, the one with large holes that many people think of as 'Swiss cheese', is only one of many regional types. Gruyère is pungent, flavourful cheese produced in the Gruyère valley. Gruyère and Emmenthal are often mixed in equal portions in the classic Swiss *fondue*. And both are eaten in a variety of other ways, ranging from simple cheese toasts to soufflés, cheese 'steaks', fried cheese, cheese and egg, and much more. Sbrinz, another distinctive Swiss cheese, is hard and crumbly, and thus excellent for grating and cooking with. Creamy Vacherin, Appenzell, and Royalp are all excellent. Authentic Swiss cheese can always be recognized by the alpine hornblower on the pack—and the word 'Switzerland' marked in red on the cheese rind.

A typically Swiss speciality for memorable occasions is *fondue bourguignonne*. Like cheese *fondue* this is another communal meal everyone dips into. A pot of oil is kept hot at the table by means of a spirit lamp or alcohol burner, and diners spear cubes of steak on long forks, and cook them in the hot oil. The meat is then dipped into a variety of sauces that decorate each plate.

Fish from Lake Geneva, the Rhône, Lakes Zurich and Neuchâtel are welcome contrasts to dairy and meat dishes. Fillets of perch are dredged in flour, then fried until golden. This is delicious with a chilled glass of Dorin. Fish is baked *au gratin*, and brought to the table with a crusty layer of melted cheese. And trout is enjoyed fresh from river and lake, served in an aromatic herbal cream sauce.

The Swiss love fresh vegetables and fruit. Asparagus is a favourite, when in season, while creamed kohlrabi is served with *Leberspiessli*, which are 'kebabs' of calf's liver, bacon, and sage leaves. *Rösti*, in its many guises, is virtually the national dish of Switzerland, and is eaten in many homes for the evening meal, with a cup of coffee (the main meal is usually taken at midday). *Rösti* is simply boiled potatoes, sliced and fried into a flat, brown, crusty cake, sometimes cooked with bacon or sausage, often served plain, at times covered with a thick layer of melted Emmenthal.

Pears, plums, cherries, and other fruits that grow in the fertile upper Rhône valley become delicious fruit pies and tarts. And in northwestern Switzerland such fruits are distilled into clean neutral spirits known as kirsch (made from cherries), eau-de-vie, or schnapps. These clean, fiery drinks are often taken in the middle of a *fondue* party, a practice known as the *coup de milieu*.

Switzerland is a curious country. Her varying regions seem distinct and utterly different from each other. And yet, somehow, there is a unifying force that consolidates them nationally. When it comes to food and drink, she has borrowed much from neighbouring countries. But, here, too, a unique national character superimposes itself over the distinctions.

Finally, perhaps, it is not so much a question of what the Swiss eat and drink, as how they eat and drink that is important. *Fondue*, probably the most typical dish of Switzerland, reflects a healthy, warming attitude to life. Basically the dish is undistinguished—simply a piping hot pot of melted cheese in which one dips cubes of bread. But tradition and ritual dictate that the *fondue* be stirred clockwise; that if a man drops a cube of bread into the pot, he forfeits a bottle of wine; that if a woman loses her bread, she forfeits a kiss. The meal lasts for hours; the *coup de milieu* is drunk; another bottle of Fendant is opened. The evening becomes an occasion. From humble origins deep in the Swiss Alps, a simple communal meal has evolved into a celebration of friends, family, neighbours, who get together to share food, drink, and exuberance. In such company, could one want more than a bubbling pot of cheese and a bottle of wine?

Quantities where necessary are given in
Metric, Imperial and US measurements.

Busecca

Ticinese Vegetable and Tripe Soup
Serves 6

100 g/4 oz bacon, finely diced
25 g/1 oz/¼ stick butter
1 onion, peeled and finely chopped
1 garlic clove, peeled and finely chopped
1 carrot, peeled and finely chopped
2 leeks, white part only, chopped
3 sticks of celery, chopped
Freshly chopped parsley
Bouquet garni
1 large tin tomatoes
500 g/1 lb tripe, boiled until tender (usually 2 or
3 hr.) and finely shredded
1 large potato, peeled and diced
Salt
Freshly ground black pepper

Fry bacon until fat begins to run. Add butter, and
gently sauté onion, garlic, carrot, leeks, and
celery. Add parsley, bouquet garni, and tomatoes. Simmer for 20 min. Add cooked and
shredded tripe and potatoes, season, and simmer
for 1 hr. Add water as necessary.
Serve hot, as a first course.

Suggested wine:
Merlot del Ticino VITI

Cheese Fondue

Serves 4

2 garlic cloves, peeled
300 ml/½ pt/1¼ cups dry white wine
400 g/14 oz/4½ cups Gruyère cheese, finely grated
400 g/14 oz/4½ cups Emmenthal cheese, finely grated
Freshly grated nutmeg
Freshly ground black pepper
Small glass kirsch

1 tsp cornflour
French bread

Rub inside of a *fondue* pot with 2 cloves of garlic.
Leave garlic in pot. Add wine, and heat gently
over a low heat. Add finely grated cheese, and
stir, in a figure eight motion, until all cheese has
dissolved. Season with nutmeg and black pepper.
When completely melted, add kirsch mixed
with cornflour. Stir thoroughly, and transfer pot
to table.
Cut French bread into 2½ cm/1 in cubes, so
each cube still has some crust attached.
The *fondue* pot sits on a small spirit burner in
the centre of the table. Each guest has a long-
handled fork with which to spear cubes of bread

Swiss *fondue*, the herdsman's pot of Gruyère and
Emmenthal, accompanied by Fendant and a *coup de
milieu* of kirsch.

and dip them into the bubbling cheese. Allow *fondue* just to simmer throughout the meal.

Suggested drinks:
Fendant, coup de milieu of kirsch

Fondue Bourguignonne

Allow about 150–250 g/6–8 oz fillet of beef for each person, and cut into 2 cm/¾ in cubes. Lightly season with salt and pepper, and place in individual bowls on the table, with an assortment of sauces, salads, and relishes.

Fill the metal *fondue* pot with about 300 ml/ ½ pt/1¼ cups of good quality vegetable oil, and heat over stove. When it begins to bubble, transfer to alcohol burner on the table.

Each person spears a cube of meat on a long fork, and dips it in the boiling oil until it is done to his or her liking. The *fondue* forks become very hot in the cooking process, so remember to transfer the cooked meat to another fork before dipping into one of the sauces.

Serve with plenty of French bread, and a variety of salads.

Many bottled sauces, such as sweet corn relish, chutney, or pickle relish, can add to the variety of sauces, without adding to the workload. Here are a few recipes for home-made sauces. Your selection should be as varied in flavour as in colour, and should decorate each plate like dabs of paint on an artist's palette.

Home-made Mayonnaise

This home-made mayonnaise can be the base for many delicious sauces by adding chopped capers, chopped fresh herbs, or spices. An electric mixer is ideal, but it can easily be made by hand with a whisk, if you have the energy.

2 egg yolks (at room temperature)
1 tsp French mustard
2 tsp wine vinegar
300 ml/½ pt/1¼ cups good quality olive oil
Salt
Freshly ground black pepper

Place egg yolks and mustard in the mixing bowl with 1 tsp wine vinegar, and mix well. Gradually add olive oil in a very thin stream (almost a drop at a time, until mixture begins to thicken), and whisk constantly. When about half the oil has been used up, add the other spoon of vinegar. Continue to add oil in a steady trickle, until it is all in. Season to taste with salt and pepper.
Serve chilled.

Hot Tabasco Sauce

150 ml/ ¼ pt/ ⅔ cup mayonnaise
3 tbsp plain yoghurt
Dash of tabasco sauce
1 tbsp tomato purée (paste)
Pinch of cayenne pepper
Salt
Freshly ground black pepper
1 tsp lemon juice

Combine all ingredients and mix well.
Serve chilled.

Garlic Butter

2 garlic cloves, peeled and chopped
50 g/2 oz/ ½ stick softened butter
Freshly chopped parsley
Salt
Freshly ground black pepper

Combine all ingredients and mix until smooth.
Serve chilled.

Curried Egg

4 hard-boiled eggs, finely chopped
3 tbsp of home-made mayonnaise
Salt
Freshly ground black pepper
1 tsp curry powder
Freshly chopped parsley

Combine all ingredients and mix well.
Serve chilled.

Suggested wines:
Dôle, Salvagnin

Geschnetzeltes

Sautéd Chopped Veal
Serves 4

50 g/2 oz/½ stick butter
1 medium onion, peeled and chopped
100 g/4 oz/¼ lb fresh mushrooms, finely chopped
500 g/1 lb fillet of veal, finely chopped
Salt
Freshly ground black pepper
Squeeze of fresh lemon juice
4 tbsp cream

Melt butter in a large frying pan, and sauté onion until soft and golden. Add mushrooms, and cook until tender. Add chopped veal, and cook for only 5 min. on a high heat. Season with salt, pepper, and lemon juice.

Add cream just before serving.

Suggested wines:
Fendant, 'Oeil de Perdrix'

Ossobuco

Braised Veal Shin Bones
Serves 6

1 kg/2 lb shin of veal, sawn by the butcher into
5 cm/2 in pieces
50 g/2 oz/½ stick butter
1 tbsp olive oil
150 ml/¼ pt/⅔ cup dry white wine
350 g/¾ lb tomatoes, peeled and chopped
150 ml/¼ pt/⅔ cup stock
Salt
Freshly ground black pepper
1 garlic clove, peeled and finely chopped
2 sprigs of parsley, finely chopped
Grated rind of 1 lemon

In a wide shallow heavy pan, brown pieces of veal in butter and oil. Once they are browned, arrange them so they remain upright and close together, to prevent marrow falling out of bones.

Add wine, and let it cook over a fairly high heat until it has almost evaporated. Add tomatoes, and allow to reduce. Add stock and

seasoning. Cover, and cook over a low heat for about 1½ hr.

Mix garlic, parsley, and lemon rind together, and sprinkle over bones just before serving.

Serve with rice.

Suggested wine:
Merlot del Ticino VITI

Zürcher Leberspiessli

Liver and Bacon Kebabs
Serves 6

750 g/1½ lb calf's liver
Salt
Freshly ground black pepper
3 sage leaves, crushed
12 thin rashers/slices of bacon
3 tbsp butter

Skin liver, and cut into strips about 4 cm/1½ in long and ½ cm/¼ in thick. Season with salt, pepper, and sage leaves.

Wrap each strip of liver in a rasher of bacon, and spear on a wooden skewer. Melt butter in a frying pan, and brown the kebabs on both sides.

Serve with *rösti*.

Suggested wines:
Dôle, Salvagnin

Rösti

Swiss Fried Potatoes
Serves 4

1 kg/2 lb potatoes
100 g/4 oz/1 stick butter
Salt
Freshly ground black pepper
150 g/5 oz/1 ½ cups Emmenthal cheese, grated

Boil potatoes in their jackets until tender. When they have cooled, peel and thinly slice. Heat butter in a large frying pan, and add potatoes, seasoning well. Turn frequently until golden brown.

Mix in 75 g/3 oz/1 cup of cheese with the potatoes, and form into a flat cake. Top with remaining cheese, cover, and fry until cheese melts.

Turn out on to a warm plate, with crusty side uppermost.

Suggested wines:
Dorin, Gamay

Zürcher Chriesitotsh

Cherry Tart

750 g/1 ½ lb red cherries (not black)
100 g/4 oz/1 stick butter
150 g/5 oz/⅔ cup sugar
6 egg yolks
100 g/4 oz/⅔ cup ground almonds
150 ml/¼ pt/⅔ cup cream
Rind of 1 lemon
100 g/¼ lb sweet plain biscuits, finely crushed
Icing (powdered) sugar

Wash, dry, and de-stalk cherries. Leave stones remaining, since this prevents them from becoming too soft during cooking—but warn your guests!

In a large mixing bowl, beat butter and sugar together until smooth. Add egg yolks, and whisk until foamy. Add almonds, cream, lemon rind, and crushed biscuits, and beat well.

Grease a 23 cm/9 in baking tin, and add one-third of the mixture. Put in a pre-heated oven, 200°C/Gas Mark 6/400°F, for 10 min. Remove, and add cherries to half-baked dough. Put remaining dough over cherries, and return to oven reduced to 180°C/Gas Mark 4/350°F, for 50 min.

Remove from oven, and allow to cool. Turn out of tin, and dust with sugar. Decorate serving dish with additional cherries.

Suggested wines:
Malvoisie, Ermitage

ITALY

PIEDMONT

VAL D'AOSTA
Aosta

L. Maggiore

GATTINARA

Novàra
Vercelli

VERMOUTH

R. Po

Turin

ASTI
SPUMANTE

Asti

R. Tanaro

Alba
BARBERA
BARBARESCO
BAROLO

CORTESE

Molare

LANGHE

VENETO

Conegliano

GRAPPA
Bassano
del Grappa

TOCAI
DEL
VENETO

L. Garda

VALPOLICELLA

Treviso

Bardolino
BARDOLINO

SOAVE
Soave

Vicenza

Venice

Peschiera

Verona

Padua

R. Adige

Mantua

Rovigo

R. Po

TUSCANY

Lucca

Pistoia

R. Arno

Florence
CHIANTI
CLASSICO

Pisa

Castellina in
Chianti

Arezzo

R. Cecina

Sienna

Chiani Valley

MONTEPULCIANO
BRUNELLO DI
MONTALCINO

Grosseto

R. Ombrone

UMBRIA

Spoleto

Amatrice

Orvieto   ORVIETO

Terni

Rieti

EST!
EST!!
EST!!!

L. Bolsena

Montefiascone
Viterbo

R. Tiber

L. Vico

Tivoli

L. Bracciano

Palestrina

FRASCATI

Rome   Frascati
Grottaferrata

SANGIOVESE
DI APRILIA

MARINO

COLLI
ALBANI

TREBBIANO
DI APRILIA

Latina

LATIUM

The ancient Romans were famous for their (excessive) achievements. Their outrageous orgiastic feasts titillated even the jaded palates of patricians and emperors. Camel's foot, roast hippopotamus, mice, and pigs stuffed with live larks appeared on the table at such occasions, disappeared just as quickly, and then, often as not, reappeared.

But hand in hand with a reputation for excess goes one of great ability to invent ideals and better institutions believed necessary for a good life. We are heirs today to their love of wine, for example, for they established some of the greatest vineyards in Italy some 2,500 years ago. And as the empire expanded, so did viticulture. Thirsty soldiers had to have their daily wine rations; lands they colonized were therefore planted with vines from home for the purpose of providing them with their daily pot. How remarkable that today some of these vineyards continue to produce wine considered to be the deepest, finest, or most complex in the world: the wines of Burgundy, Bordeaux, and the Rhineland.

Latium, the region that encompasses Rome and its environs, as a proper descendant of Rome, is not neglectful of its legacy of gastronomic marvels—albeit no one today slavers for mice in *salsa piccante* or elephant tail *ragù*. Still, as in all of Italy, food and wine are serious concerns, and no one shrugs away their importance in the total complex of man's well-being.

The gastronomy of modern Rome, however, is neither exotic nor conspicuous. To a great extent, it is a development of the workaday dietary habits of Roman citizens who lived modestly and frugally, leaving excesses to the

Entrance to a typical *cantina* in the Colli Albani.

indulgent rich. But modesty and frugality should not connote a sense of deprivation or neglect. One has only to remember Rome's history as the greatest power in the western world for over 1,000 years to recognize that the average citizen probably did not live at all badly. Archaeological evidence shows that the central market near the Forum was remarkably similar to today's markets. It consisted of a series of small shops and stalls selling staples and fresh produce—vegetables, meat, olive oil, wine, honey, and herbs. Meat was a luxury of special occasions; *pulmentum*, a gruel made of crushed grain, was eaten daily. Indeed, *polenta*, a dense mush so popular in northern Italy today, is a direct descendant of *pulmentum* (though *polenta* is made from coarsely-ground maize—not introduced to Italy until after the discovery of the New World).

If the gastronomic excesses of Imperial Rome were exceptions to the norm, they nevertheless reflect an all-consuming passion for the joys of food and drink. Certainly the Rome of today still holds Bacchus in high esteem. For meals, whether simple or elaborate, should be entertaining and enjoyable experiences. It is not mere coincidence that the word 'gusto' stems from the Latin verb *gustare*, to taste. *La vita breva, buon divertimento*—life is short, enjoy yourself—sums up the Roman attitude to living.

Nowhere is this attitude more evident than in the Colli Albani, a series of volcanic hills south of Rome, and Latium's most important wine region. The Colli Albani have long been popular with holidaying Romans; even the Pope, of course, has a summer house at Castel Gandolfo. The craters of long-extinct volcanoes have filled, creating beautiful natural lakes. Towns such as Frascati, Grottaferrata, or Albano, though popular, lively, and noisy, are unspoiled, and, if not exactly reminiscent of ancient Rome, still strangely, broodingly medieval. The local *cantine* with entrances carved into sides of ancient buildings or hills might have been here for hundreds of years, serving today, as in the past, as meeting places for all who congregate for wine, company, and conviviality. In these dark, underground dens, whole families gather bearing dinners wrapped in chequered cloths: men

to play cards, women to chat, children to be petted by friends and relations alike. Here, there is no differentiating between yours and mine—neither of children nor of food and drink.

A traditional food of this region is *porchetta*, a fragrant, tender suckling pig stuffed with generous amounts of rosemary, garlic, and *pancetta* (a type of pork fat), then roasted in a *forno di legno* (wood-fired oven). *Porchetta* is sold in roadside stands, accompanied by large rounds of *pane casareccia* (home-made bread cooked alongside the meat). How delightful is a slab of bread and a generous portion of paper-wrapped *porchetta*, when taken to a cool underground tavern where tumblers of wine are drawn directly from barrels, to eat with fingers in the company of others who are also not unmindful of goodness contained in simplicity.

This area of Colli Albani, sometimes referred to as the Castelli Romani, produces a variety of wine itself broadly known as Castelli Romani. Among the grapes grown here are Malvasia, Greco, and Trebbiano Toscano. Frascati is

Freshly roasted *porchetta*, a Roman convenience food, carved off and carried to informal wine taverns in towns such as Albano, Marino and Frascati.

probably the best known of the Castelli wines. It is congenial, firm, straw-yellow, often sold in squat, clear-glass bottles. Very young Frascati, served locally in open carafes, is generally robust, perhaps even a trifle rough, because it is traditionally fermented on the *grappa* (skins and pips), which gives the wine a certain gutsy flavour. As the wine develops, however, it becomes more supple and smooth. Much more *abboccato* (medium-sweet) Frascati used to be produced, but today the preference is primarily for dry wine. Frascati *superiore*, incidentally, is a wine with higher alcohol content.

Marino is a town perched on the very rim of the volcanic crater that now forms Lake Albano. The vineyards that produce Marino wine spread up to the town and spill over into the crater itself. This rich volcanic earth yields grapes for making fragrant, dry white wine, which, when well made, is both clean and strong. Wine from this district is also sold under the broader *denominazione* Colli Albani, although this often refers to wine produced farther away from the lake, towards Ariccia and Nemi.

Castelli Romani wine as a whole, also produced around towns such as Albano, Velletri, and Castel Gandolfo, varies both in style and quality, but these sound, primarily white thirst-quenchers provide the great bulk of everyday drinking wine for the region of Latium. It is not surprising, therefore, that they go so well with typical Roman cuisine.

Some say the farther south one goes in Italy the better the food is, and, whether or not one agrees, there are certainly dramatic differences between northern and southern styles of cooking. *Pasta asciutta* (pasta served with a sauce rather than in broth or soup) is generally favoured in the south, for example, where it is a staple food of the poor. Rich egg noodles, *polenta*, and *risotti* (rice dishes), on the other hand, are more popular in the north. Tomatoes—almost a symbol of stereotypical Italy—colour the dishes of the south, while northern dishes, by contrast, appear painted in cooler shades of green and cream. Butter is favoured as a cooking medium in the north, but olive oil is essential in the south—a tree, after all, costs less to keep than a cow.

Latium, however, is located in central Italy, and thus is able to take advantage of the best of both traditions. Southern-style pasta dishes are popular, and delicious, such as *bucatini all'amatriciana*, elbow macaroni served with a fiery tomato and hot pepper sauce covered with a layer of sharp Pecorino cheese. *Spaghetti alla carbonara* is another favourite and filling *primo piatto* (first course), a simple dish of spaghetti tossed with *pancetta* or bacon and raw egg, which cooks as it is mixed with the steaming hot noodles. Northern influence is apparent in such dishes as *gnocchi alla romana* (semolina dumplings baked in butter and cheese) or *fettuccine al burro*. *Fettuccine* are a Roman version of the flat, rich egg noodles known as *tagliatelle* in northern regions such as Emilia-Romagna (though *fettuccine* are both thinner and flatter), eaten in the simplest way possible, boiled *al dente* (that is, with some bite left in them), then dredged in abundant sweet, unsalted butter and freshly grated Parmesan cheese.

If the *cucina romana* is a balance of north and south, there are many specialities she can claim as wholly her own. *Supplì al telefono*, for example, reflect a characteristically whimsical approach to eating. These popular appetizers are little balls of left-over *risotto* stuffed with chewy Mozzarella cheese, coated in breadcrumbs, and deep-fried. When these crunchy little balls are picked up with the fingers and eaten hot, strings of melted cheese stretch out into 'wires', justifying the name 'telephone wires'. *Saltimbocca* is another traditional Roman favourite—thin slices of milk-fed veal layered with slices of air-dried mountain ham (*prosciutto*), and fresh sage leaves, rolled and secured with a toothpick, then fried in butter and oil. They are so delicious and delicate that they seem virtually to jump into the mouth, which is exactly what the name means.

Romans love to eat out, whether it is simply an ice cream in the Piazza Navona, or a full-blown picnic with several courses. Tables and chairs appear in parks throughout the city, and in favourite places for outings such as Tivoli and Ostia, whenever the weather is fine. Lunch is always the main meal of the day, and if it is to be taken out of doors, it must still be substantial. Picnic tables are spread with brightly coloured tablecloths, and plates, forks, and knives are carefully set. Flasks of wine appear, and chunks of bread are sawn off round, crusty country loaves. Marinated artichoke hearts, onions in a sweet and sour sauce (*agrodolce*), *peperoncini* (small pickled chilli peppers), or slices of fresh moist Mozzarella (the real thing here is made from buffalo milk) covered in olive oil and dusted with oregano, might be dipped into first. Thick slices of salami and other cold meats are carved off, and there is probably a selection of cold breaded veal chops, *polpettone* (meat balls), or perhaps slices of *porchetta*. A *budino di Ricotta* (Ricotta cheesecake) proudly graces the table at the end of the meal, the effort of wife and daughters the previous night.

Romans love to eat out at small local restaurants too. Though there are numerous expensive and well-known *ristoranti*, it is generally agreed that the best food comes from traditional *trattorie* and Roman *osterie*. An *osteria* is no more than a small, informal, usually family-run inn, but in this part of the country such places have a reputation for serving substantial and excellent meals. There is usually little choice of dishes, because one is virtually eating with the family. A meal might begin with a simple dish of buttered *fettucine*, *gnocchi*, perhaps a special stuffed pasta, such as *cannelloni* (large hollowed tubes of pasta filled with savoury mixtures of meat or cheese), or just a hearty bowl of *minestra* (home-made soup). A favourite to follow the first course is *abbacchio*, a local speciality of very young, milk-fed lamb. *Abbacchio* can be roasted, like *porchetta*, in a *forno di legno*, or the tiny chops can be fried or cooked on a grill. Another favourite way of preparing this exceedingly tender and delicate meat is *alla cacciatora* (hunter's style), in which the meat is stewed in oil, vinegar, rosemary, and anchovies. The robust and flavourful character of the *cucina romana* is also reflected in such characteristic dishes as *coda alla vaccinara*, a hearty oxtail stew, and *trippa alla romana*, tripe braised in a tomato and cheese sauce.

Just as the mineral-rich volcanic soil of Latium favours the vine, it also yields superb vegetables, such as artichokes, celery, beans, salad greens, tomatoes, and broccoli, and the Romans are expert in their preparation. An inventive and delicious dish originated in the ancient Jewish quarter of Rome. *Carciofi alla giudìa* are sweet, tender Roman artichokes that are flattened then deep-fried, and delicious as part of a *fritto misto* (mixed platter of fried meat and vegetables) along with fried courgette (zucchini) flowers, sweetbreads and brains, and perhaps crunchy fried fillets of *baccalà* (dried salt cod soaked for at least twenty-four hours, boiled briefly, then dipped in batter and fried in hot oil). Other vegetable dishes typical of the region are broccoli or cauliflower stewed in wine, oil, and garlic; peas or onions cooked in *agrodolce* (sweet and sour); and beans or celery braised with *pancetta* or *guanciale* (two characteristic types of pork fat used in cooking).

Latium as a region, of course, extends beyond Rome itself, and many towns or areas have contributed culinary specialities. The *amatriciana* sauce already mentioned comes from the Sabine town of Amatrice in northern Latium, from where also comes Pecorino Romano cheese. Pecorino is a dry, hard, and sharp cheese made from sheep's milk curdled with lamb's rennet (rennet comes from the stomach lining and is necessary to coagulate milk solids in the cheese-making process). This delicious cheese is just as good for cooking as it is eaten with a glass of Frascati or Marino. Ricotta is another characteristic cheese of the region, a fresh, moist curd cheese, that is used in both savoury and sweet dishes. Gorgonzola, creamy and blue-veined, also comes from Latium, and is magnificent to eat on its own after a meal, while a delicious pasta sauce is simply prepared by combining Gorgonzola with cream, butter, and fresh sage.

South of Rome, in the district known as Aprilia, once-wasted marshland has been re-claimed, and vineyards there are now producing wines from the Merlot and Sangiovese grapes (both red), and from the Trebbiano Toscano (white). In the north, another important wine district centres around Lake Bolsena, while just across the border, in the region of Umbria, delicate Orvieto wine is produced. Orvieto is insidiously attractive—flaxen, slightly sweet, its charm never seems to pall. One could go on drinking it all night (and day too). Unfortunately, however, the popular taste for light primarily dry wines means that the traditional Orvieto *abboccato* is giving way to a dry version, which, though sound enough, lacks the unique appeal of this important and well-known wine.

Wine produced in the district overlooking Lake Bolsena, near the town of Montefiascone, is perhaps not as distinguished as wine from either the Castelli Romani or Orvieto. In the twelfth century, at least, it must have been exquisite, because it was then that it earned the curious name that remains the legal *denominazione* for wine from the region: Est! Est!! Est!!!

Apparently, a German prelate named Johannes Fugger decided to make a trip to Rome, ostensibly on ecclesiastical business. Not a man to waste time, Bishop Fugger sent his trusted servant Martin ahead of him, to scout out the inns on the route with the best wine, and to mark them with the single Latin word '*est*' (it is). Where the wines were not of a standard that would satisfy the bishop's discerning palate, Martin was to warn him off with the words '*non est*'.

Martin proved more than trustworthy, and the bishop travelled in a pleasant haze, wandering from one *osteria* to the next. At each, Martin's discreetly printed '*est*' ensured him that he would not waste his noble tastebuds on inferior *vinum*.

When the bishop arrived in Montefiascone he was overjoyed to see Martin's message scrawled on a tavern door: '*Est! Est!! Est!!!*' The wine there was, as the Italians say, *ottimo*. The bishop, in fact, never made it to Rome—so delicious was the wine of Montefiascone that he stayed there until his death (untimely) from over-indulgence.

Faithful Martin erected a tombstone with a poignant epithet.

> *Est. Est. Propter Nimium*
> *Est Hic Jo. Defuk Dominus*
> *Meus Mortuus Est*

'Because of too much Est! Est!! Est!!! my master, Johannes Fugger, died here.' We feel somehow the bishop lies easy, having earned by his enthusiasm the silent admiration of even the ancient Romans.

Cleaning a small wine press after the harvest in Montefiascone, home of Est! Est!! Est!!!

Quantities where necessary are given in
Metric, Imperial and US measurements

Supplì al Telefono

Rice Balls
Serves 6

350 g/12 oz/2 $\frac{1}{2}$ cups left-over rice or risotto
(preferably Italian arborio*)*
2 eggs, beaten
175 g/6 oz Mozzarella cheese, cut into cubes
100 g/4 oz/1 $\frac{1}{3}$ cups fine dried breadcrumbs
Vegetable oil for deep frying

Stir beaten eggs into left-over rice, making sure
not to damage rice. Take about 1 tbsp of rice
mixture in the palm of your hand. Place a cube of
cheese in the middle of mixture, and top with
another spoonful. Form into a ball, so the cheese
is completely encased by rice. Then very carefully
roll in breadcrumbs. Shape rest of mixture
similarly.

Fry the *supplì* in hot oil, without crowding,
until golden brown. Remove, and drain on
kitchen towel. The cheese should have melted
just enough so that as one cuts into the crisp ball
it stretches into threads like telephone wires—
hence the name.

Suggested wines:
Castelli Romani, Est! Est!! Est!!!

Gnocchi alla Romana

Semolina Dumplings
Serves 4–6

750 ml/1 $\frac{1}{4}$ pt/3 $\frac{1}{4}$ cups milk
Pinch of nutmeg
250 g/8 oz/1 $\frac{3}{4}$ cups semolina (preferably Italian)
100 g/4 oz/1 $\frac{1}{4}$ cups freshly grated Parmesan cheese
2 eggs, beaten
Salt
Freshly ground black pepper
100 g/4 oz/1 stick butter

Heat milk, with a pinch of nutmeg, to almost
boiling point. Lower heat, and slowly dribble in
semolina, beating continuously. Stir until mixture is so thick that a spoon will stand up in it.
Remove pan from heat, and stir in half of the
Parmesan cheese, beaten eggs, salt, and pepper,
until well blended. Turn mixture on to a flat
well-buttered shallow dish or tin. Smooth out
with a palette knife to a thickness of 1 cm/$\frac{1}{4}$ in,
and leave to cool for 1 hr. in the refrigerator.

Pre-heat oven to 200°C/Gas Mark 6/400°F.
Cut out small circles, either with a pastry cutter
or a small glass, and put a layer of these overlapping each other in a shallow buttered baking
dish. Dot with butter and remaining Parmesan
cheese. Bake for 25 min., until the *gnocchi* are
crisp and golden.

Serve as *primo piatto* (first course).

Suggested wine:
Orvieto secco

Spaghetti all'Amatriciana

Spaghetti with Piquant Tomato Sauce
Serves 4

25 g/1 oz/2 tbsp butter
1 tbsp olive oil
4 rashers/slices bacon, diced
1 medium onion, peeled and finely chopped
500 g/1 lb ripe tomatoes, skinned and chopped
(or 1 large tin of Italian plum tomatoes)
1 or 2 small hot chillies, cut into rings
Salt
Freshly ground black pepper
500 g/1 lb spaghetti
Freshly grated Pecorino cheese

Melt butter and oil in a large saucepan, and add diced bacon. When it is cooked, add onion, and sauté until soft and golden. Then add tomatoes and peppers, and cook, uncovered, over a low heat for about 25 min. Season with salt and pepper.

Cook pasta until *al dente*, drain, and turn into a warm serving dish. Pour sauce over pasta, and sprinkle liberally with Pecorino cheese.

Suggested wines:
Merlot d'Aprilia, Colli Albani

Abbacchio alla Cacciatora

Roman Lamb
Serves 6

25 g/1 oz/2 tbsp lard
1 garlic clove, peeled and finely chopped
Flour seasoned with salt and black pepper
1.5 kg/3 lb leg of spring lamb, boned and cut into cubes
1 sprig fresh rosemary (or $\frac{1}{2}$ tsp dried rosemary)
1 bay leaf
300 ml/$\frac{1}{2}$ pt/1$\frac{1}{4}$ cups dry white wine
150 ml/$\frac{1}{4}$ pt/$\frac{2}{3}$ cup water
3 anchovy fillets, chopped
1 tbsp wine vinegar
Freshly chopped parsley

Melt lard in a large frying pan, add the garlic, and cook gently. Dust lamb cubes with seasoned flour, and brown them on each side in hot fat. Add rosemary, bay leaf, and wine. Bring to the boil, add water, and simmer uncovered over a low heat for 1 hr. or until tender. The cooking liquid should reduce substantially.

When the lamb is tender, remove about 3 tbsp of sauce from the pan, and mix with chopped anchovies and wine vinegar to make a smooth paste. Pour this back into the pot, and mix well. Transfer to a warm serving dish, garnish with fresh parsley, and serve hot.

Suggested wine:
Frascati, Marino

Porchetta

Stuffed Roast Pork
Serves 6–8

Porchetta is usually an entire roast suckling pig. However, a delicious home-version can be made with pork loin.

1$\frac{1}{2}$–2 kg/3–4 lb loin of pork (boned)
10 garlic cloves, peeled and crushed
2 tbsp fresh rosemary leaves, coarsely chopped
100 g/$\frac{1}{4}$ lb pancetta or
thick-cut bacon, coarsely chopped
1 tbsp sea salt
15–20 black peppercorns, coarsely crushed with mortar and pestle

In a small mixing bowl, combine crushed garlic, rosemary, *pancetta* or bacon, salt, and crushed peppercorns.

Lay the boned loin of pork out flat on a board. Spread with most of garlic seasoning mixture. Roll the loin and tie securely with string. Prick the outside of the joint, and spread with rest of seasoning mixture.

Place *porchetta* in roasting tin, and put in a pre-heated oven, 160°C/Gas Mark 3/325°F, for approximately 2$\frac{1}{2}$–3 hr.

Serve hot or cold.

Suggested wine:
Frascati

Coda alla Vaccinara

Braised Oxtail
Serves 6

3 tbsp olive oil
100 g/4 oz/¼ lb streaky bacon
1 small garlic clove, peeled and chopped
1 large onion, peeled and chopped
1.5 kg/3 lb oxtail, cut into pieces
300 ml/½ pt/1¼ cups dry white wine
1 large tin tomatoes, drained and chopped
150 ml/¼ pt/⅔ cup water
Salt
Freshly ground black pepper
1 bay leaf
Sprig of fresh thyme
Freshly chopped parsley
3–4 sticks celery, coarsely chopped

Heat olive oil in a large casserole, and gently fry bacon until brown. Add garlic and onion, and cook until golden. Turn up the heat, and add oxtail pieces, browning them on each side. Pour in wine, and allow to boil for 2 min. Then add tomatoes, water, salt, pepper, bay leaf, thyme, and parsley. Bring to the boil, then cover and simmer in a moderate oven, 180°C/Gas Mark 4/ 350°F, for 2 hr. Add chopped celery, and stir in well. Cover and cook for a further 30 min. Skim off as much fat as possible, and serve straight from the casserole.

Suggested wine:
Merlot d'Aprilia

Saltimbocca

Veal and Ham Rolls
Serves 4–6

12 thin slices veal escalope
Salt
Freshly ground black pepper
12 slices prosciutto
12 fresh sage leaves
2 tbsp butter
2 tbsp olive oil
Dry white wine

Pound veal as thinly as possible, and season with salt and black pepper. On each slice of veal lay a slice of *prosciutto*, then a fresh sage leaf. Roll up, and secure with a wooden toothpick.

Melt butter and oil in a large frying pan, and brown veal rolls on all sides, then pour a small glass of dry white wine over them. Allow to bubble up, then cover, and simmer for about 15 min. until veal is tender. Serve immediately.

Suggested wines:
Marino, Est! Est!! Est!!!

Budino di Ricotta

Ricotta Cheesecake

500 g/1 lb Ricotta cheese
4 egg yolks, well beaten
100 g/4 oz/½ cup sugar
2 tbsp candied orange peel
Juice and grated rind of 1 lemon
75 g/3 oz/½ cup ground almonds
Castor sugar

Sieve Ricotta cheese into a large bowl, and add beaten egg yolks, sugar, candied peel, lemon juice and rind, and ground almonds. Beat together well. Butter a 23 cm/9 in flan tin, and pour mixture into it. Bake in a pre-heated oven, 180°C/Gas Mark 4/350°F, for 40 min., or until cheesecake is set.

Serve hot or cold, sprinkled with sugar.

Suggested wines:
Frascati abboccato, Orvieto abboccato

Tiled roofs and ribbed vineyards in Serralunga d'Alba.

PIEDMONT

In autumn, the rolling hills of Piedmont are often covered in fog. Piedmont means 'foot of the mountain', and the Alps, which crown the region to the north and west, send early tidings of another winter. Towns such as Serralunga, La Morra, and Castiglione Falleto stand atop peaks that look across to each other over a sea of golden, red, and yellow vines that rise from half-hidden valleys. The name of this wine region's most famous grape, the Nebbiolo, is derived from the word '*nebbia*' (fog), because it is inevitably harvested well into the season of mists.

In the forests of the Langhe, under a layer of rotting yellow leaves, at the bases of poplar, birch, willow, or oak trees, a mysterious germination is taking place. Here, at certain altitudes, in certain terrain, under certain trees, and in this season only, a rare and prized fungus foments into being—the *tartufo bianco*, white truffle of Piedmont. Truffles grow underground, and cannot be planted by man. The only way to find these rare tubers is with the help of specially trained dogs, who are able to sniff and locate the truffle from the pungent aroma it emanates. Truffles seem to reappear in the same general locality year after year, and truffle hunters have passed knowledge of secret spots from generation to generation. Many hunt only at night, for fear that others will follow them to their valuable caches. Prized both for its intense, penetrating aroma and a taste that is more sensation than flavour, the truffle of Piedmont is quite unlike the black French variety of Périgord. In Piedmont, the truffle is eaten raw; shaved into razor-thin slices with a special knife, then sprinkled over *risotti*, salami, raw meat, marinated vegetables—virtually everything.

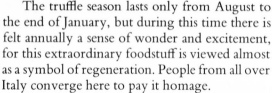

A truffle hunter and his assistant at work in the woods of Piedmont.

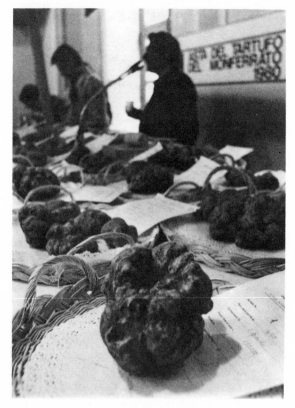

The annual truffle auction in Nizza Monferrato.

The truffle season lasts only from August to the end of January, but during this time there is felt annually a sense of wonder and excitement, for this extraordinary foodstuff is viewed almost as a symbol of regeneration. People from all over Italy converge here to pay it homage.

Auctions are held in towns such as Alba, Asti, and Nizza Monferrato. The truffle hunters (*cercatori di tartufi*) tramp into the town hall early in the morning to have their *prodotti* weighed, sniffed, classified, and given a base value (the criteria for grading are intensity of aroma, colour, size, the location of origin, and smoothness of surface, for if a truffle is very irregular there will be too much waste when it is grated into slivers). The truffles on display transfuse a throbbing, overpowering aroma. Potential customers—restaurateurs, gastronomes, and beefy men who swear by their fabled aphrodisiacal power—examine the truffles with careful, loving attention. They hold them up to their noses in cupped hands, and inhale deeply. Bidding is fast, and the prices fetched are astronomical. Afterwards the entire town celebrates with a series of feasts to honour (and consume liberally) this magical fungus.

Pots of *bagna cauda* bubble in homes and restaurants throughout the region, while freshly baked *grissini* (breadsticks) are laid on pressed linen tablecloths. (Though as much a symbol of Italy as the ubiquitous straw-covered flasks of Chianti, *grissini* in fact originated in Piedmont.) *Bagna cauda* is a strongly flavoured sauce made from anchovies, olive oil, lots of garlic, and, when available, truffles, mixed together in an earthenware crock and kept hot at the table by a spirit lamp or alcohol burner. *Grissini* and chunks of bread are dipped into the bubbling mixture along with *cardi* (an edible thistle much loved here), strips of red pepper, carrots, and celery. Tumblers of dark, tannic Barbera wash down the simple feast.

Autumn colours in the vineyards of Asti.

The food of Piedmont is basically robust and sustaining mountain fare. Game such as deer, wild boar, mountain goat, pheasant, and quail is found throughout the region. Large-capped edible mushrooms grow wild in the forests. Known as *funghi porcini*, they are either eaten fresh or are dried and used as a pungent flavouring in stews and sauces. Garlic, used sparingly in many Italian regions, is here used with unashamed abandon. Italy's greatest rice-producing area is the fertile flatlands of the Po valley, and meals often begin with steaming bowls of *risotto*. Gargantuan platters such as *bollito misto* satisfy appetites heightened by a day (or, if you are a truffle hunter, a night) spent out of doors. A proper *bollito* of Piedmont consists of a large piece of the best beef, a chicken, tongue, *cotechino* (boiling sausage), a piece of veal, and various vegetables boiled together in a large pot. It is served in stunning array on a platter with two sauces, *salsa verde*, made of parsley and anchovy, and piquant *salsa rossa*, made of fresh tomatoes. The liquid in which the meat and vegetables are cooked is reserved for making *risotto* or, perhaps, another day's soup.

Hearty mountain fare, however, is balanced by a repertoire of regional dishes that is surprisingly delicate and refined. Piedmont is adjacent to France, and the autonomous region to the north known as the Val d'Aosta is actually a French-speaking area. As well, there are culinary influences that stem from the many aristocratic families who lived in this area when it was the Kingdom of Savoy. (The Savoys were an important family, originally French, who settled in the region in the eleventh century, and played an influential part in Italian history, especially in the country's unification movement.)

In Piedmont, butter, cream, and other milk products are used extensively. The well-known Piedmont speciality, *fonduta*, resembles the cheese *fondue* from French-speaking Switzerland. But while Swiss *fondue* is made with piquant Gruyère and Emmenthal cheeses mixed with white wine and kirsch, *fonduta* is a creamy mixture of Fontina cheese, eggs, and milk, covered with a thin layer of grated truffles. Another dish that typifies this refined, richer aspect of the *cucina piemontese* is *finanziera*, which combines sweetbreads, brain, chicken giblets, and cockscomb (literally) in a creamy delicate truffle sauce. The desserts of Piedmont also reflect a deliciously indulgent character. *Zabaione*, for example, was invented by cooks in the House of Savoy, and combines Marsala, sugar, and egg yolks, gently cooked and whipped to a frothy, creamy consistency.

If the food of Piedmont ranges from the delicate to the robust, the wine is equally varied. Turin is the capital of the region, and it is also the centre for an aromatic manufactured wine known and loved throughout the world: vermouth. As in French areas where similar wines are produced, there is a plentiful supply of fragrant mountain herbs at hand, for vermouth is wine infused with a mixture of herbs, bitters, and spirits to result in a delicious *aperitivo*. The name comes from the German '*Wermut*', or wormwood, a shrub that gives the distinctive flavour to absinthe, used here along with cinnamon, nutmeg, orange and lemon peel, quinine, bark, coriander, and other herbs and ingredients. Indeed, these flavourings are much more important than the wine itself, which should be neutral and bland (and often comes from the south of Italy). Each firm jealously guards the secret recipe for its unique mixture of flavourings. There are basically three styles of vermouth: *bianco* (sweet white), *rosso* (sweet with a caramel colour that comes from burnt sugar), and *secco* (dry white). Though abroad vermouth is a popular mixer for various cocktails, in Italy it is usually taken straight, before meals, since it is believed that the mixture of herbs and bitters encourages the gastric juices to flow, and thus aids digestion.

If vermouth is an anticipatory drink, the great and serious wines of Piedmont are undoubtedly the robust red table wines that partner the *cucina piemontese* so perfectly. To confuse matters, wine is named after both central towns in particular communes (Barolo, for example), and after grape varieties (such as Barbera). The grape from which is produced the finest wine in the region (many say in all of Italy) is the Nebbiolo. Wine made from this grape is sold under the varietal name, Nebbiolo, or Nebbiolo d'Alba. But fine wines with distinct regional characteristics bear the name of the commune in which they are produced, such as Barolo, Barbaresco, Lessona, and Gattinara. The Nebbiolo is not an easy grape to cultivate, and its yield is low. It is, however, the progenitor of a magnificent family of long-lasting wines, with body, scent, and depth of flavour. Producers claim that to bring out the full character and aroma of the Nebbiolo, the temperamental grape must ripen in autumn mist—and certainly this particular requirement is met in the hills of Alba that surround the unassuming town of Barolo. Barolo is intense wine, rich in tannin, and so needs at least three to five years ageing to mellow and develop a rich baritone flavour and a characteristic heavy bouquet of violets. It is a wine to drink with strongly-flavoured game, roast meat, or the favourite of the area, *brasato al Barolo*, a joint of beef marinated in full-bodied red wine and herbs, then pot roasted on top of the stove.

Barbaresco is a wine commune farther up the Tanaro valley, towards Asti, and the wine that takes the communal name is also produced from the Nebbiolo grape. Fragrant, dry, somewhat lighter than Barolo, Barbaresco is nevertheless a full, virile wine that goes well with game and meat, and also full-flavoured cheese, such as the fermented *toma veja* from the Gressoney valley below the Italian Alps.

In the region north of Novara, wine is also produced from the Nebbiolo grape (though here it is locally called the Spanna). The best comes from the commune centred around Gattinara, and indeed some connoisseurs consider it superior even to Barolo. Like Barolo, Gattinara can be rough and unbalanced when young. However, several years of ageing (in oak and chestnut casks, and in the bottle) allow the wine to develop a deep, brick-red colour, an intense bouquet, and a mellow, lingering flavour. Wine produced at nearby Lessona and Carema, also from the Nebbiolo grape, is excellent, while any that bears the varietal *denominazione* Spanna will resemble the greater wines produced in restricted zones yet tend to be considerably less expensive.

If the Nebbiolo is the aristocrat of grapes in Piedmont, the Barbera is the workhorse. The Barbera is about twenty times as prolific as the Nebbiolo, and wine produced from this grape is sold under the varietal name, sometimes with a geographical qualification, such as Barbera d'Asti or Barbera d'Alba. Barbera is dark, dry, austere wine, with plenty of body and alcohol. More so than great Barolo, it is the wine of the land. The farmer carries a jug of it with him as he goes out for another backbreaking day of tending vines. It is knocked back with pungent *bagna cauda* or steaming platters of gelatinous boiled meats. It flows freely at festivals. And it is used generously in the kitchens, for delicious wine stews, such as *gallo al Barbera* (chicken in a dark rich wine sauce flavoured with *funghi porcini*), for sauces and rice dishes, and even in desserts (a cook we know for example, makes an exquisite *zabaione* with Barbera rather than with the traditional Marsala).

Piedmont is a land of folk festivals and celebrations. After the *vendemmia* (grape harvest), wine festivals take place in towns throughout the region. In Molare, there is an annual '*Polentone*', or *polenta* festival. During the event, this characteristic corn mush, a staple food of northern Italy, is made in copper cauldrons the size of cement mixers. Bean festivals, ox and horse races, and truffle auctions provide more occasions to celebrate the produce and products of the land.

The great Italian wine for celebrations, not surprisingly, is also a product of Piedmont: Asti Spumante. Many of the great vermouth houses make this fragrant sparkling wine and, of course, it is exported throughout the world. Asti Spumante is produced from the Muscat grape, and gains its sparkle by the *cuvée close* method, in which a secondary fermentation takes place in a stainless steel tank, prior to bottling. Considerably less expensive than the laborious *méthode champenoise* (where secondary fermentation takes place in the bottle), this method, while not producing bubbles as fine or long-lasting, nevertheless preserves the distinctive grapy bouquet of the Muscat grape, and the result is a fresh, sweetish sparkling wine that is excellent with fruit, cakes, the desserts of Piedmont, or simply on its own.

Though the red wines of Piedmont are the best known, a useful dry white wine is produced in the Monferrato hills from the white Cortese grape. Known as Cortese, Cortese di Gavi, Cortese dell'Alto Monferrato, or Gavi, this is the

Dolci (sweets) found in traditional shops like this one in
Asti are excellent with Asti Spumante.

prevalent everyday white wine of the region—
dry, fairly alcoholic, clean, and honest. It is
excellent with golden-fried freshwater fish,
funghi porcini, or *antipasto piemontese*: a selection
of cold delicacies including chopped raw meat
seasoned with lemon juice, black pepper, and
truffles; roasted red peppers cut into strips and
bathed in *bagna cauda*; white beans flavoured
with anchovy and onions; stuffed eggs; cold
meatballs; trout in aspic, and much else. A trolley
of such typical *antipasti* is often wheeled into a
room at the start of a meal, and one can spend
over an hour working through this mountainous
first course.

As well as robust heavyweights, Piedmont
also produces a variety of lighter red wines that
are drunk while still refreshingly young, and
sometimes semi-sparkling. The Grignolino grape
produces just such a fresh red wine, that goes well
with first-course dishes. Freisa is another local
grape grown extensively, and wine produced
from it is often still and dry, or semi-sparkling.

Dolcetto and Brachetto are lively young wines
that froth violently in the glass and continue to
seethe in the mouth. Dolcetto is generally dry,
while Brachetto is sweetish, and resembles the
semi-sparkling red wine of Emilia-Romagna
known as Lambrusco.

Clearly Piedmont offers a variety of wines
to suit literally every taste and occasion, from
serious, solemn red wines to vivacious, fragrant
sparklers popped open at the slightest excuse for a
celebration. Similarly, the food of this region is
varied, from the robust and hearty to the subtle
and delicate, reflecting the multi-faceted character of a rugged, mountainous land rich in both
natural produce and culinary tradition.

From the snow-covered peak of Monte
Bianco to industrial Turin, across the rice
paddies of the Po valley to the vine-clad hills of
Monferrato and the Langhe, treasures from the
earth confront a wealth of traditions, and blend
in a communal melting pot: a bubbling, inviting
bagna cauda, the endless pot of a generous land.

Quantities where necessary are given in
Metric, Imperial and US measurements.

Bagna Cauda

Hot Anchovy Dip
Serves 6

50 g/2 oz/$\frac{1}{2}$ stick butter
150 ml/$\frac{1}{4}$ pt/$\frac{2}{3}$ cup olive oil
10–15 garlic cloves, peeled and finely chopped
10 anchovy fillets, chopped
White truffles (optional)

Heat butter and oil in an earthenware pot just until they begin to foam. Add garlic, and cook gently. Then add chopped anchovies, and cook over a very low heat, stirring constantly, until they eventually dissolve. Garnish with grated truffles, if used.

The sauce is served in the dish in which it is cooked, and kept warm at the table over an alcohol burner.

Serve surrounded by raw vegetables such as sliced artichokes, broccoli, courgettes (zucchini). sweet peppers, celery, carrots, radishes, cucumber—whatever are in season. (The beauty of this dish lies in its simplicity: only the freshest and most tender vegetables should be used.) Chunks of bread and *grissini* can also be dipped into the bubbling mixture, or the sauce may be served over roasted red or green peppers.

Suggested wines:
Barbera d'Alba, Spanna, Barbaresco

Risotto al Barbera

Serves 6

12 g/$\frac{1}{2}$ oz dried mushrooms (funghi porcini)
1 onion, peeled and finely chopped
2 garlic cloves, peeled and chopped
150 ml/$\frac{1}{4}$ pt/$\frac{2}{3}$ cup olive oil
300 g/10 oz/1$\frac{1}{2}$ cups arborio rice
1 glass Barbera
1.5 l/2$\frac{1}{2}$ pt/6$\frac{1}{4}$ cups boiling beef stock
Knob of butter
Salt
Freshly ground black pepper
Freshly grated Parmesan cheese

Soak dried mushrooms in warm water for about 30 min., squeeze dry, and chop finely.

Heat olive oil in a large saucepan, and sauté onion and garlic until soft and golden. Add mushrooms and rice, and cook gently for 5–10 min. Add wine, and allow to evaporate. Then add a ladle of boiling stock, and allow rice to absorb the liquid, stirring all the while. Continue to add stock in this way until rice is tender. Stir in a little butter and a generous spoonful of Parmesan cheese.

Season, and serve immediately, with plenty of additional Parmesan cheese at hand, as a *primo piatto*.

Suggested wine:
Barbera d'Asti or Barbera d'Alba

Gallo al Barbera

Chicken Stewed in Red Wine
Serves 4

12 g/½ oz dried mushrooms (funghi porcini)
2 tbsp olive oil
1 large onion, peeled and finely chopped
2 garlic cloves, peeled and chopped
1.5 kg/3 lb chicken, cut into 6–8 pieces
½ bottle Barbera d'Asti
Salt
Freshly ground black pepper

Soak *funghi porcini* in tepid water for about 30 min., squeeze dry, and chop coarsely. Strain and reserve the water in which they soaked.

Heat olive oil in a large casserole, and cook onion and garlic until soft. Increase heat, and add chicken pieces, browning thoroughly. Add chopped *funghi porcini*, reserved mushroom water, and Barbera d'Asti. Allow wine to bubble and evaporate. Season to taste, and reduce heat. Cover tightly, and leave to simmer on top of the stove for 1–1½ hr., or until chicken is tender.

Remove chicken pieces, and arrange on a warmed serving platter. Increase heat to reduce the sauce (it should be fairly thick), adjust seasoning, then spoon over the chicken.

Serve immediately. (Left-over sauce can be served over rice.)

Suggested wines:
Barbera d'Asti, Barbera d'Alba

Brasato al Barolo

Beef in Barolo
Serves 6

1.5–2 kg/3–4 lb joint of beef
½ bottle of Barolo, or other Italian full-bodied red wine
1 large onion, peeled and sliced
1 carrot, sliced
1 stick celery, chopped
Salt
Freshly ground black pepper
1 bay leaf
Pinch of rosemary

Pinch of thyme
25 g/1 oz/2 tbsp butter
1 tbsp olive oil

Put meat in a large bowl with the wine, vegetables, and seasonings. Cover, and leave to marinate for 4 hr. or so.

Remove meat, and dry it with kitchen towel. In a large casserole, heat butter and oil, and brown meat on all sides. Strain marinade, and pour over meat. Bring to the boil, and allow to bubble until liquid has reduced. Lower heat, cover, and simmer for about 3 hr.

When ready, remove the meat, slice, and arrange on a hot serving dish. If remaining liquid is too thin, turn up heat until it has reduced and thickened. Adjust seasoning, and pour over the sliced meat.

Suggested wine:
Barolo

Costolette alla Valdostana

Veal Chops with Ham and Cheese
Serves 4

4 veal chops, trimmed
Salt
Freshly ground black pepper
Flour
1 egg, beaten
Fine dried breadcrumbs
50 g/2 oz/½ stick butter
4 thin slices ham, preferably prosciutto
4 slices Fontina cheese

Lightly pound veal chops, and season with salt and pepper. Dust with flour, then dip into beaten egg. Coat each chop generously with breadcrumbs.

Heat butter in a large frying pan, and cook chops until they are golden brown on both sides. Transfer to a heatproof dish, and lay a piece of ham and a slice of cheese on each. Place dish under a hot grill, and cook until cheese begins to melt and bubble. Serve immediately.

Suggested wines:
Cortese di Gavi, Cortese dell' Alto Monferrato

Bollito Misto

Boiled Meat and Vegetables
Serves 8–10

*1.5 kg/3 lb lean joint of beef (rolled rib roast or
rump roast)*
1 large onion, peeled and studded with 8 cloves
2 garlic cloves, peeled, but left whole
Handful freshly chopped parsley
2 sprigs of fresh thyme (or 1 tsp dried thyme)
1.5 kg/3 lb boiling chicken
*500 g/1 lb cotechino or zampone (boiling salami,
available at Italian delicatessen)*
6 large carrots, peeled and cut into quarters
6 sticks of celery, coarsely chopped
4 potatoes, peeled and quartered
Salt
Freshly ground black pepper

Place beef, onion, garlic, parsley, and thyme in a
large pot, and cover with slightly salted water.
Bring to the boil, then reduce heat. As the scum
rises to the surface, remove with a slotted spoon.

After about 1 hr. (depending on the size both
of the beef joint and the chicken: the ingredients
must be added so they will all be cooked at the
same time), add chicken to the pot. Again, bring
to the boil, skim, and reduce heat. Simmer for a
further 1 hr., then add remaining vegetables and
cotechino sausage. (If the *cotechino* is very salty
then it must be soaked first or boiled separately.)
Continue to cook until beef and chicken are
tender, and sausage is done (the vegetables
should still be firm: the beef must not be over-
cooked or it will be difficult to slice). Approxi-
mate total cooking time 3–3½ hr.

Remove meat and vegetables, and arrange on
a platter. Reserve cooking liquid. Bring to table
to carve, and serve with *salsa verde* and *salsa rossa*.

Salsa Verde Green Sauce

1 tbsp dried breadcrumbs
1 hard-boiled egg yolk
2 anchovy fillets, finely chopped
½ tsp capers, chopped
1 large bunch parsley, finely chopped
150 ml/¼ pt/⅔ cup olive oil

Salt
Freshly ground black pepper

Soak breadcrumbs in a little vinegar. In a blender
or a mortar and pestle, mix egg yolk and anchovies with breadcrumbs, parsley, and capers.
Add olive oil slowly (as in making mayonnaise)
until sauce has a fairly liquid consistency. Season.

Salsa Rossa Red Sauce

1 large onion, peeled and finely chopped
6 tbsp olive oil
300 ml/½ pt/1¼ cups dry white wine
500 g/1 lb tin tomatoes, drained and coarsely chopped
½ tsp dried chillies
Freshly ground black pepper
Salt
Juice of 1 lemon

Heat 2 tbsp of olive oil in a saucepan. Add onion,
and cook until soft and golden. Next add white
wine, increasing heat to evaporate. Then add
tomatoes and chillies. Season with salt and
pepper. Cook for about 1 hr., pressing the sauce
with the back of a wooden spoon to reduce to a
pulp. Remove from heat, stir in lemon juice and
remaining oil, and adjust seasoning.

Suggested wines:
Nebbiolo d'Alba, Barbaresco, Gattinara

Torrone di Torino

Chocolate Almond Cake
Serves 8

175 g/6 oz/1½ sticks butter
*175 g/6 oz/6 squares bitter chocolate, cut into
small pieces*
175 g/6 oz/1 cup ground almonds
175 g/6 oz/6 tbsp sugar
1 whole egg, well beaten
1 egg yolk, well beaten
175 g/6 oz plain biscuits, cut into small pieces

Lightly oil a rectangular loaf tin. Melt butter in a
saucepan until soft, and add chocolate, stirring

constantly until butter and chocolate are well mixed. Stir in ground almonds. Melt sugar in a separate pan with a little water. Then add this to the chocolate mixture. Stir in beaten eggs. Remove from heat, and add biscuits. Turn mixture into greased tin, and cover with foil. Put in the refrigerator for 24 hr. Turn on to a dish to serve and cut into slices.

Suggested wine:
Asti Spumante

Monte Bianco

Chestnut Dessert
Serves 6

750 g/1½ lb fresh chestnuts
900 ml/1½ pt/3¾ cups milk
250 g/½ lb/1⅐ cups sugar
Pinch of salt
150 ml/¼ pt/⅔ cup double cream
3 tbsp grappa Moscato

Cut a cross on the pointed end of each of the chestnuts, then boil them in water for 15–20 min., or until their skins can be peeled off easily. Drain, peel, and remove inner skins. Combine chestnuts and milk, and cook over a low heat for about 30 min., until they are tender. Drain, and mash smooth. Then beat in sugar. Force chestnut mixture through a potato ricer, or food mill, on to a serving dish. As the mixture falls, it should form into a 'mountain' shape. Chill for at least 1 hr.

Whip cream until stiff, and fold in the grappa. Drop gently over top of the chestnuts, and let spread like snow down the sides of a mountain. It should have the look of a partially covered snow peak, so do not attempt to smooth out the peaks and hollows.

Suggested wines:
Moscato d'Asti, Passito di Caluso

Budino di Piemonte

Rum Pudding
Serves 4–6

100 g/4 oz/⅔ cup sugar
3 egg yolks, beaten
2 egg whites, beaten
2 tbsp rum
50 g/2 oz/½ cup cocoa
50 g/2 oz/⅓ cup ground almonds

Melt sugar in a saucepan with 2 or 3 tbsp of water. Slowly bring to the boil, stirring constantly. When mixture begins to turn a light brown colour, pour into a buttered mould, or soufflé dish, and set aside.

In a large bowl mix beaten egg yolk with the rum. Fold in beaten egg whites, and mix well. Add cocoa and ground almonds. Pour mixture into the caramelized mould, and bake in a preheated oven, 150°C/Gas Mark 2/300°F, for 45 min.

Serve chilled.

Suggested wine:
Asti Spumante

Zabaione

Whipped Egg and Marsala
Per serving

1 egg yolk
1 tbsp sugar
2 tbsp Marsala, Barbera, or Asti Spumante

Beat egg yolk and sugar together until they are creamy. Place in the top of a double boiler (or pan that fits into another, larger pan). Heat water in lower pan, and gradually add Marsala, or wine, to egg and sugar mixture, beating constantly. The water must not boil, or this will curdle the mixture. As soon as the mixture becomes thick, spoon it into a warmed glass, and serve immediately.

Suggested wine:
Moscato, Moscato Spumante

TUSCANY

Tuscany is a proud region. Of how many sons can she boast? Michelangelo, Leonardo da Vinci, Dante, Galileo, Giotto, Petrarch, and so many others who left behind a rare concentration of works detailing man and his universe—awesome reminders of rare perceptions. The Italian language, as spoken in Tuscany, is considered the purest in this land of multifarious dialects. Cities that were once deadly rivals, today compete for the honour of being the most beautiful—the most Tuscan—in the region: Pisa, Lucca, Florence, Sienna. The land itself retains a classic, timeless dignity: raw umber hills covered with silver-grey olive trees and stumpy vines roll on to recede into a horizon punctuated by moody, bleak cypress. It is the landscape of a renaissance painting.

Tuscany is equally proud of its gastronomic heritage. Indeed, it is said fine French cuisine stems from Tuscan traditions, for when Catherine de'Medici married the future King Henry II of France, she took Italian cooks with her. There her court not only introduced new cooking methods, but also instructed the barbarians in the use of the fork. Tuscan cooking, not surprisingly, in this natal land of master artists, has always been considered an art. But like their language, the colours of a Leonardo canvas, or the form revealed in a Michelangelo sculpture, its virtue lies in its purity and simplicity.

Indeed, shrug the Tuscans, why the need for complex and cluttered methods of cooking when you have quite simply the greatest produce and ingredients at hand? The finest, most tender beef in Italy (generally agreed) or in the world (if you ask a Tuscan) comes from the massive white Chianina cattle, bred in the valleys south of

Arezzo. Virgin green olive oil from Lucca is thick, pure, and refined—the most finely flavoured in all of Italy—and essential to fine Italian cooking. Vegetables that grow in this generous garden of Italy—artichokes, fennel, courgettes (zucchini), peas, and beans—are true to their essential natures: both full-flavoured and wonderfully coloured. And the best known, if not the best, wine in Italy comes from these same rugged hills: Chianti, the very word conjures conviviality throughout the world.

With such superior raw ingredients, food needs only the simplest preparation for full pleasure. Such simplicity, however, can be deceptive. The preparation of pure and unadorned Tuscan dishes takes great culinary skill, developed, implemented, adjusted, modified over a period of centuries to suit the uncompromising taste of refined palates.

An example of Tuscan simplicity is seen in the preparation of this region's most famous speciality: *bistecca alla fiorentina* (Florentine rib steak). Though many restaurants throughout Italy offer a version of *bistecca*, it is best prepared at home, or in rustic Tuscan *trattorie*—usually small family-run restaurants, simply furnished with steel chairs and tables covered with paper tablecloths. The dominant feature of such places is the smoke-blackened brick stove-oven, in full view of the tables, with a chimney that rises at an angle into the ceiling. This temperamental and primitive charcoal and wood stove is absolutely essential for the preparation of many Tuscan specialities.

A proper *bistecca alla fiorentina* can never be cooked over anything but an open fire. Thin vine shoots, branches of herbs, soft sweet wood, or shoots from tomato plants should be laid over the bed of glowing coals. The meat used must come from the Chianina cattle. Moreover, it must come from an animal killed the moment its meat is no longer considered veal, yet before it becomes classified as beef. Such meat is called *vitellone*, and it is lean, tender, and as delicate as veal, yet as tasty as red beef. It is cut into gigantic rib steaks up to a kilo in weight ($2\frac{1}{4}$ lb).

Some say the *bistecca* must first be marinated in oil, vinegar, and herbs, but the *propio cuoco toscano* wags his finger at such heresy. The steak needs no embellishment. The cook places the *bistecca* on to the sizzling grill and cooks it briefly, turning it once only. (A fine burnt aroma of seared flesh is the hallmark of these *trattorie*.) Only after the *bistecca* has been cooked and slapped on to a plate does the cook sprinkle it with a little sea salt, freshly ground black pepper, and a spoonful of pure Tuscan olive oil.

What could be simpler? And yet to produce the genuine article is not such a simple matter.

Indeed, it is wonderful to watch the Tuscan cook in action, as he orchestrates the *forno di legno* with the skill of a maestro. At times he seems a blacksmith, tossing logs into the raging, cavernous oven, or raking the coals under the grill; then he is a butcher, wielding a heavy cleaver to separate prime rib steaks, to quarter rabbits, or to 'butterfly' spring chickens. *Pollo alla diavola* (devil's chicken) is another of his specialities: chicken marinated in coarsely crushed peppercorns, lemon juice, and oil, grilled over glowing embers until the skin is crisp and black. Rabbit, guinea fowl, or pheasant are also roasted simply in the wood-fired oven. The cook splashes the game with olive oil, then massages in a handful of coarse salt, crushed sage leaves, and rosemary. He gives it a generous squeeze or two of lemon, then slaps it into the oven, where it is roasted at an intensely high heat. Meanwhile, he busies himself slicing *prosciutto* and salami, making salads, roasting left-over *polenta*, or toasting over the fire little rounds of bread spread with a paste made from chicken liver and anchovy. These *crostini* are a popular Tuscan appetizer, and, like all the food eaten in such *trattorie*, are delicious washed down with glass after glass of young plummy Chianti, probably made from grapes grown in vineyards just across the road, the back garden, or down the street.

Chianti is ubiquitous, not just in Tuscany, but throughout the world. There are no less than 3,000 growers in this fertile region who produce and sell this wine, while there are countless numbers of families who tend vines and produce enough of it to suit their own everyday needs. Often sold in gay, familiar, straw-covered flasks, Chianti embodies the fun, giddiness, and delight that is what wine drinking, at its most basic level, is all about.

Chianti sold in flasks and open carafes in

Tuscany should be young, honest, easygoing. The flask serves to prevent the wine from being laid down to age. As well, the very method of production reflects a concern for freshness and vivacity. Chianti, after its initial fermentation, is mixed with a proportion of unfermented juice high in natural grape sugar, thus resulting in a slower secondary fermentation that continues for up to a month or longer. This process is known as the *governo*, and it results in lively, fresh wine which is slightly *frizzante* (tiny bubbles form in the bottom and on the rim of the glass, and the wine has a slight tingle). Such wine should be consumed while young, swigged back with friends, drunk out of the flask, or at one of those archetypal Italian lunches that linger into evening.

Pigeons breakfast in the Piazza del Campo, Sienna.

The hills between Florence and Sienna represent the classic Tuscan landscape. Farmhouses and ageing, peeling estates stand amid fields of vines, relieved by olive and cypress trees, and an occasional plot of wheat. Stretches of forest intersperse an asymetrical agricultural vista in which game freely roam. Unspoiled, lovely villages such as Greve, Radda in Chianti, Castellina, and a score of others, seem rarely visited, for, surprisingly, this rich land remains provincial, a sort of no man's land between two popular, historic, and very different cities. Perhaps it remains today as it was in the past, a buffer zone between Florence and Sienna, once deadly rivals, often as not at war with one another.

But now the countryside is peaceful and industrious. This is the heart of Chianti country, the region known as Chianti Classico. Though much wine is produced by the *governo* process, the finest wine of the region is quite different. Indeed, it was to differentiate between quality wine made from this central core and the vast flood of sometimes indifferent wine being sold as Chianti that the Classico region was delimited. Producers of Chianti Classico belong to a private *consorzio* whose aim is to maintain high standards of production and quality. Wine that has been approved earns the right to affix the symbol of Chianti Classico to its bottles: the *gallo nero*, or black cockerel.

Confusingly, Chianti Classico is not necessarily the best. For one thing, there are over 800 producers of Chianti Classico. Naturally there exists great variety not only in the quality but also in the style of wine produced. There are also many producers outside this central core who argue that their wine is in no way inferior to Chianti Classico. They therefore banded together to form their own *consorzio*, much like its predecessor. Their symbol, found on approved bottles of members' wines, is a *putto*, a chubby, rosy-cheeked cherub.

Chianti Classico and Chianti Putto are both fine wines. The best come in Bordeaux-shaped bottles which indicate that they are wines that improve with age. *Riserva* wine, in fact, is aged for a minimum of three years in oak, and then continues to improve in the bottle—the best for ten years or more. Unlike many Italian wines

Vineyards in the region of Chianti Classico.

that come from a single grape variety (Barbera, for example, is the name of both the grape and the wine), Chianti is produced from a blend of several different varieties. In the nineteenth century, Baron Ricasoli, whose family still produces some of the finest wines in the region, perfected a combination that became the basis for the legally authorized blend used to produce Chianti. It consists of varying proportions of Sangiovese (which gives the wine both body and alcohol), Canaiolo Nero (which contributes scent and fragrance), and Trebbiano Toscano and Malvasia del Chianti (which together lighten an otherwise harsh wine).

Chianti can be rather tough, though this is not necessarily a fault. The wine is dry, slightly acid, and relatively high in tannin. This very quality, when not in excess, or when it has mellowed through ageing, makes Chianti excellent with the simple, full-flavoured, and at times rich food of Tuscany.

Some of the finest Chianti wines are not sold as such, but rather prominently bear the name of noble Tuscan families that have made their particular, distinctive style of wine for centuries. Examples include Brolio, Antinori, and Nipozzano. Riserva Ducale is the name of the best wine produced by the Ruffino family. Another great wine that is produced outside the *zona di Chianti* is Brunello di Montalcino. The Brunello grape is a variety of the Sangiovese, the principal grape used to produce Chianti, and in this region, centred around the town of Montalcino, south of Sienna, it produces a heavy, full-bodied wine that is even stronger and more fragrant than

Chianti. Brunello, without doubt, is one of the greatest wines in Italy; it needs at least eight to ten years ageing before it is ready to drink, but after that time it will have the intensity of flavour characteristic of all great wines.

Another fine, full red wine is produced west of Montalcino, the so-called Vino Nobile di Montepulciano, which also must be aged for five years or more before it is ready to accompany such hearty dishes as the popular *primo piatto* (first course) called *pappardelle con la lepre*. *Pappardelle* are wide, flat, home-made egg noodles, and in this typical Tuscan dish they are covered in a dark, gamy sauce made from left-over hare.

Indeed, such full-bodied wines as Brunello, Vino Nobile, or Chianti *riserva* are meant to accompany robust servings of game or roast meat. But Tuscan cooking is also delicate and subtle—witness its classically simple preparation of vegetables, fish, and lightly fried meats. Though the region is undoubtedly red wine country, it also produces some notable everyday whites which accompany well such lighter food. Vernaccia di San Gimignano is both the best known and the best: a dry wine with a slightly bitter aftertaste. Much everyday white *vino da tavola* is produced from the hearty Trebbiano Toscano, and is sold simply as Toscano Bianco.

Such solid local white wines are excellent accompaniments to the seafood of the region, for Tuscany borders the Tyrrhenian Sea. In fact, Pisa was once a mighty maritime republic, ruling Sardinia, Corsica, and exerting influence over much of central Tuscany, too. Though the city eventually bowed to the supremacy of Genoa (and the river outlet to the sea subsequently silted), the Pisans remain fond of fish. Their most characteristic dish is *cieche*, elver fried in olive oil and sage. Another popular dish along the coast is *cacciucco*, a Mediterranean fish stew that resembles the *bouillabaisse* of Provence. *Cacciucco* is a splash of colour—a mixture of local fish, lobster, squid, octopus, molluscs, and other shellfish, stewed together in wine and herbs. It is best sampled on the seafront streets of Viareggio or Livorno, where, in little restaurants, cauldrons bubble and tempt. Another favourite is *fritto misto di mare*, a selection of seafood breaded or dipped in batter, fried in hot oil, and served while

Panforte, a spicy Siennese speciality, in a shop window by the Torre del Mangia.

sizzling, with a squeeze of lemon. *Fritto misto* is popular throughout Tuscany, though outside coastal areas it usually consists of a variety of meats and vegetables, such as lightly breaded veal escalopes, chicken breasts, brains and sweetbreads, artichokes, courgettes (zucchini), and even Mozzarella cheese, all deep-fried and served on a large platter. Like other Tuscan specialities, it is at once exceedingly simple, yet extremely difficult to produce perfectly, for the meat must be light and tender, not oily, while the vegetables, often dipped in batter, must still be crisp and fresh.

Indeed, the art of preparing vegetables reflects the essentially pure nature of the *cucina toscana*. *Finocchio* (fennel) from Tuscany is delicious, and it is often served raw, dipped into salt and thick olive oil, then eaten with the fingers. At other times, it is baked with Parmesan cheese, or fried in fritters, but the concern always is to keep intact its sweet, delicate anise flavour. The seeds from wild fennel are used as a seasoning, while a type of salami called *finocchiona* is flavoured with them. *Finocchiona*, along with other traditionally made salami, is cut into thin slices and served as part of a platter of *antipasto*, which will also consist of marinated artichoke hearts, *crostini* (bread

In Tuscany, making sausage – like everything else – is a fine art.

toasted and spread with chicken liver paste or tomato sauce), or perhaps something simple but unexpected like *salvie fritte*: deep fried sage leaves —crunchy, full of flavour, and deliciously different. Beautifully-shaped Tuscan artichokes are stuffed, boiled, fried, or served in cream, while carrots, aubergine (eggplant), courgette (zucchini), and cauliflower are cooked simply to retain and heighten their natural flavour.

Another dish which reveals the essential character of the Tuscans is *fagioli nel fiasco*. Sometimes teasingly called *mangiafagioli* (bean-eaters), they love the delicate, dried white haricot beans. In this favourite dish, beans are actually boiled in an empty Chianti flask. This remarkable method of cooking preserves the full aroma and flavour of the beans, which otherwise would escape in the steam. After they have so cooked, they are dressed with the best olive oil from Lucca, salt, black pepper, and crushed or chopped fresh sage. *Ribollito*, a classic bean soup, and *fagioli all'uccelletto*, white beans cooked with sage and tomatoes, both make hearty *primi piatti*.

The concept of Tuscany and a *cucina toscana* is a modern one. But because many cities were fiercely independent republics there remains a variety of specialities peculiar to certain cities or areas. The Luccans, for example, are known for their delicious cakes and desserts such as *buccellato*, a ring-shaped fruit bread. Chestnuts are gathered in the forests of the Appenines, and ground into flour to make a variety of desserts called *castagnacci*. And, of course, there is the famous *panforte* of Sienna: an exquisite flat, hard cake, made of almonds, candied fruit, and spices. Such desserts are often served with Vin Santo Toscano, a dark-brown, heavy wine, which, though sweet, has an astringent, strangely cleansing aftertaste.

Ultimately, it is the elusively simple pleasures of Tuscany that captivate: barbecued steaks that are somehow more than just barbecued steaks; *crostini* roasted over an open fire that leaves black stripes on the bread, like the marble stripes that decorate the Duomo at Sienna; humble beans dressed with precious olive oil; and bright red Chianti as warm as the Tuscan sun. Simple, modest food for a proud people. But Tuscans know better than most that sublime simplicity is often the hallmark of great artistry.

RECIPES FROM TUSCANY

Quantities where necessary are given in
Metric, Imperial and US measurements.

Salvie Fritte alla Villoresi

Fried Sage Leaves

Fresh sage leaves
(quantity depends on how much sage, patience, and
time you have—3 or 4 'sage sandwiches' makes a
novel addition to a plate of antipasti)
Anchovy paste
Flour
Water
Oil for frying

Combine flour with enough water to make a batter that is just sticky, the amount depending on how many sage leaves are on hand.

Spread a thin layer of anchovy paste on one side of half of the sage leaves. Dip leaves in batter, then sandwich them together with leaves that have no anchovy paste. Now dip this 'sage sandwich' into batter again, and place on an oiled plate. Prepare all leaves in this way.

Heat about 12 mm/½ in of oil in a frying pan. Fry the sage leaves quickly in the hot oil, then drain well on kitchen towel. Serve immediately.

Fagioli all'Uccelletto

Tuscan Beans with Sage and Tomatoes

Serves 4–6

500 g/1 lb dried white beans
3 tbsp olive oil
2 garlic cloves, peeled and finely chopped
3 fresh sage leaves (or 1 tsp dried sage)
1 tbsp tomato purée (paste)
Salt
Freshly ground black pepper
2 tbsp red wine vinegar

Put dried beans in a large bowl, cover with cold water, and leave to soak overnight. Drain and add to water in a large saucepan, and cook over a moderate heat for about 2 hr., until they are tender. Drain and set aside.

Heat oil in a large pan, add garlic and sage, and cook for 1 min. Stir in tomato purée, diluted in a little water, and the drained beans. Season, cover, and simmer over a low heat for 10–15 min. Adjust seasoning, stir in vinegar, and serve hot as an *antipasto*.

Suggested wine:
Chianti Putto, Chianti Classico

Crostini di Fegatini

Chicken Liver Spread

Serves 6

2 tbsp olive oil
25 g/1 oz/2 tbsp butter
1 small onion, peeled and finely chopped
250 g/½ lb chicken livers, cleaned and chopped
3 fresh sage leaves, chopped
1½ tbsp capers
2 or 3 anchovy fillets, chopped
Salt
Freshly ground black pepper
Butter
20 crostini *(small thick rounds of bread)*

Melt oil and butter in a frying pan, and sauté onion until soft and golden. Add chopped liver and sage leaves, and fry gently until liver is cooked, about 15 min. Remove from heat, and add capers and chopped anchovy fillets.

Pass mixture through a food mill, or processor, and add enough butter to make a creamy paste. Season. Toast the *crostini* lightly on one side, then spread the paste on to the untoasted side. Cook over open fire or put into a hot oven briefly. Serve hot as an *antipasto*.

Suggested wine:
Chianti

Pappardelle con la Lepre

Pasta with Hare Sauce
Serves 4–6

*250 g/$\frac{1}{2}$ lb left-over meat of hare or rabbit, shredded
(or left-over chicken, turkey, or game such as
pheasant, shredded)
50 g/2 oz/$\frac{1}{2}$ stick butter
2 tbsp olive oil
3 rashers/slices of bacon, cut into strips
1 medium onion, peeled and sliced
1 stick celery, cut into strips
1 garlic clove, peeled and finely chopped
12 g/$\frac{1}{2}$ oz dried mushrooms (soak first in warm
water for about 30 min., squeeze dry, and chop)
2 sprigs of fresh thyme (or $\frac{1}{2}$ tsp dried thyme)
Salt
Freshly ground black pepper
1 tbsp flour
150 ml/$\frac{1}{4}$ pt/$\frac{2}{3}$ cup red wine
300 ml/$\frac{1}{2}$ pt/1$\frac{1}{4}$ cups hot stock
500 g/1 lb wide ribbon noodles (pappardelle are
usually home-made egg noodles, about 2$\frac{1}{2}$ cm/1 in
wide—use tagliatelle as a substitute)
Parmesan cheese*

Heat butter and oil in a large saucepan, and add
bacon, onion, celery, and garlic. Cook gently,
until they have changed colour slightly. Then
add dried mushrooms, thyme, seasoning, and
finally, the hare. Cook for a few minutes, then
sprinkle on the flour. Stir in well, and pour on the
wine. Turn up heat, and allow wine to reduce.
Pour in stock, cover, and cook over a low heat
for about 1$\frac{1}{2}$ hr. The sauce should become rich
and thick in consistency. Cook noodles, drain,
and put in a serving dish. Stir in hare sauce, and
serve immediately, with Parmesan cheese.

Suggested wines:
*Chianti Classico riserva, Vino Nobile di
Montepulciano, Brunello di Montalcino*

Costolette di Maiale al Chianti

Pork Chops in Chianti
Serves 4

*4 large pork chops
1 tbsp fennel seeds
Salt
Freshly ground black pepper
3 tbsp olive oil
2 garlic cloves, peeled and chopped
150 ml/$\frac{1}{4}$ pt/$\frac{2}{3}$ cup Chianti*

Trim fat from chops, and score them lightly
across each side. Sprinkle with fennel, salt, and
pepper, and pour a little olive oil over each. Leave
to marinate for about 1 hr.

Heat oil in a large frying pan, add garlic, and
sauté. Then add chops, and brown on both sides
over a high heat. Add wine, cover, and cook over
a low heat for 30 min.

When ready, remove chops from pan, and
set aside on a warm serving dish. Turn up heat,
and reduce liquid by half. Adjust seasoning, pour
sauce over chops, and serve immediately.

Suggested wine:
Chianti Classico

Pollo alla Diavola

Devil's Chicken
Serves 4

*1 roasting chicken
1 tbsp black peppercorns
3 tbsp lemon juice
3 tbsp olive oil
Salt*

Cut chicken into quarters, and pound them as
flat as possible. Crush peppercorns in mortar and
pestle. Rub peppercorns into the chicken, then
place in a deep dish. Pour over lemon juice and
olive oil. Cover, and allow to marinate for 1–2
hr., basting from time to time.

Prepare charcoal barbecue. When ready,
sprinkle chicken pieces liberally with coarse sea
salt, and place on grill. Cook until skin has turned

brown, then turn over and cook other side, brushing with marinade liquid occasionally so the meat does not dry. Turn two or three times, continuing to baste. It will take about 30–45 min. Garnish with lemon wedges.

Suggested wines:
Chianti Putto, Chianti Classico

Finocchi al Formaggio

Fennel Baked with Cheese
Serves 4

4 medium fennel bulbs
50 g/2 oz/$\frac{1}{2}$ stick butter
Salt
Freshly ground black pepper
3 tbsp freshly grated Parmesan cheese
Knob of butter

Discard any bruised leaves and surplus stem from fennel bulbs, and cut each in half, lengthwise. Wash thoroughly in cold water. Put fennel halves in a large saucepan, and fill with cold salted water. Bring to the boil, and cook until tender. Drain well, and place in a well-buttered shallow earthenware dish. Season with salt and pepper, and dot with butter. Sprinkle liberally with Parmesan cheese, and bake in a fairly hot oven, 200°C/Gas Mark 6/400°F, until top is golden brown. Serve hot.

Suggested wines:
Vernaccia di S. Gimignano, Toscano Bianco

Piselli alla Fiorentina

Florentine Peas
Serves 4–6

2 tbsp olive oil
1 garlic clove, peeled and chopped
1 small mild onion, peeled and finely chopped
50 g/2 oz ham, diced (preferably prosciutto)
500 g/1 lb fresh peas (frozen peas can be used, but they should be thoroughly defrosted beforehand)
Salt

Freshly ground black pepper
2 tbsp freshly chopped parsley
3 tbsp water

Heat olive oil in a saucepan, and add garlic and onion. Sauté until soft and golden. Next add ham, and cook gently for 1 min. Then add peas, salt, pepper, parsley, and water. Cook until tender, about 5–10 min. (less if using frozen peas). Serve immediately.

Panforte

Siennese Nougat

100 g/4 oz/1 cup shelled almonds
100 g/4 oz/1 cup shelled hazelnuts
50 g/2 oz/$\frac{1}{2}$ cup flour
25 g/1 oz/$\frac{1}{4}$ cup cocoa
2 tsp cinnamon
$\frac{1}{2}$ tsp allspice
100 g/$\frac{1}{4}$ lb/$\frac{1}{2}$ cup honey
4 tbsp sugar
250 g/$\frac{1}{2}$ lb candied fruit, finely chopped
1 tbsp grated orange rind
1 tbsp grated lemon rind
Juice of 1 lemon
Icing (powdered) sugar

Pre-heat oven to 150°C/Gas Mark 2/300°F. Put almonds and hazelnuts in a greased shallow pan, and bake until golden, about 20 min., and set aside.

Meanwhile, sift flour together with cocoa, cinnamon, and allspice. Mix well. Put honey and sugar in a saucepan, and cook over a low heat for about 10–15 min., stirring constantly. Remove from heat, and mix into flour mixture. Then add candied fruit, orange and lemon rind and juice, and roasted nuts, combining them together well. Grease a round baking tin, and turn the mixture into it. Bake in a slow oven, 140°C/Gas Mark 1/275°F, until it is firm, about 50 min. Remove from the oven, turn out, and sprinkle liberally with icing sugar.

Suggested wine:
Vin Santo Toscano

Fish market by the Rialto.

VENETO

For centuries, the Rialto has been the commercial heart of Venice. It is still market and forum; a place to meet friends, down a quick Punt e Mes or grappa, complain about last week's *acqu'alta*, buy artichokes and oranges, or arrange a surreptitious rendezvous. Its shops and stalls are stocked with goods essential to life Venetian style: sweet, fragrant *prosciutto di San Daniele*, homemade *tortellini*, Parmigiano Reggiano, milk-fed veal, glassware from Murano, lace tablecloths from Burano, and stainless steel *espresso* coffeemakers, of which most families have at least half a dozen in varying sizes. The vendors, with their reputation of Venetian cunning, appeal to the aesthetic sensibilities of the people, arranging *radicchio* and fennel, artichokes and zucchini, oranges, pears, and juicy grapes with as much attention to colour and composition as in a painting by Giovanni Bellini.

In all the bustle and commotion, the most exciting corner, perhaps, is the adjoining fish market, where the mysteries of the murky Venetian lagoon are displayed in garish, licentious abandon—gaping, great-mouthed *rospo* (monkfish), long, squirming eels, inky squid, pink shrimp and scampi, tiny live crabs, Venetian *peoci* (mussels), small scallops, and cuttlefish. Giant tuna weighing hundreds of pounds hang by their tails to be centre-cut into thick, firm steaks for grilling. Red and grey mullet, freshwater sardines, hake, flat round sole, sea bass, and river trout are carried in continuously from flat barges that bob upon the Grand Canal, while men in boots hose down the slippery area and sing out the bargains of the day.

Exotic produce used to flow into this great market from every corner of a vast Venetian

A floating market in Venice.

The Bardolino country above Lake Garda.

empire. It was the youthful Venetian Marco Polo who boasted of the splendid glories of the court of Kublai Khan; and until da Gama discovered a sea route to the Indies, Venice held a virtual monopoly on the fabled riches of the Orient. Closer to home, the tentacles of Venetian power drew in the Dalmatian and Grecian coasts, indeed the eastern Mediterranean.

Today, the region known as Veneto includes towns that were once under Venetian control and protection, such as Verona, Padua, Vicenza, Treviso, Belluno, and Bassano del Grappa. For the Venetian Republic ruled over most of what is now north-eastern Italy. It is large, wealthy, and relatively modern. And Venetian influence still subtly holds—in archi-

Tortellini – hand-made with loving care.

During an outdoor festival in Verona, *polenta*, a staple
corn mush, is roasted and served with sausage.

tecture, language, social behaviour, and, not least of all, styles of cooking and eating.

The *cucina veneta* is distinctive. Its most important starch is *polenta*, a characteristic maize porridge which is stiff enough to turn on to a board and slice. It is usually served as an accompaniment to meat or fish, sometimes baked with sauce or sausages, or even deep-fried until crunchy. Corn was introduced to Venice during the city's seafaring days and quickly became a favourite of rich and poor alike. The food in Veneto generally is an expression of democracy, with many dishes (like *polenta*) loved by all. In Venice, as well as throughout Veneto, a style of cooking emerged which combines the sophistication of Venice with a down-to-earth practicality that is Veneto.

The food can seem exotic—*seppia alla veneziana*, for example: squid stewed in its own ink. The resulting dish is as black and murky as an underworld lagoon. When it is served with its usual accompaniment of yellow *polenta*, the visual effect is, to say the least, overwhelming. Yet the squid is sweet and delicate—not at all the imagined taste of black and yellow. *Carpaccio* is another Venetian favourite—thin slices of raw fillet steak served with olive oil and lemon, or a whisky and horseradish sauce. The ugly monkfish, so menacing in the market, is prized for just its tail. Known as *coda di rospo*, it is typically grilled in abundant butter, and tastes as fine (almost) as lobster. Fat eel from the lagoon is at its most delicious slow-roasted in ovens (it used to be cooked overnight in the kilns of Murano).

In fact, most dishes are simplicity itself. When young Henry III of France visited Venice in 1574, the official banquet consisted of over a thousand dishes (so the chroniclers say). But one that no doubt took pride of place was a humble peasant dish known colloquially as *risi e bisi* (Venetian dialect for rice and peas). Made of rice from the Po valley cooked with tender little peas that grow near the banks of the Venetian lagoon, this dish still graces dinner tables—grand or simple—throughout the province.

If the food of Veneto is at once sophisticated yet down-to-earth, the same is true of her wines. Exciting and imaginative, they are also simple and modest—the lifeblood of the people.

Recioto di Soave or the rare Picolit, for example, would not have been out of place on the banquet table of the most discriminating doge. The modest table wines of Veneto, on the other hand, known only by the grape used to produce them (Merlot del Veneto, Tocai del Veneto, Cabernet del Veneto), when drunk with a home-cooked meal, taste as honest as wine should be.

Veneto is one of the most important wine regions in Italy. Its popular and best-known wines come from vineyards in the hills above Verona that fan down to the shores of Lake Garda. Here the vines are in perfect harmony with the gentle land. On grassy plains and terraced hills, trained to a dependence on old-fashioned pergolas, they grow high, spreading wide dappled canopies of foliage. Romantic and pastoral though these vineyards are, such old-fashioned cultivation makes impossible the wide-scale use of modern machinery.

Soave, which takes its name from a small, walled town about fifteen miles east of Verona, is a fresh, sound wine made principally from the Garganega grape. Within the Soave area is a smaller Classico zone where slightly stronger and, in theory, superior wines are produced (the harvest of grapes in the Classico zone usually begins somewhat later than in the rest of the region). Much wine is made in local co-operatives, which results in large-scale standardization; but at least many of the small growers are, under this system, guaranteed a price for their grapes. The wine is made with modern, up-to-date equipment, and the product is generally good—firm, fairly high in alcohol: a plentiful wine, which is thus relatively inexpensive. Of course, though, there are Soaves and there are Soaves. The very best possess body, aroma, and strength which combine in a forceful, dry wine that is excellent with food.

Valpolicella is produced in the hills north of Verona and east of the river Adige; Valpantena is a neighbouring sub-district; Bardolino's vineyards rise from the little tourist town of the same name on the banks of Lake Garda. All three areas produce red wine. Though grapes grown in these areas are similar, the result, from the redder, heavier soil of Valpolicella is, not surprisingly, a slightly heavier, softer wine with a fresh aroma

Home for lunch Venetian style . . .

and a bright ruby colour. When still young, the wine may be slightly *frizzante* as well as a touch sweet. Bardolino is paler in colour, drier and lighter than its neighbours, not an obvious or a great wine, but an appealing, always drinkable one that rarely disappoints. The even paler Chiaretto Classico comes from the same region. Too dark to be a rosé, too light to be a red wine, it is a fragrant favourite with prawns and other shellfish.

A different type of wine altogether, though made from the grapes of these same hills, is Recioto. It comes from selected grapes—the 'ear of the bunch' (*recce* is Venetian dialect for ear)—which have received more sun than the rest, and

so are that much riper. They are semi-dried in racks to concentrate the sugar further, and are finally pressed sometime during the new year. The resulting wine can be either red or white, and the region from which it comes is usually designated, as in Recioto di Soave or Recioto della Valpolicella. There are also two styles of wine: Recioto, a full, sweet red or white dessert wine; and Recioto Amarone, austere red wine that partners roast meat, game, and strong cheese.

Wine is produced throughout Veneto. From near Vicenza and Breganze come a variety of sound reds and whites, including Garganega di Gambellara, Breganze Pinot Bianco, Breganze Pinot Nero, and Breganze Vespaiolo. There is

also a growing number of vineyards in the Colli Euganei near Padua. Yet another important wine centre is found in the province of Treviso, north of Venice. Long concerned with the production of quality wines, Treviso is the home of Italy's first school specializing in oenology: the Viticultural Research Institute, at Conegliano.

Prosecco di Conegliano is an elegant and unique wine, sadly exported only in small quantities, since the Venetians (who never miss a bargain) consume all they can get their hands on. The wine takes its name from the grape Prosecco (grown throughout the region), which is so versatile that it can produce either sweet or dry, still or sparkling wine. The still, dry wine is clean, strong, and firm, an elegant partner to shellfish and fish. Sparkling Prosecco, on the other hand, is a perfect wine for a celebration; here in Veneto it is preferred to Italy's better known wine for special occasions—less flowery, more austere than Asti Spumante.

The Treviso province is also the source of considerable amounts of honest, uncomplicated table wines, sold in screw-topped bottles or by the cask, that are found in homes, bars, and restaurants throughout the region. In wine-producing regions themselves, after all, it is honest, robust and cheery table wines—wines such as Merlot, Tocai, Cabernet or Riesling Italico—that are most often encountered, naturally and unselfconsciously forming an harmonious partnership with the foods of the land.

It is really not possible to speak of the *cucina veneta* without mentioning rice, because it is the staple in the north, much more so even than pasta. *Arborio*, which grows in the fertile Po river valley, is a medium-grain variety ideally suited for *risotto*; in fact, no other type so lends itself to being cooked in stock with the addition of numerous and various ingredients. In Veneto, *risotto* appears steaming on the table, made with sausages, chicken meat and liver, mushrooms, tripe, vegetables such as artichoke and asparagus, and, of course, fish and other fruits of the sea. Typical are *risotto di scampi* (rice cooked with large shrimps, butter, garlic, and brandy), *risotto alla finanziera* (with sweetbreads, chicken giblets, and wine), *risotto di pesce* (with fish, shellfish, and fish stock)—and, of course, the famous *risi e bisi*.

Risotto is always eaten as a *primo piatto* (first course), as are *pasta e fagioli* (a thick, hearty macaroni and bean soup), *tortellini in brodo* (stuffed pasta served in consommé), *zuppa di trippa* (tripe soup), *zuppa di pesce* (fish soup), *gnocchi* (potato or semolina dumplings), and other pasta dishes or soups. They can, however, be preceded by or replaced with *antipasto* (literally, before the meal). *Prosciutto di San Daniele*, an air-dried raw mountain ham which is sliced razor-thin is one excellent example; another is *insalata di mare*—a seafood salad of baby squid, firm white fish, octopus, shrimp, clams, mussels, and crayfish, served on a bed of lettuce with an oil and lemon dressing.

The *secondo piatto*, which follows, is apt to be fish, although there are also delicious meat specialities. Freshwater trout, carp, sardines, and eel from Lake Garda are eaten simply grilled and served with lemon wedges. *Fritto misto di mare* is an extravagant mixed platter of lightly fried fish, squid, scallops, and mussels. Fish such as sea bass and tuna are fried or grilled, then dredged with virgin olive oil, and served with lemon and parsley. Curiously, despite the abundance of such wonderful fresh fish, the people of Veneto have a passion for dried salt cod (a passion shared by so many others on the Continent). Despite the fact that it is no longer cheap, and its preparation takes several days, they still eat great quantities of it. Known as *baccalà*, it comes hard

as rock, and must be soaked in water for up to forty-eight hours. Then, in the classic preparation (*alla vicentina*), it is stewed slowly in onions and milk.

Meat specialities of Veneto include *spezzatino di vitello* (a veal goulash reminder of the Austrians who occupied Venice for part of the nineteenth century), *fegato alla veneziana* (thin strips of calves' liver fried with onions), and various roasted game birds, such as partridge, pigeon, duck, and quail, served with *polenta*. Meaty turkey breasts are carved into slabs for frying, and are served with a special fruit mustard that is also good with pork steaks, veal *escalopes*, and, on Christmas Day, boiled capon and *cotechino* (a boiling sausage).

As in the rest of Italy, meals often end with fruit—but nowhere in the world is it as good as here: a juicy peach, black cherries, or an orange-red 'blood' orange all that a sweet tooth could ask for. Sweets and pastries appear on special occasions, and are usually bought from the *pasticcerie* that specialize in elaborate creations as beautiful to look at as they are to eat. As a matter of course, they are meticulously gift-wrapped in beautiful paper and ribbons; it is a smug pleasure to be invited by friends for a home-cooked meal when such specially-wrapped treasures can be proffered. From dark raisin-and-nut slabs of cake to light, airy confections, the list is endless. One particular Venetian favourite is *tiramesú*, a rich chocolate cream cake (in Venetian dialect the name means 'pick-me-up', in acknowledgement of the alleged restorative powers of its filling of *zabaione*).

Veneto is a region with a magnificent past, a region that has lived hard and well. Though today Venice might benefit from a physical 'restorative', this city is not dying. On the contrary, it throbs with life—at five in the morning when fishing boats unload their nocturnal prizes on the Rialto; at noon when the squeals of children going home from school by boat or water-bus announce the midday meal; and at dusk when elderly ladies and gentlemen, arms linked, make a formal *passeggiata* along the Zattere, seeing and being seen by all who matter. Indeed, the way of life found throughout Veneto is unsinkable.

Quantities where necessary are given in
Metric, Imperial and US measurements.

Risi e Bisi

Rice and Peas

Serves 4

50 g/2 oz/$\frac{1}{2}$ stick butter
2 tbsp olive oil
250 g/$\frac{1}{2}$ lb/1$\frac{1}{4}$ cups arborio rice
2 tbsp freshly chopped parsley
1 medium onion, peeled and finely chopped
75 g/3 oz bacon or ham, diced
1.8 l/3 pt/7$\frac{1}{2}$ cups boiling chicken stock
250 g/$\frac{1}{2}$ lb fresh peas (use frozen if fresh are not
available, but reduce their cooking time)
Freshly grated Parmesan cheese

Heat butter and oil in a large saucepan. Add rice,
parsley, onion, and ham, and fry gently until
onion is soft and golden. Start to add boiling
stock, a ladleful at a time, stirring constantly. As
the liquid is absorbed, continue to add more stock.
After about 10 min., add peas (later, if frozen).
Add as much stock in this way, until rice is cooked but still *al dente*. The dish should be fairly
moist. Season to taste, and stir in Parmesan
cheese.

Serve piping hot, with extra Parmesan, as a
primo piatto (first course).

Suggested wine:
Soave Classico

Pasta e Fagioli

Macaroni and Bean Soup

Serves 6–8

250 g/$\frac{1}{2}$ lb beans (small red beans
mottled with black, red speckled, or
kidney beans), soaked overnight
1 smoked ham bone or bacon joint (if very salty,
soak overnight)
1 large onion, peeled and chopped

1 stick of celery, chopped
1 large carrot, chopped
2.4 l/4 pt/10 cups cold water
Salt
Freshly ground black pepper
3 tbsp olive oil
250 g/$\frac{1}{2}$ lb macaroni
Freshly grated Parmesan cheese

Add soaked beans, ham bone, and chopped
vegetables to a large pot. Pour on water, and
bring slowly to the boil. Skim, then reduce heat,
and simmer for 2$\frac{1}{2}$ hr.

When cooked, remove ham bone, and either
take off meat and add to the soup or serve separately. (In Veneto, in fact, the meat might be
served as the main course after the soup.) Season,
stir in olive oil, then add macaroni. Cook until
pasta is *al dente*. Stir in Parmesan cheese, and
serve immediately.

Suggested wine:
Merlot del Veneto

Spaghetti al Tonno

Spaghetti with Tuna

Serves 4–6

6 tbsp olive oil
1 small onion, peeled and finely chopped
2 garlic cloves, peeled and sliced
Generous handful of freshly chopped parsley
150 ml/$\frac{1}{4}$ pt/$\frac{2}{3}$ cup dry white wine
1 large tin of tuna, drained and flaked
(or 250 g/$\frac{1}{2}$ lb fresh tuna)
Salt
Freshly ground black pepper
500 g/1 lb spaghetti

Heat oil in a large saucepan. Add onion and garlic, and fry gently until onion begins to turn

colour. Next add parsley and white wine. Bring to the boil, and allow to reduce by about half. Then add tuna and cook gently for a further 10 min. Season.

Meanwhile, cook the spaghetti *al dente*. Serve in bowls, with a spoonful of sauce on each serving, as a *primo piatto*.

Suggested wines:
Prosecco di Conegliano, Soave

Insalata di Mare

Seafood Salad
Serves 6–8

2 dozen mussels or clams
6 tbsp olive oil
1 cleaned squid, cut into rings or strips
1 fillet of cod or other white fish, cooked and cut into pieces
3 dozen prawns, cooked and shelled
Cockles, scallops, winkles, or any other shellfish
2 tbsp lemon juice
Salt
Freshly ground black pepper
Freshly chopped parsley
Lemon wedges to garnish

Heat one-third of olive oil in a large frying pan, and add scrubbed and dried mussels or clams or other shellfish. Cover and cook until shells open. Discard any that do not. Transfer to a bowl, and allow to cool.

In same pan, cook the squid for 20 min., or until tender. Remove, and allow to cool.

Combine mussels, squid, fish, prawns, and other shellfish on a large serving platter. Mix olive oil with lemon juice; season, and dress seafood. Garnish with chopped parsley and lemon wedges, and chill before serving.

Suggested wines:
Chiaretto Classico, Soave Classico

Baccalà alla Vicentina

Salt Fish Venetian Style
Serves 4–6

500 g/1 lb salt cod
4 tbsp olive oil
3 medium onions, peeled and chopped
2 garlic cloves, peeled and chopped
Handful freshly chopped parsley
3 tbsp seasoned flour
2 tbsp freshly grated Parmesan cheese
300 ml/$\frac{1}{2}$ pt/$1\frac{1}{4}$ cups milk
Salt
Freshly ground black pepper

Soak salt cod in several changes of water for 24–48 hr., depending on how hard it is. Boil for 2 hr. Skin and bone the fish, and chop into small chunks.

Heat oil in an ovenproof casserole, and fry onion and garlic until it begins to change colour. Add parsley. Roll pieces of chopped fish in seasoned flour, and add to fried onion and garlic mixture. Fry for a few minutes, adding more oil if necessary. Stir in grated cheese, then pour over the milk. Season. Transfer to a pre-heated low oven, 140°C/Gas Mark 1/275°F, and cook for 4–5 hr.

Serve hot, with *polenta*.

Suggested wine:
Tocai del Veneto

Scampi alla Griglia

Grilled Giant Prawns
Serves 6

24 raw giant prawns (jumbo shrimp)
Olive oil
Lemon juice
Handful of finely chopped parsley
Salt
Freshly ground black pepper
Lemon wedges to garnish

Ideally, this Venetian speciality should be cooked on a charcoal grill.

Slit the prawns down the back, de-vein and flatten. Rub them with olive oil, and season with salt and pepper. Grill for 3 min. on each side, then sprinkle with lemon juice and chopped parsley, and serve hot, garnished with lemon wedges.

They should be peeled at the table, so provide finger bowls and napkins.

Suggested wine:
Chiaretto Classico

Carpaccio con la Salsa di 'Whisky'

Raw Fillet Steak with Whisky Sauce
Serves 6

750 g/1 ½ lb best-quality fillet steak, sliced razor-thin (by butcher if possible)

Arrange slices of beef on a platter, or on individual plates, and serve as a *primo piatto* with the following whisky sauce.

Whisky Sauce
600 ml/1 pt/2 ½ cups cream
50 g/2 oz grated fresh horseradish
Generous shot of Scotch whisky

Mix all ingredients together, and allow to blend for about 1 hr. in the refrigerator.
Serve over *carpaccio*.

Suggested wines:
Valpolicella, Raboso

Fegato alla Veneziana

Liver and Onions Venetian Style
Serves 4

3 tbsp olive oil
Knob of butter
3 medium onions, peeled and thinly sliced
1 tbsp freshly chopped parsley
500 g/1 lb calf's liver, thinly sliced
Salt
Freshly ground black pepper

Heat olive oil and butter in a large frying pan. Add onions and parsley, and cover the pan. Cook over a low heat for 45 min., until onions are soft and golden (but not browned).

Turn up heat, and add sliced liver. Season well, and cook for a few minutes only.

Serve immediately, with *polenta* or fried bread.

Suggested wines:
Valpantena, Bardolino

Polenta

Cornmeal Mush
Serves 6

500 g/1 lb coarse yellow polenta *flour*
1.8 l/3 pt/7 ½ cups cold water
2 tbsp salt

Bring salted water to a boil, then allow to simmer steadily. Take some of the *polenta* flour, and dribble it very slowly into the water. Stir continuously, with a long wooden spoon, to avoid lumps. Continue to add flour in a steady thin stream.

When mixture is smooth and begins to thicken, turn heat down, put lid on the pan, and continue to cook for 20 to 30 min. The *polenta* is ready when it pulls away from the sides of the pot.

Dampen a large wooden board, and with a wet spatula loosen the *polenta* from sides of the pot. Turn it out on to the board, and shape it either into cake form or rectangle.

Polenta is served as an accompaniment to main dishes in Veneto (roast meat, fish, stews). Left-over *polenta* can be sliced and grilled, or fried, then served with a sauce or Italian sausage.

THE IBERIAN PENINSULA

RIOJA

RIOJA ALAVESA
Laguardia
Haro
R. Tiron
R. Oja
ALTA
Cenicero
R. Najerilla
NAVARRA
R. Ebro
Logroño
R. Iregua
R. Lexa
San Adrian
Calahorra
Alfaro
RIOJA BAJA
R. Cidacos
Arnedo
R. Alamo

MINHO
VINHO VERDE
Oporto
TRAS-OS-MONTES
ROSÉ
ALTO DOURO
PORT
R. Douro
DÃO
BAIRRADA
R. Dão
Coimbra
Covilhã
Abrantes
R. Tegus
BUCELLAS
COLARES
Lisbon
Carcavelos
MOSCATEL DE SETÚBAL
Setúbal
Elvas
ALENTEJO
R. Guadiana
ALGARVE
Portimão
Lagoa
Faro

PORTUGAL

R. Guadalquivir
MANZANILLA
Sanlúcar de Barrameda
SHERRY
Jerez de la Frontera
R. Guadalete
Puerto de Santa María

JEREZ

PORTUGAL

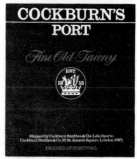

In the busy old quarter of Oporto, there is a maze of steep, carless alleys that rise from a street of warehouses on the waterfront. Houses with glass-less windows are linked by lines of handwashed laundry, and the stone streets echo the squeals of barefoot children, yapping dogs, and squawking chickens.

It is early morning, but the market—an endless line of little stalls along the banks of the Dòuro—is already in top gear. Ancient trucks heave around corners and push through the crowd, sloshing water from their cargoes of ice-packed fish. The trucks shudder to a halt, men and women load the dripping crates on their heads, and hurry off to their stalls to display the gleaming silvery catch. Elsewhere, sweet melons, bunches of fat grapes, oranges as big as grape-fruit, lemons, limes, and mountains of tomatoes are piled high. A woman is shredding the large *couve* cabbages used to make the ever-present *caldo verde* soup. Fresh dates and plump figs, almonds from the Algarve, and juicy green olives all indicate the verdant richness of this agricultural land.

By lunchtime, gaping doorways, the sound of laughter, and the smell of no-nonsense cook-ing beckon. Behind the colourful plastic strips that serve as doors in many little restaurants of this city, people are feasting on bowls of *dobrada à moda do Porto*, accompanied by clay jugs of fresh, mouth-puckering Vinho Verde.

This national dish is a one-pot meal that com-bines tripe, chick-peas, sometimes chicken, *chouriço*, and vegetables. It originated in the fifteenth century, when Prince Henry the Navi-gator, the half-English hero from Oporto, had all the cattle in the city slaughtered and the meat

Street scene in Oporto.

salted in preparation for his expedition to Ceuta. He left the unfortunate inhabitants of Oporto only the tripe and offal, yet such was the ingenuity of these tough people who had learned to make do with adversity that they turned meagre pickings into a favourite food.

Portuguese food, like Portuguese wine, tastes of the land itself, exuding a scent of lemon blossom, sea breeze, and brilliant sunshine, all collected in an almond shell. Despite increasing tourism and a growing economy, both food and wine remain virile, simple, and wholesome. Yet, because Portugal once led the world in her voyages of exploration, exotic and unexpected elements have also been inherited—fierce *piri-piri* peppers from Africa, cardamom and cinnamon from the Indies, tomatoes and potatoes from the New World.

While fresh fruit and vegetables, pork, chicken, and game all feature in Portuguese cooking, seafood takes pride of place. Nowhere here is more than a few hours from the sea, and lakes, streams, and rivers abound. Up and down the coast, cast-iron barbecues called *fogareiros* sizzle with juicy fresh sole, red mullet, sea bass, turbot, eel, giant prawns, and fresh sardines. They are sprinkled with sea salt, brushed with olive oil, and served simply with fried potatoes and a tomato and onion salad.

In the busy fishing town of Portimão in the Algarve, sardine boats chug in daily. Their shimmering baskets of wriggling fish are tossed up to men along the quay who wait with trays and trucks of ice. The tiniest sardines are packed off to the tinning factories. The rest—shiny silver fish as large as small mackerel—are packed in wooden boxes and loaded on to trucks, scooters, motorcycles, and bicycles. Like morning milk deliveries, they are then rushed from house to house for daily consumption.

Across the road from the fishing boats, iron braziers blaze, and the acrid, bitter smell of grilled sardines mixes with the colourful noise of the waterfront. The sardines are cooked until their skins are almost black, then slapped on to a slab of crusty bread. The fish juice and thick olive oil soak into the bread as it is washed down with full-bodied, heady red wine from the local co-operative. Though other fish dishes in Portugal

Tripe and chick-peas, the basis for a favourite Portuguese dish.

are generally accompanied by white wine, sardines, as well as *bacalhau* (the dried salt cod so loved by the Portuguese) go best with red.

Vinho Verde is probably Portugal's most distinctive wine. The perfect companion to relaxed conversation and casual good times, this slightly sparkling, slightly sour wine has stamina too, and partners both fresh or rich and spicy foods. The name means 'green wine', a reference not to its colour but to the fact that it is made from slightly under-ripe grapes. In fact, almost seventy per cent of Vinho Verde is red, although little of this is exported.

The wine is produced in the northern Minho region, an area that has a close affinity with the Spanish province of Galicia, just across the border, where 'green wine' is also made. Because this is Portugal's most densely populated area, however, land is precious, therefore vines are trained high above the ground, either on wires or on natural supports such as sycamore or poplar trees. Often, they grow so high that the harvesters have to climb ladders to get to the fruit. Wrapped around branches, the drooping bunches present to the uniniatiated a surprising illusion of grape-bearing trees. Working these vineyards is labour-intensive, but such unorthodox practice serves another important purpose. If the vines were closer to the earth, the grapes would gather too much heat from the burning ground and so become over-ripe and produce coarse wine. Training the vines to climb high, however, exposes the grapes to a cool breeze from the Atlantic. Harvested in early autumn, before they are fully ripe, they thus have a low sugar content

and a high acidity. Some of the resulting wines are so fresh, young, and high in acid that they are surprisingly mouth-puckering. With most, however, the malic acid is softened by a secondary fermentation (malo-lactic) which takes place after the wines are bottled, throwing off carbon dioxide as a by-product. Thus, they also have a natural semi-sparkle that goes well with their sharp freshness.

The Dão region, north of Coimbra, is another important wine-producing area, spread over almost 1,000 square miles. Much wine here is produced in large co-operatives, though this takes nothing from the area's reputation for quality and reliability. Blended from a variety of grapes little known outside Portugal, red Dão is characterized by a full, velvety quality, which

Eating grilled sardines on the waterfront at Portimão.

Fish, the Portuguese staff of life.

comes in part from a high natural glycerine content. In an area as large as the Dão, with its multifarious soil and climate, there are, necessarily, many different styles of wine. The family trait of robust smoothness is always present, however, and it is rightly regarded as Portugal's most important table wine. Excellent white Dão is produced from grapes grown higher up the terraced mountains. Well-balanced and attractive, it should be drunk while young and fresh.

The vineyards of Colares, on the coast west of Lisbon, are unlike any other in the world. Because the vines are grown in deep sand dunes (in dug trenches) they escaped the devastation caused in the last century by the dread *phylloxera*, which virtually destroyed most of the vineyards in Europe. Once the insect has taken hold of a plant, there is no alternative but to destroy it and replant with native stock grafted on to aphid-resistant roots. And this has been done in most vineyards throughout the Continent. The pest, fortunately, could not penetrate the sand in which the vines of Colares grow. If they are not threatened in this way, however, there is still the danger today from land developers. The red wine of Colares is interesting: it has an assertive astringency and a unique flavour that is worth safeguarding.

Though the system of demarcated regions (*região demarcada*) in Portugal is supposed to work similarly to the French *appellation d'origine contrôlée*, in fact over half of Portugal's wine comes from undemarcated regions, much of it good and well worth trying. One of Portugal's best-known wines, Mateus rosé, comes from an undemarcated region. Demand is so high for this refreshing pink wine that almost the entire grape harvest of its home province of Trás-os-Montes is given over to its production. Taken with a light lunch on a blistering summer afternoon, cool Portuguese rosé reliably transforms a hot, heavy day into a lighter, breezier one. Other blended wines are sold under brand names, and are also worth seeking. *Reserva* and *garrafeira* are general quality terms; *engarrafado na origem*, the Portuguese equivalent of 'estate bottled', is another mark of distinction.

Good and relatively inexpensive sparkling wine is made in the northern area of Bairrada,

Cork groves in the Alentejo. The bark is stripped without damage to the trees.

much of it by the laborious *méthode champenoise*. It is good value and a perfect partner to the rich food of the region, such as suckling pig.

Meals in Portugal often start (and finish) with soup. The most popular and prevalent is the simple *caldo verde* which is no more than potatoes boiled in water, with finely shredded cabbage, garlic, and olive oil. A variety of interesting and filling soups are known as *açordas*. The simplest takes just a thick slab of wholewheat bread, boiling water, olive oil, garlic, and fresh coriander. Sometimes, as a treat, a raw egg is broken into the resulting soup. Portuguese *gazpacho* is another 'bread' soup—a mixture of coarse bread, chopped tomatoes, onion, cucumber, coriander, and green peppers, served cold.

Though beef tends to be tough in Portugal, pork is superb. In the great cork oak groves of the Alentejo, herds of pigs thrive on a diet of acorns

Bark from the cork oak is stripped and left in piles along
the road in the Alentejo; Portugal is the most important
cork-producing country in the world.

and white truffles which give their meat an exquisite flavour. One dish which demonstrates the inventiveness of Portuguese cooking is *amêijoas na cataplana*, which combines bite-sized cubes of pork with clams in the shell simmered in a *refogado*—a sauce of garlic, onion, tomato, olive oil, and coriander. If at all possible, the dish should be cooked in a *cataplana*, a copper or tin saucer-shaped cooking vessel, which works along the lines of a (primitive) pressure cooker.

The virile simplicity of Portuguese cooking is evident in the *cozido*. No fussy measurements or recipe here; a *cozido* is always a new encounter because every cook in the land prepares it differently, using whatever ingredients are at hand. Chicken, bacon, beef, perhaps sausage (such as *chouriço* or *morcela*) vegetables, rice, and chick-peas all add up to a rib-sticking feast that keeps winter out, if winter should become a

problem. A warm red Dão is the wine to drink with this.

A similar national dish made from fish is the *caldeirada de peixe*, a Portuguese *bouillabaisse* utilizing whatever the daily fish market has on offer. On the southern Algarve, for example, fresh sardines, cherne, bream, and sea bass are used, along with *piri-piri* peppers, onion, tomato, garlic, and parsley. The result is exciting—and fiery. A chilled and refreshing white wine such as Bucellas (which bears a slight resemblance to the light wines of the Rhine) does well to cool things down, as does Portuguese *sangria*, a drink of red wine, brandy, port, soda, and fresh fruit. It is a powerful thirst-quencher.

The Portuguese have a sweet tooth, and the most popular desserts are variations of egg custard, the ubiquitous *pudim flan*. Other sweets are rice-based, and in the Algarve there are elaborate sculpted creations made from ground almonds and figs.

Portugal's most famous wine, port, is a natural after-dinner drink—but it is not that widely drunk in the country itself. It was the British taste for this sweet, fortified wine that helped build a national industry. Indeed, port does seem more suited to northern climates and temperaments than to this warmer, gentler country.

Port is produced in the famed lodges of Vila Nova de Gaia, where the names of firms are written in white on sloping, sunbaked roofs—Sandeman, Cockburn, Croft, Taylor, alongside Ferreira, Fonseca and others—reminders of the British families who settled on the banks of the Douro to start the great port dynasties.

Grapes for this wine are grown in a strictly defined area of the Alto Douro, a steep stretch of land with miserable soil, blistering summer sun, and cold, foggy winters. The vineyards lie on tortuous terraces that descend to the narrow river gorge. They must be harvested by hand—backbreaking work in such inhospitable terrain—and the grapes taken to isolated *quintas* high in the Alto Douro. In many of these *quintas* that mysterious transformation of grape into wine begins in the oldest way possible: with the human treading of the grapes in ancient stone troughs to the dizzy rhythm of traditional folk-singing. The port trade came into its own when England, at war with France, signed the Methuen Treaty, an agreement with Portugal under which preference was given to Portuguese wine in exchange for an English monopoly on wool. Since the wine of the Alto Douro, however, was naturally dry and harsh, brandy was added to the new wine to stop the natural fermentation, thus making it possible for port to retain a high natural sugar content. This young, raw, slightly fortified wine eventually makes its way down-river to the shippers' lodges in Vila Nova de Gaia, where the delicate and skilful processes of blending and maturing it into the many types of port takes place.

Most ports are made by this careful and complex blending of a variety of wines to produce trade brands that are confidently consistent year after year. The result is a wine of remarkable range and versatility. White port, made from white grapes, though not exported widely, is the driest, and thus makes an unusual aperitif. Ruby port, as the name suggests, is full-coloured, rich, and fairly young wine that is blended and aged in oak for not less than five years. Tawny port is also a blended wine aged in wood, though for considerably longer periods (sometimes twenty years or more) than ruby. As it ages, its colour fades to a light gold or pale onion peel hue, and it develops mellowness and complexity.

Vintage port, unlike the blends, is produced only in exceptional years, from grapes of a single year only. It is further distinguished through being aged in wood for only two or three years, then transferred to bottle, and laid to rest for the slow, silent fifteen, twenty, thirty years, and often more, that allow it to reach a full richness and fragrance that is unrivalled. As it ages, the wine sheds a heavy crust. For this reason the bottle has to be handled with extreme care, in storage, transportation, and serving. Such wine must always be carefully decanted before drinking. Crusted port is wine from better-than-average harvests which, like vintage, gains its full character through long periods of bottle ageing. It too must be handled with extreme care. Late-bottled vintage, on the other hand, is single-year wine aged in oak for five to fifteen years before bottling. The wine both sheds its crust in the cask, and matures much sooner. Though late-bottled vintage is easier to care for and serve, some argue that with this most traditional of wines, the ritual is integral to the enjoyment of it.

Another world-renowned dessert wine comes from vineyards south of Lisbon. Moscatel de Setúbal has a heavy perfumed bouquet and deep amber colour that evokes the atmosphere and aroma of Portugal's lush countryside.

Even in January, in the Algarve, almond blossoms carpet the land. But in harsher climates to the north, people huddle together for warmth, and hardy fishermen brave the icy waters of the Atlantic. Whether in the rugged Trás-os-Montes province, the verdant Minho where vines seem to grow on trees, the baked golden plains of the Alentejo, or the wind-carved cliffs of the Algarve, the intrinsic character of Portuguese food and wine is an inheritance of the land.

RECISES FROM PORTUGAL

Quantities where necessary are given in
Metric, Imperial and US measurements.

Caldo Verde

Cabbage and Potato Soup
Serves 6

5 medium potatoes
1.5 l/2 ½ pt/6 ¼ cups water
3 whole cloves of garlic, peeled
4 tbsp olive oil
350 g/¾ lb cabbage or kale, finely shredded
Salt
Freshly ground black pepper

Peel and cut up potatoes, and boil in salted water,
with garlic. When soft, mash, and add olive oil
and cabbage. Boil uncovered for about 3 min.
Season to taste, and serve in bowls, with a drop of
olive oil in bottom of each.

Suggested wines:
Colares, red Dão

Dobrada à Modo do Porto

Tripe and Chick Peas
Serves 6

500 g/1 lb chick-peas (soaked overnight)
1 kg/2 lb honeycomb tripe, washed thoroughly
Salt
Freshly ground black pepper
1 bay leaf
3 tsp cumin
Freshly chopped parsley
2 tbsp olive oil
2 onions, peeled and sliced
2 garlic cloves, peeled and crushed
4 large tomatoes, chopped (or 1 large tin)
250 g/8 oz/½ lb chouriço, sliced

Put chick-peas in a large saucepan, and cover
with salted water. Cook for 2 hr., or until tender.
Drain, and set aside. Meanwhile, cut tripe into

smallish pieces, and put in a large saucepan, with
plenty of salted water. Add black pepper, bay
leaf, cumin, and parsley. Bring to the boil, and
simmer for 2 hr., or until tender. Drain and set
aside.

Heat oil in a casserole, and sauté onions and
garlic until soft and golden. Add tomatoes, and
cook for a further 5 min. Add chick-peas, tripe,
and sausage, and cook for a further 45–60 min.
Adjust seasoning, and serve hot.

Suggested wine:
Vinho Verde

Amêijoas na Cataplana

Pork and Clams
Serves 6

1.5 kg/3 lb clams (substitute large-shelled fresh
cockles if necessary)
2 tbsp olive oil
2 large onions, peeled and chopped
2 garlic cloves, peeled and finely chopped
1 kg/2 lb pork fillet, cut into 2 ½ cm/1 in cubes
150 ml/¼ pt/⅔ cup dry white wine
4 or 5 fresh tomatoes (or 1 medium tin)
Handful finely chopped coriander (or parsley)
1 tsp cayenne pepper
Salt
Freshly ground black pepper

Wash clams or cockles thoroughly under running water, and discard any that do not open
when tapped (which means they are dead). Soak
overnight in salt water, if necessary, to expel
sand.

Heat olive oil in a cataplana, or large casserole.
Fry onions and garlic until soft and golden. Add
pork, and brown on all sides. Add clams or
cockles and dry white wine. Increase heat, and
cook briskly, shaking pot until wine has reduced.
Add tomatoes, coriander (or parsley), cayenne

pepper, salt, and black pepper. Cover tightly, and simmer for 30–40 min., or until pork is tender.

Bring *cataplana* to the table, and open when guests are seated.

Suggested wines:
Portuguese rosé, white Dão

Bacalhau à Portuguesa

Portuguese Salt Cod
Serves 4–6

750 g/1 $\frac{1}{2}$ lb dried salt cod
5 tbsp olive oil
1 large onion, peeled and chopped
2 garlic cloves, peeled and chopped
2 green peppers, sliced
5 tomatoes, sliced (or 1 large tin)
Salt
Freshly ground black pepper
1 tsp piri-piri (or cayenne to taste)
500 g/1 lb potatoes, thinly sliced

Soak salt cod for 24–48 hr., changing the water frequently. Then simmer in just enough water to cover until tender (2–3 hr.). Drain, remove skin and bones, and flake.

Heat olive oil in a saucepan, and fry onion, garlic, and green peppers until soft. Add tomatoes, seasoning, and *piri-piri*. Simmer for 20 min.

In a casserole, layer sliced potatoes, flaked salt cod, and tomato mixture. Sprinkle with olive oil, then bake in a moderate oven, 180°C/Gas Mark 4/350°F, for about 45 min., or until potatoes are done.

Suggested wines:
Red Dão reserva, robust red table wines such as Lagoa or Serradayres

Lulas Recheadas

Stuffed Squid
Serves 4

4 medium squid
2 tbsp olive oil
100 g/ $\frac{1}{4}$ lb chopped ham
75 g/3 oz/1 cup fresh white breadcrumbs
2 hard-boiled eggs, chopped
1 egg

Sauce
1 tbsp olive oil
1 large onion, peeled and finely chopped
2 garlic cloves, peeled and chopped
4 fresh tomatoes, chopped
2 tbsp tomato purée (paste)
1 bay leaf
1 sprig of marjoram
Salt
Freshly ground black pepper
Freshly chopped parsley

Pull heads of squid away from tentacles. Remove and discard inner organs. Reach into body cavity, and remove and discard the plastic-like spine. Wash thoroughly. Chop tentacles, and wing flesh.

Heat oil, and gently fry chopped ham, chopped tentacles, and wing flesh. Remove from heat, add breadcrumbs and chopped egg. Mix well, season, and bind with egg. Stuff mixture into squid bodies, and close opening with skewers or cocktail sticks.

Meanwhile, heat oil in a saucepan, and fry onion and garlic until soft. Add tomatoes, herbs, and seasoning, and allow to simmer.

Transfer squid to a casserole, and pour over the sauce. Cover, and bake in a pre-heated moderate oven, 180°C/Gas Mark 4/350°F, for about 35 min., or until squid are tender.

Serve with rice.

Suggested wines:
Red or white Dão

Iscas

Lisbon Liver
Serves 6

1 kg/2 lb lamb's liver, thinly sliced
300 ml/ $\frac{1}{2}$ pt/1 $\frac{1}{4}$ cups dry white wine
3 tbsp white wine vinegar
5 garlic cloves, peeled and crushed
2 bay leaves
Salt
Freshly ground black pepper
4 tbsp olive oil
175 g/6 oz smoked bacon, diced

In a shallow dish, cover liver with wine, vinegar, garlic, bay leaves, salt, and pepper. Cover dish, and leave to marinate overnight.

Remove liver, and pat dry. Reserve marinade. Heat olive oil in a large frying pan, and add liver and bacon. Cook over a fairly high heat until tender. Remove, and keep warm. Pour marinade into pan. Bring to the boil, and reduce a little. Adjust seasoning. Remove bay leaves, and pour over liver and bacon.

Serve immediately, with fried sliced potatoes.

Suggested wines:
Bucellas, Vinho Verde

Bolo Algarvio

Almond Tart

250 g/ $\frac{1}{2}$ lb/1 $\frac{1}{2}$ cups sugar
150 ml/ $\frac{1}{4}$ pt/ $\frac{2}{3}$ cup water
250 g/ $\frac{1}{2}$ lb/1 $\frac{1}{3}$ cups ground almonds
4 egg yolks
2 egg whites
50 g/2 oz/ $\frac{1}{2}$ stick butter
2 $\frac{1}{2}$ tbsp flour
1 tsp cinnamon
50 g/2 oz/ $\frac{1}{3}$ cup whole almonds

Add sugar to water in a large saucepan, bring to the boil, and stir until dissolved. Continue to boil for 5 min., then remove from heat. Meanwhile, beat the egg whites until they are stiff enough to hold peaks.

Add the ground almonds, egg yolks, and beaten egg white to the sugar water mixture. Return to a gentle heat, and gently stir in the butter, flour, and cinnamon, until well mixed. Continue to stir until the mixture forms a caramel-consistency paste. Remove from heat.

Meanwhile, grease an 18 cm/7 in flan tin. Add the mixture to the baking tin, and decorate with whole almonds and cinnamon. Bake in a moderate oven, 150°C/Gas Mark 2/300°F, until evenly browned (about 40 min.). Remove, and chill in refrigerator until ready to serve.

Suggested wine:
Moscatel de Setúbal

Pudim Flan

Caramel Custard
Serves 6

6 tsp soft brown sugar
100 g/4 oz/ $\frac{1}{2}$ cup sugar
6 eggs
900 ml/1 $\frac{1}{2}$ pt/3 $\frac{3}{4}$ cups milk
1 $\frac{1}{2}$ tbsp coffee essence or strong coffee

Put a heaped teaspoon of brown sugar into 6 individual ramekins.

In a large bowl, beat sugar and eggs together until yellow and frothy. Bring milk to the boil, and gradually add it to the egg mixture, beating continuously. Add coffee essence.

Pour this mixture into ramekins, and place in a roasting tin. Add enough water to come halfway up the sides of the dishes. Bake in a moderate oven, 180°C/Gas Mark 4/350°F, until just set, about 45 min. To test, stick a skewer into the custard: if it comes out clean, the custard is done. Remove from oven, and allow to cool.

The indoor market in Logroño offers a variety of
piquant paprika-flavoured sausages which colour the
hearty stews of this region.

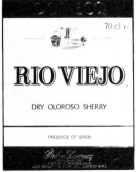

In Spain, breakfast is usually a light affair. The midday meal is not served before two or three —even as late as four—in the afternoon. A normal time for the evening meal is nine-thirty or ten o'clock, though many find even this a trifle early. These lengthy stomach-grumbling gaps between meals, however, can be stopped most pleasantly: it is the custom here, when hunger pangs first strike, to head straight for the nearest bar. There, virtually the entire surface of the bar-top is covered with plates bearing a variety of appetizing morsels. As *copita* after *copita* of cool *fino* sherry, or tiny squat tumblers of thick red wine are downed in endless succession, the floor soon becomes littered with discarded toothpicks and crumpled paper napkins. For no self-respecting Spaniard would dream of drinking his mid-morning or early-evening glass of wine without first munching on a grilled prawn, a bit of fried fish, or even just an olive.

These bite-sized snacks are known in the south as *tapas*; the word means 'cover' because in dusty Andalusia a lid, saucer, or even a piece of bread was placed over wine glasses. An enterprising proprietor conceived the idea of attracting customers by putting an appetizer on each lid. And so the tradition began. In the north, such snacks go by the name of *banderillas*, after the flag-bedecked darts used to stab and enrage a bull in the *corrida de toros*. Not surprisingly, the bar-top *banderillas* are toothpicks speared on to such tasty morsels as *tortillas* (pieces of cold Spanish omelette), *chiperones* (minute ink-fish fried in boiling olive oil), pickles, marinated mushrooms, artichokes, carrots, grilled prawns, pieces of cheese, deep-fried fish, *chorizo* (a spicy paprika-flavoured sausage), *boquerones* (fresh anchovies

marinated in vinegar and onions), cod's roe in tomato-flavoured mayonnaise, sea snails, and *jamón serrano* (air-dried mountain ham, almost black in colour, stringy, yet deliciously sweet). These snacks, selected one by one, induce a powerful thirst, and some Spaniards toss back fifteen or twenty tumblers of wine in quick succession, while satisfying their gnawing morning or early-evening hunger.

Spain produces vast amounts of strong, inexpensive, and powerful *vino corriente*, everyday wine that slakes an incessant national thirst. Such wines have long been known abroad, too. But Spain is also an important producer of quality wines that Spanish and foreign *aficionados* are turning to increasingly with enjoyment. Travellers in the north, for example, discover the delights of the light, tart, semi-sparkling 'green wines' of Galicia, which are opposite in character to the alcoholic heavyweights produced in the central plain of La Mancha. Panadés, a region near Barcelona, produces fragrant, fruity white wines, and intense yet delicate red wines, as well as a variety of excellent and distinctive *méthode champenoise* sparklers. Wines from the far south, produced from grapes grown on the dusty slopes near Jerez de la Frontera, have been known and loved for centuries. Indeed, this one region alone demonstrates the remarkable variety of Spanish wines, because sherry can be delicate, pale, and exceedingly fine, or dark, buttery, and reassuringly warm. In the north, meanwhile, bordering the Basque country, the region known as the Rioja produces red and white table wines of depth and elegance that are as exciting as any found in Europe.

The variety of Spanish wines is but a reflection of the extremes of a country in which geography, climate, attitudes, and food vary markedly from region to region. Spain is not solely a country of bullfights and flamenco dancing, any more than Spanish wine is solely alcoholic and inexpensive. Spain's two greatest wine regions exemplify the country's variety. Moreover, the wines of Rioja and Jerez, different though they are, exist in harmony, each with its own place.

The two regions are a study in contrast. Jerez lies within Andalusia, land of *sol y sombra*, where

The Palomino grape, at home in the élite chalk soil of Macharnudo, above Jerez de la Frontera.

the midnight air is perfumed with the heavy scent of orange blossom, and the whitewashed mosques and buildings that are the legacy of centuries of Moorish occupation match the snow-white *albariza pagos*—the elite chalk hills on which the finest Palomino grapes grow. In summer, the stuffy, humid Levant blows from the Sahara, and the region's usual heat is compounded by an oppressive heaviness. At such times, one can do little more than seek relief in the tulip-shaped form of *copitas* of *fino* sherry, or in jugs of fruit-filled *sangria*, and bowls of ice-cold *gazpacho*.

The Rioja, on the other hand, located mainly in historic Old Castile, has an entirely different character. The Ebro valley is rich, covered with fields of vines as well as peppers, potatoes, beans, cabbage, and asparagus. Towns such as Logroño have a northern industriousness, not the languid southern shrug of *mañana*. Winters here are surprisingly harsh, and icy winds blow from the Sierra de Cantabria. Then, warmth is provided by oak fires, while rich warm stews and roasted meat, plus the comfort of mellow oak-aged red wines help keep out the cold.

Sherry is probably the most versatile wine in the world. Indeed, it is remarkable that so many types of wine can be produced from the same grapes grown on the same soils. The sherry region extends between two rivers, Guadalquivir and Guadalete, a triangular area of land between the towns of Jerez de la Frontera, Puerto de Santa María, and Sanlúcar de Barrameda (Christopher Columbus sailed from this port on his third voyage to the New World). The grapes used to produce sherry are the Palomino, Pedro Ximénez, and Moscatel (the last two serving primarily to sweeten blends).

After the grapes have been harvested and pressed (usually in early September), they undergo their first, tumultuous, fermentation, which converts sugar into alcohol, grape juice into wine. They are soon categorized by both quality and style, for they early develop distinct characteristics. Some of these wines, for example, are lighter and more fragrant, others heavier and more full-bodied. The lighter wines will eventually become dry, pale *fino* and darker *amontillado* wines; the fuller are destined to become *oloroso* and cream sherry. *Fino* gains its unique character from a yeast known as *flor* which grows unpredictably on the surface of some wines and eventually dissolves to contribute inimitable flavour and bouquet. Wines in the *oloroso* family, on the other hand, are fortified with alcohol up to a defined level to ensure the yeast will not survive.

The young wines from both the *fino* and *oloroso* families, after about a year, join a *criadera*, a 'nursery' for the raising of wines. For sherry is always blended, which means there is continuity and consistency in style and quality, year after year, rather than an individuality, either good or bad, which comes from a single-year vintage. This is achieved in part by a fascinating method of blending known as the *solera* system. Most wines are aged statically; that is, they develop and mature through time in barrel or bottle.

Sherry, on the other hand, is aged dynamically. Barrels of wine of similar style are organized on scales of varying ages. As a certain quantity of wine is drawn off from the oldest scale (the *solera* itself) to be blended, bottled, and sold, the barrels are replenished with wine from the next oldest scale, then these are in turn replenished with still younger wine. The process repeats itself throughout the chain, with the youngest wines blending with the next youngest and being blended in turn with wine from a new year. The rationale behind the *solera* system is that small quantities of young wine gradually mixed with larger quantities of older wine will absorb its style and character.

Wines drawn from the different *soleras* themselves (the word means 'foundation') are finally blended, both with each other, and with wines for sweetening and adding colour. Thus the various wines recognized by brand names throughout the world are produced consistently year after year. The usual types of wine are *manzanilla* (a dry *fino*, produced only in Sanlúcar de Barrameda; the proximity of the Atlantic is supposed to give the wine a brisk tang and pungency); *fino* (pale, elegant, and fragrant; it must be drunk soon after a bottle is opened, because it quickly loses its exhilarating freshness); *amontillado* (dry to medium dry, dark, and with a deep, nutty flavour); *oloroso* (usually medium sweet, though old dry *oloroso* is available and can be magnificent); and finally cream sherry (very sweet, full, and rich, for which *olorosos* are also the basis).

The cuisine of the sherry region reflects the influence of waves of invaders who entered the Iberian peninsula at this southern outpost. The Greeks, for example, planted the vine, while the Romans brought garlic; the Moors introduced saffron, nutmeg, pepper, and other spices, and also planted the lush *huertas*—fruit gardens of almond and orange groves that give to the land such poetic fragrance when they are in bloom.

Tapas, naturally, are eaten here throughout the day. Another popular and fast snack is any variety of small fish, such as fresh sardines and anchovies, ink-fish, squid cut into rings, and baby sole, dredged in flour then quickly fried in boiling olive oil. Paper-wrapped packets are picked up from any of a number of fried fish stands, *freidurías*, in Jerez or Cadiz, and either taken home, or eaten in the cool shade of an orange tree. Here the coast offers many varieties of seafood; *gambas* (large prawns or jumbo shrimp), *chiperones* (baby squid), and fresh fish steaks are often cooked *a la plancha*, that is, directly on an oiled, flat, and very hot griddle, until golden and sizzling. In this dusty southern land olive trees grow where nothing else can and thus olive oil is used for frying, the favourite method of cooking.

As in most wine regions, the local product usually finds its way into the cooking pot, and sherry is no exception. Mussels are steamed in this fragrant wine, while kidneys simmered in a rich sauce made with *fino* (*riñones al Jerez*) are equally delicious. Wild duck from the marshes above Sanlúcar is also excellent stewed in sherry and flavoured with fleshy green olives. And a vinegar made from sherry is used as a fragrant seasoning or dressing—some say it's the best vinegar in the world.

Traditionally, dry and medium-dry sherries are drunk as aperitifs, with *tapas*, and with soups. Cold *gazpacho* is the most famous, while another cold favourite is made from almonds and grapes: *sopa de almendras*. Hot vegetable soups are eaten in winter, as well as rich fish broths such as *sopa de pescado*, a fisherman's brew made with whatever has been freshly caught that morning. Simple soups combining fish and rice are thrown together quickly and effortlessly—though nothing beats *sopa al cuarto de hora*, 'quarter-of-an-hour soup', because it takes just that time to chop onions, ham, garlic, and parsley and simmer them together with local clams, hard-boiled egg, and sherry.

Though fish dominates the cuisine, small game birds such as partridge and quail are also favoured. Partridge is a particularly savoury treat when prepared *a la torera*, or bullfighter's style, stuffed with bacon and anchovies, then stewed in white wine. Chicken is good too, simply stewed with green olives and a glass or two of sherry. Meat such as pork steaks or beef is cooked *a la plancha*, or else sautéed in wine.

Would one drink sherry with such dishes? Some here might. *Aficionados* believe it is the best aperitif in the world, can be drunk throughout a

A cathedral-like *bodega* in Jerez.

meal, and finally is the logical after-dinner choice, too. It is, of course, a matter of taste; indeed the table wines of the Rioja are equally suited to accompany such foods. Thus sherry and Rioja serve to complement one another.

The Rioja is divided into three districts: Rioja Alta, to the north and west of Lorgoño; Rioja Alavesa, north of the Ebro river between Haro and Logroño; and Rioja Baja, extending south and east from Logroño, through Calahorra to Alfaro. Soil composition and climate vary considerably from one district to the next, so wines with distinct characteristics come from each. The wine of the Rioja Alavesa, for example, is *muy bonito*—very pretty and delicate, with a fine balance of fruit, alcohol, and oak, which gives the wine an elegant vibrancy. Wine from the Rioja Alta, on the other hand, is somewhat sturdier, and good examples continue to develop subtle nuances in flavour and bouquet through prolonged barrel and bottle ageing of twenty years and more. Wine from the Rioja Baja usually has a higher alcoholic content and correspondingly less finesse, since the climate is considerably drier and hotter. There are exceptions, of course, to these generalizations. Though the Baja is often considered the 'ugly sister' of the Rioja, for example, sound and good wine does come from here. And the wine of the Baja is useful, too, in adding body and strength to the wines of the Rioja Alta and Alavesa through judicious blending.

The soft, mellow flavour of oak is the most obvious characteristic of Rioja wine. The barrels in which the wine ages should be approximately 225 litres in volume (the exact size varies from barrel to barrel, since each is traditionally hand-crafted from North American oak). This is important because in a larger barrel not enough of the wine would come in contact with the wood, while a smaller one would impart too much of the flavour of oak. All red wines that receive the official Rioja stamp of authenticity must spend a minimum of two years in the barrel; many, in fact, are aged for considerably longer. A wine designated *reserva*, for example, must have at least five years of barrel ageing, while a *gran reserva* needs at least eight.

As in other fine wine districts, cellar work in the Rioja is labour-intensive. During the first year, for example, the wine is continually racked. Red wine, in particular, as it ages, throws a heavy sediment of dead yeast cells and other solid matter. The wine is transferred to clean barrels in order to take it off its sediment, and thus to result in clearer, brighter wine. Even in the second year, racking usually takes place at least twice, though for the further ageing of *reserva* and *gran reserva* wines it is probably only necessary to rack once a year. What this means from a consumer's point of view is that Rioja wine is exceptionally bright; even with the oldest wines it is rarely necessary to decant them, because there is virtually no sediment left in the wine.

There are numerous styles of wine produced in the Rioja, ranging from young and light to robust and powerful. The oldest and greatest wines are the designated *reservas* and *gran reservas*. Younger wine with less barrel ageing is designated *vino de crianza*. Styles of wine are often indicated by differing bottle shapes. A straight-sided Bordeaux-type bottle indicates a lighter wine (the word *clarete* is often used, too). Bottles with sloping shoulders similar to those found in Burgundy, on the other hand, coupled with the descriptive word *tinto*, indicate a deeper, darker, and more full-bodied style. But these are broad guidelines only, because the wines of the Rioja are really quite different in character from their French counterparts.

Though the Rioja is primarily known for its mellow, oak-aged red wines, a variety of excellent white and pink wines are also produced here. Traditionally even the white wines of this region were matured in oak casks for four or even five years at least, resulting in deep, gold to amber wines tasting of oak, not grape; many bodegas today, however, are concentrating on the production of light, fresh, crisp wines made primarily from the Viura grape. These, as well as the light, young, sprightly *rosados* (rosé) are especially good with fish and shellfish, such as *cangrejos*, a much-loved freshwater lobster found in the Ebro and in the Rio Oja, the tiny tributary that gives the region its name.

Although the Rioja is inland, the area has a rich tradition of fish dishes, because Haro was once a market for the distribution of fish to

Cleaning and disinfecting oak barrels.

Racking, i.e. transferring wine off its
sediment to clean barrels.

Checking the clarity of wine during racking.

The best wines of Rioja are wrapped in
metal mesh, a traditional guarantee
of authenticity.

A worker wraps oak with a reed known as
anea; this stopper will be used as a bung in
the traditional Rioja barrel.

The all-important *bacalao* (dried salt cod) has a shop of
its own in Logroño.

oven. It is so tender that when served in tiny
restaurants in Haro or along the Calle Laurel, in
Logroño, it can be torn apart into pieces with
two forks. Roast kid and suckling pig are cooked
in the same manner; all are superb with the fine
reserva and *gran reserva* wines.

Game comes from the foothills of the Sierra
de Cantabria; hare, partridge, grouse, and wild
boar are hunted in season. In winter, invigorating,
blood-warming food helps keep out the cold.
Pimientos are roasted over open fires until their
skins turn black, then are peeled, cut into strips,
and stewed with chunks of garlic in olive oil.
Equally warming are *alubias con chorizo*, tiny
white beans cooked with *chorizo*, and flavoured
with paprika to colour the soup a pale orange.
Patatas riojanas combine potatoes with *chorizo*,
garlic, and *pimientos*, while *menestra* is a vegetable
stew of peas, beans, potatoes, celery, and *acelgas*
(a coarse, dark, lettuce-like green) all boiled
separately to preserve colour and taste, then
simmered in a saffron-scented sauce of onions,
garlic, tomatoes, bacon, and ham.

The influence of the Basque region permeates
this northern province, and indeed its food here
is as exciting as any found in Spain. One unusual
Basque speciality encountered in the Rioja is
angulas, a wooden bowl filled with what appear
to be thickish noodles but are in fact elvers caught
in the region's many rivers, fried quickly in garlic
and olive oil. Another Basque favourite is a
dessert called *cuajada*, a type of junket made from
curdled ewe's milk, served in a wooden bowl.

Spaniards love their many cheeses, and a
chunk made from goat's or ewe's milk, together
with a bowl of fresh fruit, often rounds off the
midday meal. Indeed, a hard cheese such as
Manchego is superb with a goblet of Rioja.
Desserts such as *flan* (caramel custard) or the
riojanito (a marzipan sweet) might round off a
meal. A glass of sweet *oloroso* sherry, on the other
hand, is itself as perfect a finish as any could ask
for.

And so full circle to the wines of Jerez. From
the Basque country in the north to Cadiz in the
far south, the wines and foods of Rioja and Jerez
are vibrantly alive, whether cool or soothingly
warm, in harmony, one with the other—like sea
and sky, mountain and plain.

central Spain. River crab is cooked in a sauce
made from oil, red peppers, tomato, and garlic,
while fresh river trout is grilled over a fire made
from vine shoots. And as is the case throughout
Spain—indeed Europe—*bacalao* (salted codfish)
is a great favourite, here prepared *a la riojana*—
stewed with olive oil, garlic, and *pimientos*, the
firm red peppers so characteristic of the cuisine
here, whether used whole, or ground into
pungent powder. Although the white wine is
good and plentiful, many here are just as content to drink the fine red wines of the region with
such forthright food.

Indeed, the red wines of the Rioja really come
into their own when accompanied by the robust
but basically simple foods of the region. A great
speciality is *cordero asado*, milk-fed lamb (*lechazo*),
which is simply roasted in an oak-fired baker's

Piles of squash and melons for sale by a road in Andalusia.

Quantities where necessary are given in
Metric, Imperial and US measurements.

Tapas

An attractive and impressive array of *tapas* can be put together with very little effort. Ham, salami, or *chorizo* cubed and speared on toothpicks; marinated artichoke hearts; large prawns in the shell; small crusts of bread spread with meat paste; fresh dates wrapped in ham; dried figs; toasted almonds; stuffed olives; cubes of cheese; fried slices of aubergine (eggplant); cubes of deep-fried fish or squid rings; marinated mushrooms; stuffed eggs; *tortilla*. Here are recipes for a few simple ones.

Hongos a la Vinagreta
Marinated Mushrooms
1 kg/2 lb large firm mushrooms
300 ml/$\frac{1}{2}$ pint/1$\frac{1}{4}$ cups wine or cider vinegar
150 ml/$\frac{1}{4}$ pint/$\frac{2}{3}$ cup olive oil
10 black peppercorns
2 garlic cloves, peeled and crushed
Sprig of fresh dill (or $\frac{1}{2}$ tsp dried dill)
Salt

Wash mushrooms gently. Place in a large screw-topped jar, or in 2 jars. Combine and simmer remaining ingredients in a saucepan for about 15 min. Add this liquid to the jar, cover tightly, and leave for at least 1 day.

Serve on a platter, with toothpicks speared through the stems.

Huevos Rellenos
Stuffed Eggs
8 hard-boiled eggs
150 ml/$\frac{1}{4}$ pint/$\frac{2}{3}$ cup mayonnaise
Salt
Freshly ground black pepper
1 or more of the following: dry mustard, tomato purée (paste), cayenne pepper, Worcestershire sauce, anchovy paste, chopped pickles, capers.

Slice eggs in half lengthwise. Carefully remove egg yolks without damaging the whites. Mix egg yolks with mayonnaise, salt, and black pepper. Then add any of the suggested flavourings. Mix well, and stuff into egg whites just before serving. Decorate with sliced olives, chopped peppers, or anchovy fillets.

Tortilla
Spanish Omelette
3 tbsp olive oil
2 large onions, peeled and chopped
2 large potatoes, peeled and diced
6 eggs
Salt
Freshly ground black pepper

Heat oil in a large frying pan. Add onion and potatoes. Cover and cook gently for 20–25 min.

Meanwhile, beat eggs in a large mixing bowl. When vegetables are tender, remove them with a slotted spoon, add to beaten eggs, and mix well. Discard most of the fat from the frying pan, and re-heat pan. Pour in egg mixture, lower the heat, and cook until it begins to set. Now, place frying pan under a pre-heated grill, and brown the top of the *tortilla*.

When cooked, it should be as solid as a cake. Cut into wedges, and eat hot or cold.

Calamares Fritos
Fried Squid Rings
500 g/1 lb small squid
Enough water and flour batter to coat squid
Oil for deep frying
Lemon

Wash the squid and remove the ink bags, tentacles, and plastic-like spine. Cut the bodies into thin rings, dry thoroughly, and dip into batter. Deep fry until crisp, and serve hot with quarters of the lemon.

Suggested wine with *tapas*:
Fino sherry

Gazpacho

Chilled Summer Soup
Serves 4

3 tbsp fresh white breadcrumbs
4 large ripe tomatoes, peeled and finely chopped
½ cucumber, peeled and finely chopped
3 green peppers, de-seeded and finely chopped
1 onion, peeled and finely chopped
4 tbsp olive oil
900 ml/1½ pints/3¾ cups cold water
10 almonds, crushed
2 garlic cloves, peeled and crushed
3 tbsp wine vinegar
Salt
Freshly ground black pepper

Put breadcrumbs, tomatoes, cucumber, green peppers, onion, and olive oil in a large bowl. Stir in cold water, and leave for 1 hr.

Purée the mixture, and season to taste. Add almonds, garlic, and wine vinegar. Chill for several hours, and serve with some of the cut-up cucumbers, pepper, and onion as garnish.

Suggested wines:
Sangria, Fino sherry

Mejillones a Jerez

Mussels in Sherry
Serves 4

2.4 litres/4 pints mussels
2 garlic cloves, peeled and crushed
3 tbsp olive oil
1 onion, peeled and chopped
1 tbsp flour
150 ml/¼ pint/⅔ cup fino sherry
Freshly chopped parsley

Scrape and scrub mussels under running cold water. Remove beards. Put into a large bucket of cold water, add a handful of bran, and leave overnight.

Wash mussels well. Boil 2½ cm/1 in of water in a large wide saucepan. Add mussels, and cook briskly until shells open, about 10 min. Drain,

reserve cooking liquid, and discard any that have not opened.

Meanwhile, heat oil in a large frying pan, and sauté onions and garlic until soft and golden. Sprinkle with flour, and cook for further 5 min. Stir in strained mussel stock, mussels, and sherry. Heat gently for 2 or 3 min., and serve immediately, with parsley, as a first course.

Suggested wines:
Fino sherry, white Rioja

Alubias con Chorizo

Beans with Spiced Pepper Sausage
Serves 6

1.5 litres/2½ pints/6¼ cups cold water
500 g/1 lb haricot beans (soaked in water overnight)
1 onion, peeled and chopped
3 garlic cloves, 2 crushed, the other left whole
200 g/7 oz chorizo, cut into 2½ cm/1 in pieces
2 tbsp sweet paprika
2 tbsp olive oil
Freshly chopped parsley
Salt

Put water in a large saucepan. Add beans, onion, whole garlic clove, and *chorizo*. Bring to the boil, and simmer, partially covered, for 3–4 min.

Heat oil in a frying pan, and sauté crushed garlic. Remove from heat, and stir in paprika. Add this to the beans and *chorizo*. Add parsley, and cook for about 1½ hr., or until tender. Season with salt halfway through cooking.

Serve in bowls, as a first course.

Suggested wine:
Rioja reserva

Pimientos a la Riojana

Stewed Red Peppers
Serves 4

3 large red sweet peppers
3 garlic cloves, peeled and cut into 2 or 3 pieces
150 ml/ $\frac{1}{4}$ pt/ $\frac{2}{3}$ cup olive oil

Roast peppers over an open fire or gas flame until their skins turn completely black. Peel under running water, and cut into strips.

Heat olive oil in a saucepan. Add garlic, and stew gently. Add peppers, and cook for further 5 min.

Serve as a first course, or as a side dish.

Suggested wine:
Rioja Alta tinto

Cordero Asado

Roast Baby Lamb
Serves 4

1.5 kg/3 lb shoulder of spring lamb
Salt
Freshly ground black pepper
1 garlic clove, peeled
150 ml/ $\frac{1}{4}$ pt/ $\frac{2}{3}$ cup red Rioja

Season lamb with salt and pepper, and rub with garlic. Place in an earthenware pan, and add wine. Bake in a pre-heated oven, 200°C/Gas Mark 6/400°F, for 20 min., then reduce temperature to 180°C/Gas Mark 4/350°F, for remaining time, about 45–60 min., or until lamb is browned on the outside and very tender. Baste with pan juices from time to time.

Serve straight from earthenware pan, and tear into pieces at the table with knife and fork.

Suggested wines:
Rioja Alavesa reserva or gran reserva

Perdices a la Torera

Bullfighter's Partridge
Serves 2

2 partridges (or 1 small chicken, pheasant,
or rabbit)
50 g/2 oz bacon, finely chopped
50 g/2 oz anchovies, finely chopped
2 large tomatoes, sliced
1 large green pepper, chopped
1 tbsp freshly chopped parsley
Salt
Freshly ground black pepper
150 ml/ $\frac{1}{4}$ pt/ $\frac{2}{3}$ cup dry white wine
2 slices ham

Stuff partridges with bacon and anchovies, then put them in an ovenproof casserole, surrounded by tomatoes and green pepper. Add parsley, and season with salt and pepper. Pour on wine, and cook in a moderate oven, 180°C/Gas Mark 4/350°F, for 1 hr. Add a little more wine if necessary, although amount of liquid should be small.

Fry ham slices just before the partridges are done. Place them on the ham, and serve immediately.

Suggested wines:
Dry oloroso, white Rioja

Menestra de Verduras

Mixed Vegetable Stew
Serves 6

250 g/½ lb broad beans, shelled
250 g/½ lb fresh peas, shelled
250 g/½ lb potatoes, peeled and chopped
2 tbsp olive oil
1 onion, peeled and chopped
50 g/2 oz bacon, diced
50 g/2 oz ham, diced
3 stalks celery, cut into short lengths
2 bay leaves
150 ml/¼ pt/⅔ cup light red Rioja
2 large tomatoes, peeled and chopped
2 garlic cloves, peeled
Large pinch of saffron
6 white peppercorns
Freshly chopped parsley
Outer leave of 1 coarse lettuce, chopped
3 hard-boiled eggs, sliced

Boil broad beans, peas, and potatoes all separately. Cook until just tender, drain, and set aside. Heat oil in a large casserole, and sauté onion until soft and golden. Add bacon, ham, celery, and bay leaves, and cook for further 5–10 min. Add wine, and allow to reduce a little. Stir in tomatoes, then add cooked beans, peas, and potatoes. Mix well. Meanwhile, pound garlic, saffron, and pepper together in a mortar. Add a little water, and add this to casserole. Add parsley and lettuce. Season with salt. Cover, and cook gently for 10 min. Add a little water, if necessary, to prevent sticking.

Serve hot, decorated with slices of hard-boiled eggs, as a first course.

Suggested wines:
Rioja vino de crianza, rosado (rosé)

Crema de Chocolate

Chocolate Mousse
Serves 6

250 g/8oz/8 squares dark chocolate
25 g/1 oz/¼ stick butter
1 tsp vanilla essence
Grated rind and juice of 1 orange
4 egg yolks, beaten
4 egg whites, beaten until stiff
150 ml/¼ pt/⅔ cup double cream
50 g/2 oz/½ cup chopped almonds

Gently melt chocolate and butter in a saucepan. When thoroughly melted, remove from heat and blend in vanilla, orange rind and juice. Beat in egg yolks, one at a time. Gently fold in egg whites. Pour into a glass bowl, or 6 individual glasses, and chill for about 4 hr.

Serve decorated with whipped cream and chopped almonds.

THE BALKANS

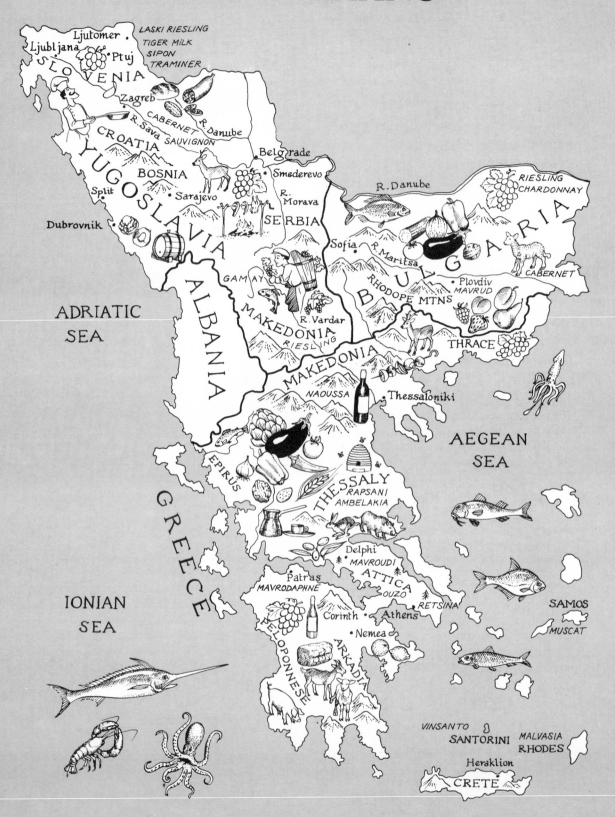

LASKI RIESLING
TIGER MILK
SIPON
TRAMINER

Ljutomer
Ljubljana
Ptuj
SLOVENIA
Zagreb
CABERNET
R. Sava SAUVIGNON
R. Danube
CROATIA
YUGOSLAVIA
BOSNIA
Split
Sarajevo
Dubrovnik
Belgrade
Smederevo
R. Morava
SERBIA
Sofia
GAMAY
MAKEDONIA
RIESLING
R. Vardar
MAKEDONIA

R. Danube
RIESLING
CHARDONNAY
B U L G A R I A
R. Maritsa
Plovdiv
MAVRUD
RHODOPE MTNS
CABERNET
THRACE

ALBANIA

ADRIATIC
SEA

NAOUSSA
Thessaloniki

AEGEAN
SEA

EPIRUS
THESSALY
RAPSANI
AMBELAKIA

GREECE

Delphi
MAVROUDI
ATTICA
OUZO
RETSINA

IONIAN
SEA

Patras
MAVRODAPHNE
Corinth
Athens
Nemea
PELOPONNESE
ARKADIA

SAMOS
MUSCAT

VINSANTO
SANTORINI
MALVASIA
RHODES

Heraklion
CRETE

GREECE

It is a balmy, close evening, and moonlight rests on wine-dark waters. The outdoor tables of the *taverna* are loaded with a feast of *orektika*—appetisers such as *taramosaláta*, cold meat balls, plump olives, fried fish, rings of squid, yoghurt and cucumber, tomatoes stuffed with rice and pine nuts, and much else. Ouzo is drunk out of assorted small or chipped tumblers. Its heady anise aroma mixes with the acidity of the charcoal grill, the warm secret musk of wild *rigani*, sage, rosemary, mimosa, and a thousand other scents of summer. In the distance, the whining, twanging cadence of the *bouzouki* mingles with the night, and we are left to contemplate the unchanged elements of this ancient and rugged land.

More so than anywhere else in Europe, Greek food and wine are linked to a way of life that is at once indigenous and timeless. The sea of olive trees that extends below Delphi to the Gulf of Corinth is said to have belonged once to the god Apollo. Sheep and shaggy goats still clamber over rocky Arkadia, ancient land of myths and legends. Weathered fishermen brave Poseidon's wrath, with fishing methods unchanged for centuries. And olive oil, wild herbs, honey, nuts, and wine are the basis of a cooking style with roots several thousand years old.

The vineyards of Greece are timeless. The legend of Dionysus, god of wine, is traced from the earliest age throughout Mediterranean lands. Certain vineyards were already famous for their wine as early as the ninth century BC. The Greeks also took the vine with them to lands they colonized. Thus, many vineyards in Italy, the Rhône valley, Jerez de la Frontera, and Málaga are of Greek origin. And when the Romans came

to Greece they took back with them not only Greek wine, which was highly esteemed, but also Greek viticulture.

The Greeks have always known the importance of wine and food as a warm and civilizing influence. Nearly 3,000 years ago, Homer's hero Odysseus, longing to return to his home in Ithaka, asserted, 'There is no moment more pleasurable than when guests and feasters sit at a table laden with breads and meats, and listen to the voice of the singer, while the wine steward draws wine from the mixing bowl to pour into each cup in turn. This is the best of all occasions.'

The vine today grows in seeming haphazard abundance on the Greek mainland, and on many of the islands, providing a variety of red, white, and pink table wines, dry or sweet, frail or heavyweight. Though Greek wine today makes few claims to greatness, it is honest and clean, and contributes wholeheartedly to the festive atmosphere of a Greek meal.

The most individual and distinctive type of wine is undoubtedly retsina, much of which comes from the region of Attica, above Athens. It is quite unlike any other wine in the world, because during fermentation, pine resin is infused, imparting to it a distinctive sappy flavour. The ancient Greeks drank similar wine, as evidenced by archaeological finds of pine resin in clay wine jugs or mixing bowls. Some believe the pine resin was added to the wine because of its preservative property. Once there, it remained, and indeed retsina is a favourite throughout Greece as a sharp counterpart to the country's rather rich and oily food. Most retsina is white, though there is also an agreeable light-pink variety called kokkineli. Both are delicious with grilled meats, oily dips, and rich or salty Greek cheese, because strange though the wine tastes on its own, in conjunction with the foods it is meant to accompany it is perfectly natural and appetizing.

The Peloponnese, an unwieldy southern protuberance that extends below the Gulf of Corinth, is another important wine region. The peninsula boasts some of the most famous and important ruins of ancient Greece—Mycenae, Epidaurus, Olympia, Sparta, Corinth, and many others. The gnarled vines placidly, almost indifferently growing amid the columned ruins of that Golden Age remind that yesterday and today are intertwined.

Full-bodied red wine has been produced in vineyards in and around Nemea for at least 2,500 years. The wine is well-made, deep, dark, and strong; maturation in oak casks gives it an attractive mellow softness. Nemea is popular both in Greece and abroad since more Greek wine is now being exported. Fine dessert wine is produced in vineyards around Patras. Muscat de Patras is one such, while Mavrodaphne is a sweet red wine—thick, dark, and heady. Makedonia, to the north, produces what many consider to be the best red wine in Greece, Naoussa, deep, extremely dark and powerful, and astringently dry. Rapsani and Ambelakia (both red) come from Thessalia, while from near ancient Delphi comes Mavroudi, another well-liked red.

Most of the islands produce enough table wine for local consumption. Crete, for example, produces a variety of heavy golden or dark red wines, some of which are fortified. Malvasia, another sweet dessert wine, is the speciality of the island of Rhodes. The volcanic island of Santorini produces mineral-rich Vinsanto, while the island of Samos still boasts the Muscat for which Byron called, 'Fill high the bowl with Samian wine!'

Greece is a land of rugged honesty, which her wine reflects. Life is hard here, but Greek food too makes do with ingredients and produce abundantly at hand.

Greek cooking is based on olive oil, not surprisingly, since this tough tree is native to the eastern Mediterranean. Symbol of peace, crown to the victor in Olympic or Delphic games, it appears everywhere, an important element in everyday life. The oil from its fruit is green, heavy, and strongly flavoured, and lends an unmistakable scent to any dish prepared with it. Olives are gathered by laying a system of nets under the trees. The fruit is then crushed, and the oil extracted in a centrifuge. Meat and fish are fried in olive oil; game is marinated in it; salads are dressed with it; vegetables are preserved in it; dips are garnished with it; and at times it seems virtually everything is bathed in it, for flavour if nothing else. And the olive fruit itself, of course, is eaten in great quantity. Green olives, by the

The ruins of Delphi, the site of the legendary oracle.

The sparse countryside of Arkadia in the central Peloponnese.

The rugged country around Mycenae.

way, are unripe olives that turn black as they ripen, but, green or black, they must be treated in brine before they are edible.

Seafood plays an important role in the diet of the Greeks. The warm Aegean yields a colourful catch of octopus, squid, red and grey mullet, sea bass, sea bream, swordfish, and much else. Trout, carp, crayfish, and eels come from freshwater lakes and rivers. And dried salt cod, as in other Mediterranean countries, is also a favourite.

The hot Mediterranean sun ripens vegetables and fruit until they are bursting with a freshness and flavour that simple cooking enhances. Aubergines (eggplants), beans, peas, and artichokes accompany main dishes. Large, firm tomatoes, cabbage leaves, courgettes (zucchini), and vine leaves are often stuffed with mixtures of rice, ground lamb, herbs, spices, and nuts, cooked in stock, then bathed in a simple lemon and egg sauce (avgolémono). Indeed, vegetables often combine with meat in delicious ways. Since meat is relatively scarce, inventive dishes make do with little of it. Moussaká, for example, combines ground lamb and aubergine in a flavourful white sauce.

Pungent wild herbs like rigani (a type of oregano), as well as lemon juice, garlic, dill seed, anise, and cumin season the food. Sesame seeds, sunflower seeds, almonds, pistachio nuts, walnuts, and pine kernels, combine with fragrant mountain honey, cinnamon, and rose or orange flower water to produce a variety of sticky cakes, pastries, and confectionery. Baklava, made with layers of thin phyllo pastry, honey, butter, and nuts, or kataifi, which are like balls of honey-soaked shredded wheat, are not usually eaten as desserts, but rather accompany a cup of murky, muddy, extremely sweet coffee brewed in an individual pot of ancient beaten copper.

Greek meals are never rushed. One is led effortlessly into them. The feast of orektika, appetizers that always precede the meal, serves as much to set the pace of an evening as to sustain. Indeed, an hour, two hours, even longer can be spent nibbling olives and nuts, taramosaláta (dip made from smoked cod's roe), hummus (purée of chick-peas and garlic), tzatziki (yoghurt and cucumber), cold stuffed dolmathes (vine leaves), tyrópitta (layered cheese pie), bits of fried fish, wild onions, or salted sardines. Ouzo, that clear anise-flavoured spirit that turns cloudy when mixed with water, makes a persuasive aperitif that livens and animates conversation.

Lamb and pork are often simply cooked over a charcoal fire, threaded on to skewers (souvlakia) and basted with lemon juice and oil, then sprinkled with rosemary or rigani. A sprig of fresh herbs is placed in the fire to give the air, as well as the food, a beautiful charred scent of the mountains. Fish is likewise barbecued out of doors.

Greek summer salad relies upon freshness for its flavour—chunks of tomato, slices of green and red pepper, large mild onions and cucumber are combined with salty Feta cheese, dusted with rigani, and doused liberally with olive oil. Greek cheese, usually made from sheep's or goat's milk, is both delicious to eat on its own and used extensively in the kitchen. Apart from crumbly Feta, Kasseri (firm and mild) is good with coarse bread and a glass of wine, while Myzithra (a sort of fresh cottage cheese) is used to make savoury pies and sweets. Greek yoghurt, also made from sheep's milk, is thick, creamy, and luxurious. A supremely simple dessert is homemade yoghurt with honey, dried figs, and chopped nuts. Another is yoghurt with fruit —strawberries, peaches, oranges, grapes, melons.

This country is at once rocky and sparse, lush and warm. While the Turks were still 'cooking' by placing a slab of meat between their saddle and the horse, then riding like the devil, the ancient Greeks developed a simple, practical cuisine to conform with the full-flavoured ingredients and produce available. Greek cooking (and cooks) travelled far afield. When the Turks eventually conquered the Balkan Peninsula, Greek dishes acquired Turkish names, but survived intact to modern times. Greeks today can boast of an indigenous cooking style that, having influenced European cuisine profoundly, remains distinct, exciting, active.

The charcoal fire, so elemental, fills the night air with its irresistible perfume. And sappy, fresh retsina, tasting of pine, not grape, whets the appetite in anticipation of the simple, special meal that always follows—as constant as the Aegean, conversation, company, and warmth: the essence of Greek hospitality.

The olive groves of Amphissa below Delphi which lead to the Gulf of Corinth.

Olives are harvested by laying an intricate system of nets under the trees to catch the fruit.

The wide variety of olives for sale in the central market in Athens.

A shop in Athens selling olives and oil.

RECIPES FROM GREECE

Quantities where necessary are given in
Metric, Imperial and US measurements.

Taramosaláta

Smoked Fish Roe Dip
Serves 4–6

250 g/½ lb smoked cod's roe
100 g/4 oz/4 slices soft white bread, crustless
300 ml/½ pt/1¼ cups Greek olive oil
Juice of 1 or 2 lemons
1 garlic clove, peeled and crushed
Freshly chopped parsley
Freshly ground black pepper

Remove skin from cod's roe, and mash to a pulp
in a mixing bowl. Soak bread in warm water
until soft. Squeeze dry, and crumble into the roe.
Combine the two, mixing well. Gradually add
oil until mixture has the consistency of a purée.
Add crushed garlic and enough lemon juice to
loosen it. Season. The paste should be pearly pink
and smooth.

Serve chilled and garnished with chopped
parsley.

Serve as *orektika* with ouzo

Tzatziki

Cucumber and Yoghurt Salad
Serves 4–6

1 small cucumber, peeled and thinly sliced
300 ml/½ pt/1¼ cups natural yoghurt
Juice of ½ lemon
1 garlic clove, peeled and crushed
1 tbsp Greek olive oil
Salt

Combine all ingredients together, and serve
chilled.

Serve as *orektika* with ouzo

Pitta

Greek Pocket Bread
Makes 8–10

1 tsp sugar
25 g/1 oz active dry yeast
300 ml/½ pt/1¼ cups tepid water
500 g/1 lb/3½ cups flour
1½ tsp salt
3 tbsp olive oil

Dissolve sugar and yeast in tepid water, and mix
well. Allow to stand in a warm spot for 5 min.

Combine flour and salt together in a large
bowl. Rub oil into flour with fingertips until it is
all worked in. Make a well in the middle of the
flour and pour in yeast mixture. Form into a
dough, and knead for 5 min. Turn ball of dough
on to a floured board, cover with a damp cloth,
and leave in warm place for 1 hr.

Divide it into about 8 equal pieces, and roll
out each piece of dough into a circle about 5 mm/
¼ in thick. Put them on to greased baking trays,
and cook in a hot oven, 240°C/Gas Mark 8/
450°F, for 8 min., or until golden.

Eat with *tzatziki, taramosaláta* and *hummus*.

Tirontomáta

Greek Salad
Serves 6

6 tomatoes, cut into wedges
1 cucumber, cut into chunks
1 onion, peeled and thinly sliced
2 green peppers, sliced into rings
6 tbsp olive oil
2 tbsp wine vinegar
Salt
Freshly ground black pepper
250 g/$\frac{1}{2}$ lb Feta cheese
2 dozen black olives
Oregano

Put all the vegetables in a large salad bowl. Mix together olive oil, wine vinegar, salt and pepper, and pour over the salad. Toss well. Cut cheese into small chunks, and lay on top of the salad. Add olives, and dust with oregano.

Suggested wine:
Retsina

Avgolémono

Egg and Lemon Soup
Serves 4

1.2 l/2 pt/5 cups home-made chicken stock
50 g/2 oz/$\frac{1}{3}$ cup rice
2 egg yolks
Juice of 1$\frac{1}{2}$ lemons
Salt
Freshly ground black pepper

Bring chicken stock to the boil. Add rice, cover, and simmer for about 25 min. Meanwhile, beat egg yolks well, and gradually whisk in lemon juice. When they are well mixed, gradually add 150 ml/$\frac{1}{4}$ pt/$\frac{2}{3}$ cup of the hot stock. When rice is cooked, add the egg and lemon sauce, stirring continuously. Continue to cook over a very low heat until the soup is hot, but do not boil. Serve at once.

Suggested wine:
Retsina

Souvlakia

Lamb on Skewers
Serves 6

1 leg of lamb, boned (approx. 1.5 kg/3 lb)
Salt
Freshly ground black pepper
Marjoram
6 tomatoes, quartered
18 small bay leaves
2 medium onions, peeled and cut into chunks
100 ml/$\frac{1}{5}$ pt/$\frac{1}{2}$ cup olive oil
Juice of 1 lemon
Oregano
1 lettuce, chopped
Lemon wedges

Cut lamb into 2$\frac{1}{2}$ cm/1 in cubes, and season with salt, pepper, and marjoram. Thread on to long skewers alternately the meat, tomatoes, bay leaves, and chunks of onion. Brush with olive oil and lemon juice, and sprinkle with oregano. Grill over a charcoal fire, and serve on a thick bed of chopped lettuce garnished with lemon wedges. (There should be enough lamb for about 12 skewers.)

Suggested wine:
Retsina

Dolmathes

Stuffed Vine leaves
Serves 6

30 vine leaves
5 tbsp olive oil
1 large onion, peeled and finely chopped
90 g/3 oz/½ cup rice
Finely chopped fresh parsley
Finely chopped fresh mint
50 g/2 oz/⅓ cup currants
2 tbsp pine nuts
1 tbsp finely chopped dill
Juice of 1 lemon
Salt
Freshly ground black pepper
Slices of lemon for garnish

Wash vine leaves well in cold water to remove brine. Pour boiling water over them, drain, and dry on kitchen towel. Heat 2 tbsp oil in a large frying pan. Add onion, and sauté until soft and golden. Add rice, cover, and cook for 5 min. Then add parsley, mint, currants, pine nuts, and dill. Season to taste.

Cover bottom of a shallow pan with layer of vine leaves. Stuff remaining leaves by placing spoonful of the rice mixture in the centre of the leaf, shiny surface downwards. Fold leaf, like an envelope, over the mixture, and roll up, tucking edges in neatly. (Do not roll too tightly, or put too much stuffing in, as rice will expand.)

Layer stuffed leaves in pan with folded side face down. Pour over them 3 tbsp olive oil, lemon juice, and enough hot water to cover. Place a heavy plate upside down over the *dolmathes* to prevent from opening. Cover, bring to the boil, and simmer over a low heat for 45 min. Allow to cool in the saucepan. Garnish with slices of lemon.

Serve chilled, with yoghurt, or hot, with egg and lemon sauce.

Suggested wines:
Dry white table wine (Demestica, Hymettus), Retsina

Styphatho

Beef and Onion Stew
Serves 4–6

1 kg/2 lb lean chuck steak cut into 2½ cm/1 in cubes
2 tbsp olive oil
Salt
Freshly ground black pepper
150 ml/¼ pt/⅔ cup red wine
4 tbsp red wine vinegar
1 bay leaf
1 tsp rosemary
6 black peppercorns
1 tsp allspice
3 tbsp tomato purée (paste)
1 tbsp honey
1 kg/2 lb small white onions, peeled
2 garlic cloves, peeled and chopped
Freshly chopped parsley

In a heavy-bottomed casserole, brown meat in olive oil. Season well. Add wine, vinegar, seasonings, tomato purée, and honey. Add enough water to cover meat comfortably. Bring to the boil, cover, and simmer until meat is just tender (about 1½ hr).

Meanwhile, sauté onions and garlic in olive oil until a light golden colour. Add to the pot, and continue to simmer until onions are tender, but not over-cooked.

Serve garnished with parsley.

Suggested wines:
Naoussa or Nemea

Moussaká

Baked Aubergine
Serves 4–6

2 medium aubergines (egg plants)
4 tbsp olive oil
1 large onion, peeled and chopped
1 garlic clove, peeled and crushed
500 g/1 lb minced (ground) lamb
1 tsp cinnamon
1 tbsp oregano
Freshly chopped parsley
Salt
Freshly ground black pepper
1 large tin tomatoes
2 tbsp toasted breadcrumbs

For the sauce
25 g/1 oz/2 tbsp butter
1 tbsp flour
450 ml/$\frac{3}{4}$ pt/2 cups hot milk
Salt
Freshly ground black pepper
2 egg yolks
100 g/4 oz/1 cup grated cheese

Thinly slice aubergines lengthwise. Salt, and leave to stand for about 1 hr. Pat dry. Heat oil in a large frying pan, and fry slices until soft and slightly brown on both sides. Remove from pan, and drain on kitchen towel. Add more oil to pan, and repeat until all slices have been fried. Sauté onion and garlic until golden. Add lamb, and fry until browned. Add cinnamon, oregano, parsley, salt, and pepper. Stir in tomatoes. Bring to the boil, and allow to simmer for about 45 min. Grease a large ovenproof dish, and sprinkle bottom with toasted breadcrumbs. Then put in alternate layers of aubergine slices and meat.

To prepare the sauce, melt butter in a saucepan, and stir in flour. Cook over a low heat for 2 min., stirring constantly. Remove from heat, and gradually stir in hot milk. Return pan to heat, bring to the boil, stirring constantly. Simmer until sauce thickens. Season to taste. Remove from heat, and stir beaten egg yolks into sauce. Add two-thirds of the cheese, and mix well. Spoon sauce over aubergines and meat. Sprinkle with remaining cheese, and bake in a moderate oven, 180°C/Gas Mark 4/350°F, for 45 min., until top is golden.

Serve piping hot, with a salad.

Suggested wines:
Nemea, Mavroudi

Baklava

Pastry Filled with Nuts and Honey
Makes about 2 doz

500 g/1 lb phyllo (this layered pastry can be bought already made from many specialist shops)
350 g/12 oz/1$\frac{1}{2}$ cups melted butter
500 g/1 lb walnuts or almonds, finely chopped
100 g/4 oz/$\frac{1}{2}$ cup sugar
1 tbsp cinnamon

For the syrup
500 g/1 lb/2 cups honey
300 ml/$\frac{1}{2}$ pt/1$\frac{1}{4}$ cups water
Juice of 1 lemon
3 cloves
1 tsp cinnamon

Butter the bottom and sides of a large baking pan about 40 cm × 30 cm/16 in × 12 in. Lay a sheet of *phyllo* in it, and brush with melted butter. Place a second pastry sheet on top of the first, and butter again. In this way, butter about 8 layers of *phyllo*. Mix nuts with sugar and cinnamon. Sprinkle over top *phyllo*. Over this, place a sheet of *phyllo*, butter it, and sprinkle with nut mixture. Repeat until all nuts have been used up. Over all this, layer and butter 8 more pastry sheets. Brush top with remaining butter, and with a sharp knife trim edges. Cut diagonal lines across pan to make diamond shapes. Bake the *baklava* in a moderate oven, 180°C/Gas Mark 4/350°F, for about 1 hr., or until golden.

To prepare the syrup, boil honey, water, lemon, cloves, and cinnamon together for 10 min. Then spoon the hot syrup over cooked *baklava*. Allow to stand for several hours before serving. Do not refrigerate, but keep in a cool place.

Suggested drink:
Greek coffee

Down below the ragged rim of the Austrian Alps, east of Venice and Trieste, are lands that seem to lie beyond the pale of the rest of Europe. Slovenia, the Yugoslav republic closest to Italy and Austria, and former province of the Habsburg Empire, is familiarly western, its capital city Ljubljana not too dissimilar from other modern European cities. Parts of the Dalmatian coast, too, once ruled by the Venetian Republic, have that slow-paced, heavenly-scented feel of the Mediterranean. But what of inland Croatia, steamy, exotic Serbia, Makedonia, or Bosnia, whose native son Gavrilo Princip sparked off a world war when, in a fit of nationalist fervour, he assassinated the Habsburg heir, Archduke Franz Ferdinand?

What, too, of the Bulgarian People's Republic, a 1,300-year-old nation bordered on the east by the Black Sea and Turkey? Long before the Roman legions came, a civilization known as the Thracians inhabited this European outpost, and produced staggeringly beautiful artefacts of gold. For centuries the dusty plain named after them was the most important trade route in Europe. It led to Byzantium, eastern capital of the Roman Empire, later named Constantinople, and today known as Istanbul, a city poised literally between Europe and Asia. Not only did the Romans advance over this strategic land route, so also did Attila the Hun, opportunistic crusaders, and finally, expanding from the east, the Turks themselves, who ruled Bulgaria and parts of Yugoslavia for no less than five centuries.

It was the Turkish occupation, as much as anything, that kept southern Yugoslavia and all of Bulgaria separated from the rest of Europe, and even today it colours the peculiar atmosphere

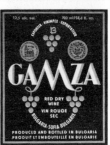

and flavour of these two countries. Indeed it was the frantic, too often frustrated desire to break from a centuries-old yoke of imperialism (Turkish, Austro-Hungarian, Venetian) that fomented such turbulence earlier this century. Today Yugoslavia and Bulgaria are developing Communist states that bear not only the rifts, tears, and scars of their vivid pasts, but also the warmth and complex richness of their Balkan heritage.

The food of these two countries reflects this heteromix and is quite simply among the most exciting, direct, and wholesome found anywhere in Europe. In Slovenia the influence of Vienna is apparent in dishes such as *ljubljanski zrezek* (veal escalope layered with ham and egg, breaded, and fried), which is no more than a variation of the famous *Weiner Schnitzel*. Fondness for *Strudel*, pastries, and pancakes (*palacinke*) are also culinary reminders of Austro-Hungarian dominance. In Makedonia, on the other hand, the flavours of Greece (not surprisingly, in the home province of Alexander the Great) mingle

with dishes introduced by the Muslims. Pasta, *risotto*, and rich fish soups and stews have crossed the Adriatic from Italy and appear equally at home on the Dalmatian table. Serbian food is exciting and rich, combining fiery fish stews and soups reminiscent of those found in Hungary (the Danube, after all, passes through Belgrade as well as Budapest) with grilled meats and cooked vegetable dishes. In Bulgaria, a rich and flavourful Balkan cuisine relies on lamb, combinations of meat and peppers, aubergines, tomatoes, spices and seasonings, and cheese and yoghurt. In this farthest outpost of Europe, Turkish—not Slavic—influence is veiled behind the spicy, intriguing scents that emanate from the kitchen.

Turkish domination of the Balkans may well have been profound. A fondness for desserts made from honey and nuts remains in both countries as well as a taste for murky, supersweet, and almost chewy *turska kava* (Turkish coffee), made in long-handled ancient copper pots. Despite the Muslim ban on alcohol, however, today both Yugoslavia and Bulgaria produce a variety of sound and solid table wines that go perfectly with the varied foods of these lands. An added bonus for us is that these wines are distinct and readily available abroad—and also relatively inexpensive.

One of the best known of such wines is Laski Riesling, a popular, medium-dry, white thirst-quencher that comes from Slovenian vineyards in wine communes such as Ljutomer, Maribor, and Ptuj. This wine region, which is a virtual extension of the Styrian vineyards of southern Austria, has probably been cultivated since Roman days at least. So pleasant is the area that ingenious crusaders who had taken a holy vow to fight the infidel stopped short in these vine-covered hills, founded their own 'Jerusalem', and stayed to live in a land that still seems not far short of the promised one. The tiny town of Jerusalem, just a few miles from Ljutomer (the town that gives its name to many of the region's wines), is perched atop one of a series of green and rounded hills that stretch to the Austrian border, and the vineyards on these slopes are some of the region's best. If it is not quite a land of milk and honey, it is certainly one of good food and wine.

Cleaning barrels in preparation for new wine near Ljutomer.

The soft, fruity, and primarily white wines

Alfresco lunch in a garden in Slovenia.

produced here and in other nearby communes wash down home-made salami, air-dried ham and cold smoked meats, coarse country bread, pickled cucumbers, and tomatoes. (Though many claim that pickled vegetables should never be served with wine, such caveats are rarely heeded in wine districts like this; indeed, on a midsummer day, eating and drinking out of doors at a table set up in a farmyard, such subtle and delicate distinctions are of no importance whatsoever.)

As well as the popular Laski Riesling, which is the Italian or Welsch grape variety, a pungent, almost overpoweringly aromatic wine is produced from the Gewürztraminer (Traminec). This distinctive, unmistakable grape produces wine that may lack the delicacy of that produced from the same grape in Alsace, but which more than makes up for it in richness and fruity aroma. Indeed, some of the best wines of this lush region, such as Tigrovo Mleko (Tiger Milk) are golden wines produced from late-picked grapes with a luscious natural sweetness and a low acidity. Wines produced from the Sauvignon, Beli Burgundec (Pinot Blanc), and Sipon (Hungarian Furmint), on the other hand, are crisp, forceful, and refreshing. The sweeter wines accompany Viennese- and Hungarian-inspired sweetmeats and pastries, while the dry wines are perfect partners to charcoal-grilled specialities such as *čevapčiči* (skewered pork and veal meatballs), *ražnjici* (cubes of skewered meat), and *pljeskavica*

On Sunday mornings, deep in Bulgaria's Rila mountains, people come from miles to worship in the Rilski Monastery.

ripen within sight of the Danube, or perhaps a flask of simple *crno vino* (red wine), deep, dark red, and powerful.

Such robust and honest table wines are made throughout Yugoslavia, some from native grapes, others from more familiar imports such as Cabernet, Pinot Noir, and Gamay. In Bulgaria, too, wines produced from grapes originating in classic European vineyards are gaining favour. Cabernet Sauvignon, from the Suhindol district in central Bulgaria, is rich and aromatic, an unmistakable reminder of wine produced from this small, tough-skinned grape in Bordeaux and California. The Chardonnay, the great white grape of Burgundy and Champagne, thrives in vineyards near the Black Sea, where it produces firm, sound, white wine with a character of its own—fragrant, strong, even a little coarse, but eminently drinkable. Even that temperamental aristocrat, the Rhine Riesling, has adjusted to a climate almost perfectly suited to vine growing.

The most distinctive Bulgarian wine comes from a native variety, the deep, dark red Mavrud, grown on the lower slopes of the Rhodope mountains, above the Thracian plain, near Assenovgrad and Plovdiv. Mavrud is big, intense wine, which needs ageing to mellow a raw yet rich bouquet and flavour—a fitting partner to such characteristic Bulgar fare as *ghivetch*, a delicious lamb, vegetable, and hot pepper stew much loved here, that appears in a variety of guises throughout the Balkans (the word comes from the Turkish *güveç*, which is an earthenware cooking dish).

The Bulgars, of course, have a national passion for yoghurt. Indeed, the name of the bacteria responsible for this lactic fermentation, *lactobacillus bulgaricus*, indicates its origins, or at least its importance in the diet here. Bulgars are almost notorious for their longevity, and the huge quantities of yoghurt consumed, in conjunction with a well-balanced diet of raw and cooked vegetables and fruit, are believed to account at least in part for this. Bulgarian yoghurt is thick, tangy, and creamy, and is usually made from sheep's or goat's milk. Combined with cucumbers, chopped walnuts, garlic, and oil, it becomes a favourite chilled soup known as

(highly seasoned meat patties), all served hot off the grill with mounds of chopped raw onions and a mouth-searing red pepper purée.

Grilling meats over an open fire was, of course, one of the earliest ways of cooking. Throughout the Balkans, however, and in Serbia especially, this primitive method has been developed to perfection. There is something irresistibly basic about meat juices and fats dripping into a spitting, open fire—and nothing seems to whet the appetite quite like the smell of charred meat in anticipation of a Serbian 'mixed grill' of veal or pork chops, a slab of chicken breast, and a slice of tender calf's liver, speared together with a quartered raw onion, crunchy slices of green pepper, and searing hot chilli peppers. It is even more delicious with a carafe of strong, cool, white Smederevo, produced from grapes that

Harvesting Mavrud grapes on the Thracian plain near Assenovgrad.

A rural scene in Bulgaria; many of the country roads are still cobbled.

tarator. It is also used to enrich stews, as a dressing for cooked vegetables such as beetroot or aubergine, as a sauce for fish such as carp, and even in sweets and cakes. And, as if that were not enough, a heady and highly alcoholic version is a favourite pick-me-up. Hard, sourish cheeses are enjoyed in both Yugoslavia and Bulgaria, such as Kajmak from Serbia, which is both eaten on its own and used to make a layered cheese pie called *gibanica sa sirom*. In Bulgaria, sour goat's cheese is finely grated and piled over sliced tomatoes, cucumber, chopped raw onion, and hot peppers to make *shopska salata*, which often begins a meal.

Fruit is plentiful in both countries, and apricots, plums, raspberries, strawberries, pears, and peaches are all used to make delicious jams, jellies, *compotes*, and desserts. *Slatko*, a Serbian speciality of whole small fruit, such as plums or berries, cooked slowly in their own juices, is often served, as a gesture of hospitality, with a glass of water. In Bulgaria, one can spend joyous afternoons, communicating with new friends (in hilarious confusion, since a horizontal nod in this topsy-turvy Balkan state means '*da*'—yes—and a vertical shake is negative: '*ne*') while dipping occasionally into huge communal pots of home-made rose-hip jam. The drink to accompany this humble, sticky jam feast is not wine at all, but slívova, a frighteningly strong plum brandy, also popular in Yugoslavia, where it is known as sljivovica.

Yugoslavia and Bulgaria are foreign and faraway, their customs different from our own, and indeed the rest of Europe's. But they are not really 'beyond the pale' in any pejorative sense; rather, they are important and integral elements in the always varied, always exciting and rich tapestry woven of the wine lands of Europe.

Quantities where necessary are given in
Metric, Imperial and US measurements.

Shopska Salata

Bulgarian Summer Salad
Serves 4

1 large red or green pepper
4 medium tomatoes, finely diced
½ cucumber, peeled and finely diced
1 small onion, peeled and finely chopped
1 small hot chilli, seeded and chopped
2 tbsp sunflower oil
1 tbsp wine vinegar
Freshly chopped parsley
Salt
Freshly ground black pepper
100 g/¼ lb goat cheese or Feta cheese

Roast red or green pepper on a fork over a flame
until skin is black. Peel, seed, and chop coarsely.
Make a dressing from oil, salt, pepper, parsley,
and vinegar. Mix all chopped vegetables together, and dress.

Arrange individually on small plates, and
finely grate cheese over top.

Suggested wine:
Bulgarian Chardonnay

Yoghurt

1.2 l/2 pt/5 cups milk
2 tbsp plain commercial yoghurt

In a saucepan, bring milk just to a boil. Remove
from heat, and set aside to cool until lukewarm.
In a cup, mix commercial yoghurt with a few
spoonfuls of the warm milk, until a smooth paste
is formed. Add this to the milk and stir until
thoroughly mixed.

The simplest and perhaps most effective way
of making yoghurt is to use a wide-mouthed
thermos flask. Warm flask first by rinsing with
warm water, then pour in the lukewarm milk

mixture and screw lid on immediately. Leave for
about 5 hr., or until mixture sets.

Serve chilled.

This method of incubation is effective because a thermos acts as an insulator. Conse-
quently, the mixture will maintain the same
temperature at which it was poured in. Electric
yoghurt makers are available, and these too are
very effective.

Tarator

Chilled Yoghurt and Cucumber Soup
Serves 4

2 medium cucumbers, peeled and diced
Salt
900 ml/1½ pt/3¾ cups natural yoghurt
3 garlic cloves, peeled and crushed
50 g/2 oz/½ cup walnuts, finely chopped
2 tbsp sunflower (or olive) oil
1 tbsp finely chopped dill (or ½ tsp dried dill)

Place diced cucumbers in a bowl, and sprinkle
with salt. Set aside for 30 min.

In a large bowl, mix all ingredients together.

Chill, and serve in individual bowls, with a
few ice cubes in each.

Suggested wine:
Bulgarian Rhine Riesling

Srpski Ajvar

Serbian Pepper and Aubergine Dip
Serves 4–6

1 medium aubergine (eggplant)
3 medium green peppers
2 garlic cloves, peeled and crushed
5 tbsp oil
2 tbsp vinegar
Salt
Freshly ground black pepper
Freshly chopped parsley

Prick aubergine in several places. Put on a baking tray, with green peppers, in a pre-heated oven, 240°C/Gas Mark 8/450°F. Bake peppers for about 20 min., and aubergines for 30 min. Remove and set aside to cool.

Peel and finely chop aubergine. Clean, deseed, and finely chop peppers. Mix vegetables with oil, vinegar, garlic, salt, pepper, and parsley.

Chill, and serve as an appetizer, with bread.

Suggested wines:
Ljutomer Riesling, Beli Burgundec

Čevapčiči

Skewered Lamb and Pork
Serves 6 as an appetizer

500 g/1 lb minced (ground) pork
500 g/1 lb minced (ground) lamb
Salt
Freshly ground black pepper
2 onions, peeled and finely chopped

Put pork and lamb into a large bowl, and season well with salt and pepper. Mix well, then shape into small sausages, and thread 4 or 5 to a skewer. Cook over a charcoal barbecue, or under a grill, turning once, until cooked. Serve with finely chopped onions and red pepper purée.

Red Pepper Purée

3 sweet red peppers
1 small hot red pepper, seeded and finely chopped
2 tbsp olive oil
Salt

Roast sweet peppers on a fork over a flame until skin is black. Peel, seed, and chop finely. Pound or liquidize with hot red pepper, and gradually add olive oil until a smooth paste is formed. Season with salt.

Serve with *čevapčiči*.

Suggested wines:
Yugoslavian Pinot Noir, Gamay

Ljubljanski Zrezek

Breaded Veal Escalope with Ham and Egg
Serves 4

6 eggs
50 g/2 oz/½ stick butter
4 slices of ham
4 veal escalopes, pounded thinly and dredged in seasoned flour
75 g/3 oz/1 cup fine white breadcrumbs
100 g/4 oz/½ cup lard (or half butter and oil)

Beat 4 eggs individually, and fry in butter, turning once (each egg should be more or less the size of the veal escalope). Set aside.

Layer each seasoned escalope with a slice of ham, and fried egg. Fold over once, and secure with wooden skewer. Beat the 2 remaining eggs with a little water. Dip escalopes in egg, and roll in breadcrumbs. Let stand for 30 min.

Heat lard (or butter and oil) in a large frying pan. Fry escalopes until golden. Drain, and serve at once.

Suggested wine:
Ljutomer Riesling

Ghivetch

Lamb and Vegetable Casserole
Serves 6

4 tbsp oil
2 medium onions, peeled and finely chopped
1 kg/2 lb shoulder of lamb, cut into 3½ cm/1½ in cubes
1 tsp dried hot chillies
Salt
Freshly ground black pepper
Water
4 medium potatoes, peeled and sliced
1 medium aubergine (eggplant), cut into cubes
3 large green peppers, sliced into rings
250 g/½ lb green beans
500 g/1 lb tomatoes, peeled and sliced
3 eggs, beaten
3 tbsp yoghurt
Freshly chopped parsley

Heat half of the oil in a large casserole. Add onions, and sauté until soft and golden. Add lamb, and brown on all sides. Mix in chillies, salt, and pepper. Pour on enough water just to cover the meat. Cover, and cook slowly for 1 hr. Add potatoes, aubergine, green peppers, and beans to the casserole, with enough water to cover ingredients, and cook in a pre-heated oven, 180°C/Gas Mark 4/350°F for further 1 hr. Place tomato slices on top, and cook for a further 10 min. Mix eggs, yoghurt, and parsley together. Pour over the casserole, and return to oven, uncovered, until eggs have set, and turned golden.

Serve immediately, from the casserole.

Suggested wines:
Suhindol Cabernet, Mavrud

Slatko

Plum Compote
Serves 6

1 kg/2 lb plums
500 g/1 lb/2⅓ cups sugar
2 tbsp lemon juice
1 cinnamon stick
Water

Wash, slice in half, and stone the plums. Combine sugar, lemon juice, cinnamon, and fruit in a large saucepan. Add enough water just to cover the fruit. Cook slowly, covered, for 30 min., or until plums are tender but not soft. Remove from heat, and discard cinnamon stick.

Serve chilled.

Suggested drink:
Sljivovica, Tigrovo Mleko

ACKNOWLEDGEMENTS

Many people have assisted us in the production of this book; members of the British wine trade and professional organizations who helped us arrange meetings with principals, contributed advice, encouraged the project, and read and commented on drafts of chapters; friends and new acquaintances who introduced tastes, shared recipes and their homes; and countless others throughout Europe who gladly and proudly shared their way of life with us. It is not possible to mention everybody, but we would particularly like to thank the following companies, organizations, individuals, friends, and family who all made this book possible. (Numbers in brackets indicate the page numbers of related photographs.)

'Antonio's', Albufeira (179); 'Au Rocher', Béhuard (64); 'Aux Deux France', Strasbourg (17); Balkantourist; Mrs Eva Ban, Eger Wine Combine, Eger; Katalin Bencze, Monimpex, Budapest; R. Berthaut et Fils, Fromagerie de la Perriere, Epoisses (41); Mr Kurt Bettin, German Food Centre; Tim Bleach, The Direct Sunday Times Wine Club; Mme Brissaud, Veuve Clicquot-Ponsardin (55); John Brogan, Senate Public Relations; 'La Camargue', Aigues-Mortes; Fiona Campbell, Deinhard & Co. Ltd, London; Centre d'Information du Vin d'Alsace; Bruno Ceretto, Casa Vinicola Ceretto, Alba; 'Cesco' and Bill (144); Luis Charters, Portuguese Government Trade Office; Château Margaux (26); Château Mouton-Rothschild; 'Le Cherche-Midi', Charleval; Fsco Cinzano & Cia SpA, Santa Vittoria d'Alba; 'Lucienne Clergue', Colmar (24); Comité Interprofessionnel des Vins des Côtes du Rhône; Comité Interprofessionnel des Vins du Pays Nantais; Comité Interprofessionnel des Vins de Touraine; Conseil Interprofessionnel des Vins d'Anjou et de Saumur; Conseil Interprofessionnel des Vins de Bordeaux; Paola and Franco Contin, Padua; M. Decourcel, Paul Bouchard et Cie, Beaune; Dopff 'Au Moulin', Riquewihr; Mr Gobor Egressy, Tokaji A'llgard, Sátoraljaújhely (121); Falorni & Bencistà, Greve in Chianti (158); George and Teresa Fischer and family, Budapest; Mr Geoffrey Godbert, Wines from Germany Information Service; Gratien & Meyer, Saumur; Grey-Poupon, Dijon (41); Peter and Sondra Gross; Paul Habekost; John Hawes, Laymont & Shaw Ltd, Truro; Hedges & Butler; Johnny Hugel, Hugel et Fils, Riquewihr (18,20); Mme Joly, La Coulée de Serrant; Mr M. D. King, Bouchard Aîné Ltd; Herr Helmut Kolroser, Oemolk, Vienna; M. J. B. Lanson, Lanson Père et Fils; Karl Liebetrau, Deinhard & Co., Koblenz (96, 97); M. Hervé Liégent, 'Le Vigneron', Reims (48); Mr J. Lipitch, R & C Vintners; 'La Maison des Têtes', Colmar; Catherine Manac'h, Food and Wine from France; Graf Matuschka-Greiffenclau, Schloss Vollrads, Oestrich-Winkel; Giuseppe Marchiori; Mme L. Danvers, M. Henri Perrier and Chef Joseph Thuet, Maître Cuisinier de France, Moët et Chandon, Epernay (51, 52, 54, 55); David Palengat, Luis Gordon & Sons Ltd; Paco Perez, Pedro Domecq SA (188, 190–91); 'Le Pistou', Châteauneuf-du-Pape; Pommery & Greno (54); Port Rene, Charcuterie Fine, Chablis (45); Prückel, Vienna (86); 'Les Pyrénées', Arcachon (29); Maite and Jan Read; 'Le Relais du Médoc', Lamarque; 'Restaurant Gaitan', Jerez de la Frontera; 'Restaurant Terete', Haro; 'Restaurant Walderdorff', Mainz; Pierre Riffault, aux Egrots, Sancerre; La Rioja Alta SA (193); Rioja Wine Information Centre; 'Ristorante Da Italo', Nizza Monferrato; Hotel Sacher, Vienna; Nadya Samsova (217); Ulla and Johann Schenk, Maikammer; Debbie Scott, Col. Buckmaster, The Champagne Bureau; M. Simonnet, Chablis; Sociedad General de Viñas SA, Elciego (Domecq Domain) (193); Herbert and Elizabeth Spalinger (128); Herr Steiner, Burgenländischer Winzerverband, Rust; Swiss National Tourist Office; M. P. Le Tixerant, Comité Interprofessionnel du Vin de Champagne; 'Tre Caci', Florence; Mr R. Trestini, Ashlyns-Trestini; Contessa Cristina Villoresi de Loche, Villa Villoresi, Florence; Herr Joseph Walpen, Provins Valais; Winzergenossenschaft Dinstlgut Loiben, Wachau; Robin Yapp, Yapp Bros, Mere.

We would especially like to thank: Phyllis Hanes and John Young, *The Christian Science Monitor*; our editor Andrew Mylett for his thoroughness, patience, and kindness; Uncle Larry Kim for encouragement and much-valued practical advice; Jean Jordan, Steve and Ann Jordan for help with testing recipes; Lori Ohliger for inspiration and invaluable assistance in editing and manuscript preparation; and Tiny Jordan for his constant trust and belief.

INDEX